A POLITICAL BIOGRAPHY OF AUNG SAN SUU KYI

This book is the first political biography of Aung San Suu Kyi covering both her years in opposition and all her years in power from 2016 onwards. It offers a new interpretation of Aung San Suu Kyi by presenting a balanced and thorough account of Suu Kyi's policies.

In the last 30 years there has not been a person in global politics who has risen so high and fallen so low – and so quickly – as Aung San Suu Kyi. Using postcolonial theory and introducing the new concept of 'a hybrid politician', this book explains apparent inconsistencies of Suu Kyi's agenda. It demonstrates that Suu Kyi considers herself a democrat and yet, rules autocratically. Immersed in her country's tradition of policymaking, she has at the same time been influenced by foreign concepts, both Western and Asian. Drawing on first-hand research, including talks with Suu Kyi, conversations with her supporters and rivals, observations of Suu Kyi's behaviour during intergovernmental talks as well as an extensive number of sources and fieldwork in Myanmar, the author argues that Suu Kyi's case shows both the strengths and limits of hybridity. This brings Suu Kyi priceless political assets such as visibility, recognition and support while proving that such a model of leadership has its restrictions.

A timely biography of the Nobel Peace Prize Laureate as she appears at the International Court of Justice to defend her country against charges of genocide committed against the Rohingya Muslim minority, this book will be of interest to students and researchers of Myanmar politics, Southeast Asian politics, Asian politics, Political Science more generally, Postcolonial Studies, Cultural Studies and Leadership Studies.

Michał Lubina is Associate Professor of Political Science at Jagiellonian University, Poland. He is the author of seven books, including *The Moral Democracy: The Political ⸺ ⸺ ⸺nd China: A Political Marriage of C⸺*

POLITICS IN ASIA

A POLITICAL BIOGRAPHY OF AUNG SAN SUU KYI

A Hybrid Politician

Michał Lubina

Routledge
Taylor & Francis Group

LONDON AND NEW YORK

First published 2021
by Routledge
2 Park Square, Milton Park, Abingdon, Oxon OX14 4RN

and by Routledge
52 Vanderbilt Avenue, New York, NY 10017

Routledge is an imprint of the Taylor & Francis Group, an informa business

British Library Cataloguing in Publication Data
A catalogue record for this book is available from the British Library

Library of Congress Cataloging-in-Publication Data
Names: Lubina, Michał, author.
Title: A political biography of Aung San Suu Kyi : a hybrid politician /
    Michał Lubina.
Description: Abingdon, Oxon ; New York, NY : Routledge, 2021. | Series:
    Politics in Asia | Includes bibliographical references and index.
    Identifiers: LCCN 2020015596 | ISBN 9780367469160 (hardback) | ISBN
    9780367463847 (paperback) | ISBN 9781003031956 (ebook)
Subjects: LCSH: Aung San Suu Kyi. | Women political
    activists–Burma–Biography. | Women politicians–Burma–Biography. |
    Women political prisoners–Burma–Biography. | Women Nobel Prize
    winners–Burma–Biography. | Burma–Politics and government–1988-
Classification: LCC DS530.68.A85 L83 2021 | DDC 959.105092 [B]–dc23
LC record available at https://lccn.loc.gov/2020015596

ISBN: 978-0-367-46916-0 (hbk)
ISBN: 978-0-367-46384-7 (pbk)
ISBN: 978-1-003-03195-6 (ebk)

Typeset in Bembo
by Taylor & Francis Books

MIX
Paper from
responsible sources
FSC
www.fsc.org   FSC™ C013985

Printed in the United Kingdom
by Henry Ling Limited

CONTENTS

ACKNOWLEDGEMENTS

It is proper to start acknowledgments from mentioning Daw Aung San Suu Kyi. I want to thank her once again for agreeing to talk to me. The first time was in Warsaw in September 2013, on the sidelines of her meetings with top Polish politicians and during a dinner, which she hosted for civil society activists. The second time, was through an individual, one-to-one interview in Naypyidaw in February 2015. These encounters were priceless for me to understand her as a politician. Although I'm not uncritical of her, I must admit she is the most classy politician I have ever met. She is a person that intellectually and aesthetically belongs to bygone era. She resides in times where politics was not necessarily less brutal, but certainly better mannered.

My dear wife, Magdalena Kozłowska was once again extremely supportive, empathetic, patient and understanding about my work: this is my eighth book she has had to cope with. It was during our home 'seminars' that the central idea for this book – the concept of hybridity –was developed. Professor Salvatore Babones from University of Sydney never ceased to encourage me to carry on, never mind what, and not to give up. When I almost capitulated on this project, he did not. So, without him, quite literally, this book would not have materialized. In a similar manner I want to thank Dorothea Schaefter from Routledge, who risked and trusted an unknown scholar and, by doing so, she made this book possible. If there was one person who helped the most during my book-writing it was Derek Tonkin, a former British diplomat, Ambassador to Southeast Asian countries. Our regular correspondence about Myanmar was priceless. His intellectual guidance, valuable advice, sober comments and recommendations all helped immeasurably. Derek also read the full manuscript and without his comments it would have been much less of a book. Anna Zongollowicz is yet another person I feel grateful towards. I miss our discussions about Suu Kyi in Yangon and Bangkok. Ania read the two first chapters of this book and her comments not only spared me a few errors but influenced some important ideas. A writer and journalist Mon Mon Myat has been relentless in her defence of Suu Kyi, which I respect. Meetings and correspondence with her served as a counterbalance for critical voices about Myanmar's leader, which I gathered from elsewhere. She tried her best to convince me of the ontological benevolence of Suu Kyi. Our honest disagreements about Suu Kyi helped us both make our arguments stronger. Conversations with Chosein Yamahata, a professor from Aichi Gakuin University in Nagoya, Japan, are always refreshing and nonobvious. His unique perspective brought in many new ideas. I appreciate all time he spent explaining Burmese politics to me and all the conferences, panels and forums he organized. Ye Min Zaw, the Burmese language translator of my previous book (on Suu Kyi's political thought), is the person I would talk to (or rather – listen to) about Rakhine and Shan. Ye has two rare features: insider's knowledge and nonobvious conclusions. Khin Zaw Win is the personification of a Burmese intellectual for me. His intellectual integrity, thoroughness and courage make every conversation with him a real pleasure. A widely recognized expert on Southeast Asia, Bridget Welsh generously shared her insights about Myanmar each time I had a chance to catch her between Kuala Lumpur and Europe. Discussions with her are always intellectually stimulating. Debbie Stothard offered many helpful insights during the beginnings of my interest in Suu Kyi. Thanks to Professor Adam Jelonek, the Director of Institute of Middle and Far East, Jagiellonian University, since 2011 I have been able to lecture at probably the only course on Myanmar in Eastern Europe. Professor Bogdan Góralczyk, former Polish Ambassador to Myanmar helped me when I made my first steps in researching Myanmar. Professor Jerzy Bayer, another former Ambassador to Myanmar, told me a word or two about his fascinating conversations with Suu Kyi. Ambassador Jacek Perlin, former Polish envoy to Myanmar, secured – he, and only he – my second, individual meeting with Suu Kyi. Radek Pyffel, the former Alternate Director of AIIB, used his contacts to bring me into some of Suu Kyi's meetings with top Polish politicians in 2013. Watching her behaviour behind closed doors was eye-opener and perhaps the single most valuable experience I gathered while researching her.

Also, I want to thank the following people: Than Than Myint, Aung Tun Thet, Kyaw Yin Hlaing, Daryl Lim, Hai Mann Zu Zue, Maung Than Htun Aung, Aung Tun Oo, Aye Aye Aung, Phyo Wai Lin, Moe Pwint Phyu, Saw Chit Thet Tun, Sar Yar Poine, Soe Myint Aung, Mutu Suresh, Gun Maw, Zahkung Zau Ja, Hseng Lintner, Robert Anderson, Andrzej Bolesta, David Camroux, Kenton Clymer, Rodion Ebbighausen, Michael Griffits, Ronan Lee, Jacques Leider, Mariangela Manu Mihai, Patrick McCormick, Marion Sabrié, Mandy Sadan, Wolfram Schaffar, Thomas Schaffner, David I. Steinberg, Esther Tenberg, Mirosław Zasada and Hans-Bernd Zöllner. Conversations and/or correspondence with them helped me in my research and influenced it in one way or another; in how I see Suu Kyi and Myanmar. Finally, I want to thank two anonymous reviewers, my other editor Alexandra de Brauw and especially my proof-readers Alison Jones and Anna Kostka who all helped to make this a better book.

All mistakes and errors are entirely my fault.

The book was written in 2019 and in early 2020.

INTRODUCTION

In the last 30 years there has not been a person in global politics who has risen so high and fallen so low – and so quickly – as Aung San Suu Kyi. Her spectacular fall from grace calls for closer examination. Unfortunately, to this day, this phenomenon has not been properly addressed. This serious gap should certainly be filled at the academic level. This book explores the multitude of narratives that attempt to settle, once and for all, discussions around Suu Kyi's political actions and decisions, asking such questions as: Are these sufficient in their explanations? Do the existing narratives on Suu Kyi explain her behaviour to our satisfaction? The answers are negative. These narratives, based on too few variables, reduce Suu Kyi's behaviour to one explanation, whereas a multidimensional outlook is required to move beyond the existing paradigms and clichés. This book, based on voluminous sources – two talks with Suu Kyi (as well as conversations with her supporters and rivals) – aims to push past these clichés. Furthermore, this academic gap will be addressed through the researcher's observation of Suu Kyi's behaviour during intergovernmental talks as well as the experience of 10 years of researching Myanmar and 16 research trips there. By means of postcolonial theory, this work will try to explain Suu Kyi's behaviour.

The puzzle

Aung San Suu Kyi's story has achieved great fame and has been written about in countless articles and several biographies. Most of these works, however, deal with the pre-2015 period when Suu Kyi was still considered a democracy icon, and express more about the expectations foreigners projected onto her than about her.[1] After ascending to power and especially after taking the Tatmadaw and the people's side on the Rohingya crisis, Suu Kyi became universally criticised in the West. Yet – with few notable exceptions – little has been written in depth explaining her behaviour in politics. To the global world Suu Kyi has become both a disappointment and a puzzle. The deep sense of discontent over Suu Kyi in the West has indeed become universal (it permeated even academic circles) and has contributed to a general disinterest in her. The number of articles and books about her has decreased dramatically, as have conference presentations. One may even dare to speculate that in the same manner as it was fashionable to research Suu Kyi in the 1990s and 2000s, since the mid-2010s it has become passé to do so. However, Suu Kyi has also become a puzzle: her actions make her something of an enigma to the outside world (though one may claim that she has always been one). Before the 2010s, Suu Kyi was not always well understood outside of Myanmar policies. Her opposition to the military rule, house arrest, choice of politics over her family, made Suu Kyi a personification of democratic values, if not a symbol of good and morality in politics. How is it then, that this beacon of hope, who was supposed to be "the living symbol of the Universal Declaration of Human Rights",[2] a person who had "a message for our planet"[3] and should have been granted "Freedom to Lead", could now silently endorse crimes against humanity, if not genocide, conducted in her own country? How is it, that this democracy icon rules in an effectively authoritarian way, with an iron grip, without tolerating any dissident voices and by jailing journalists and censoring press? How can yesterday's nemesis of the Tatmadaw now cohabitate with the army? And why is she unsuccessful in governance? Why was there such fundamental incoherence between the actions of Suu Kyi and the international expectations of her? The list of questions and accusations is long and the critical, anti-Suu Kyi intellectual mood has contributed to the end of the pre-2010s mainstream narrative of Suu Kyi as a democracy icon leading the forces of good against an evil military.

Instead, several new narratives emerged. The first may be called 'the Lord Acton approach': this narrative – quite popular, if not the most popular – claims that power corrupted Aung San Suu Kyi. Hence all these (Western media) voices that had at first called on Suu Kyi to 'wake up' and speak in defence of the Rohyinga changed to strong moral condemnation when she failed to do so – expressing disbelief at her lack of action, considering it a 'betrayal of values' and accusing her of 'becoming a politician'.[4] Some have even gone so far as to accuse Suu Kyi of harbouring anti-Muslim resentment, if not outright racism.[5] This narrative is intellectually coherent. According to it, Suu Kyi had liberal, universalist ideas but she betrayed them due to political interests once she gained power. This narrative may have a point, as power indeed corrupts universally and there is no reason to believe that even the very disciplined Suu Kyi is free from the temptations of power. One may doubt, too, whether Suu Kyi has anyone in her milieu brave enough to whisper "Hominem te memento!" in her ear. Nevertheless, this narrative is shallow and does not take into consideration many domestic variables (the logic behind her confrontation with the Tatmadaw and the different interpretation of democracy and human rights in Burma). Most importantly, this narrative is unable to grasp why the people in Burma are not judging Suu Kyi for her 'betrayal' of democratic values (they do not, because there is something different at play). Finally, this narrative is quite a convenient one for all those who glorified Suu Kyi before and who condemn her now. Accepting this narrative liberates them from a guilty conscience, which may ask why Suu Kyi had been promoted as the symbol of morality in politics for more than 25 years and why so many turned a blind eye when her authoritarianism was quite clearly already visible in the 1990s. Yet it is fair to say that there are voices that critically examine the West's past admiration: for example, the idea that the pre-2010s beatification of Aung San Suu Kyi offered the Tatmadaw generals "an easy route back to legitimacy"[6] or critique of the notion of "a personal betrayal" targeted at Suu Kyi.[7]

The other major narrative of Suu Kyi after 2015 may be called 'the Machiavellian approach'. The easy way to resolve the puzzle around Suu Kyi is to portray her as a realist politician, who fought only for personal power and changed her tactics in accordance with her political interests. In this narrative, the Rohingya crisis only revealed what had previously been hidden: Suu Kyi's apparent true nature – that of a political realist.[8] In its radical form, this narrative leads to accusations of hypocrisy: presenting liberal ideals to the outside world and governing without taking notice of these ideals at home. In the more moderate form, the message is more or less the following: Suu Kyi hasn't changed, but after the Rohingya crisis the world belatedly realised that yesterday's democracy icon is a political realist, closer to Indira Gandhi than to Mahatma Gandhi.[9] The realist approach is true to some extent. There was an (un)healthy dose of idealization of Suu Kyi in the 1990s and 2000s in the West. The current global condemnation of Suu Kyi after 2012 is directly proportional to the former admiration. Moreover, Suu Kyi's behaviour in power after 2016 strips away any democratic illusions people may have had before that time that she would bring to Burma a different, and better, version of politics: her governance style is closer to a precolonial Burman pattern of governance than to that of a democratically elected modern politician. And, of course, hypocrisy is the inevitable fellow traveller of politics everywhere and anywhere. So, there are solid grounds to make Suu Kyi a Henry Kissinger in a *hta mein* (female sarong). Yet, it would not do her justice: her policymaking is more about a personal sense of duty and obligation than about a desire for power. And, more importantly, it would narrow the scope of research concerning this astonishing and complex individual to power politics and political manoeuvring, consequently not showing the picture in its full extent. For example, the realist approach fails to explain why Suu Kyi had not struck a deal with the generals earlier (in the 1990s or early 2000s), even though the conditions offered to her upon entering the ruling politico-military establishment of Myanmar were no worse than those in 2011/2012. The realist way can greatly help, but cannot explain her stubborn stance, her personal approach to politics, her sense of duty and mission, or her choices as well as many other 'soft' variables.

There are voices that try to combine the 'betrayal' narrative with that of the 'power-hungry' one. Hanna Beech in her stylish journalistic piece laments the speed and the scale of Suu Kyi's transformation. She suggests that Suu Kyi has cheated the world ("she allowed herself to be misread"), making her a demonical,

Tartuffe-style politician.[10] Beech's article reads really well (and the poignant image of Suu Kyi's mean dog Taichito stays for long in one's memory),[11] yet it offers little value in terms of clarifying Suu Kyi's motives and actions. In a significant and widely commented upon article ("What Happened to Aung San Suu Kyi?") Ben Rhodes offers an intellectually honest attempt to unravel the puzzle of Suu Kyi. Rhodes rightly acknowledges that Suu Kyi is multidimensional: "the idealist, the activist, the politician, the cold pragmatist". He offers no small amount of self-criticism and critique of the Western view on Burma and portrays her as both a Burmese Machiavelli and a renegade democrat who dreams to be a queen. At the same time, between the lines Rhodes tries to defend the Obama administration's policy in Myanmar.[12]

Other voices, outside these narratives, show Suu Kyi as an inexperienced politician who entered real politics but was no match for the Realpolitik-veterans from the Tatmadaw and/or failed in confrontation with the grim reality. According to one of her biographers, whose piece must be considered a desperate attempt to save the pre-2010s narrative on Suu Kyi, stated that she made a critical mistake by accepting the army-made 2008 Constitution and all that followed was a tragic consequence of this error. She gained little (in terms of real power) and lost everything (in terms of her global image). As a consequence, she should resign to save her legacy[13] (which, of course, she never has). An equally futile attempt to justify Suu Kyi's actions from the previous idealised paradigm comes from Nilanjana Sengupta. In her otherwise excellent book Sengupta admits that in the case of the Rohingya crisis Suu Kyi's pragmatism was "showed in a bad light", just once. Nevertheless, Sengupta tries to justify Suu Kyi's stance by linking her rationale to Havel's concepts and to Engaged Buddhism.[14] More appealing, yet still scanty, is the characterological interpretation of Suu Kyi being a stubborn politician, whose inflexibility was an asset during house arrest but has now become a burden.[15]

Researchers have offered more sophisticated explanations on Suu Kyi. An 'old Burma hand', Andrew Selth, in his insightful articles on Suu Kyi's governance, showed how ill-prepared she was to rule the country, how she created many of her own problems and even how she had "little understanding of how a democracy worked in practice". Consequently, he suggests her governance resembles a "rickety old bus".[16] Another Myanmar expert, Mary Callahan, illustrated how Suu Kyi shied away from "the messy daily" politics and instead occasionally offered public sermons on duties, which allowed her "to maintain her status as a political icon" in Myanmar.[17] Selth's and Callahan's pieces are very valuable, yet they answer only in part the Suu Kyi puzzle, as they concentrate on Myanmar current affairs only.

There is also, naturally, the Burmese narrative, or rather the narrative of the majority of society (excluding the Tatmadaw and a few disillusioned dissidents). It is a 'Mother Suu' narrative, or 'the mother of the nation' story. By her actions, most importantly sacrificing family to her political cause, Suu Kyi was able to create a compassionate, motherly image within society and link her struggle with symbolic motherhood. Because of that, her supporters saw all political actions as a form of personal sacrifice, similar to those of a mother who sacrifices herself for the good of her children.[18] This has proved to be (so far) an unparalleled winning strategy, as it shelters Suu Kyi from scant, sceptical domestic voices over her ability to govern successfully. The Burmese public's anger and rejection of Western criticism is best demonstrated by the slogan "We stand with Aung San Suu Kyi". This 'mother of the nation' narrative obviously bypasses the contradictions between Suu Kyi's pre-2012 image and her subsequent actions. In this narrative, everything is explained by her commitment to the country. As such this narrative, although valuable in its own way – because it shows the emotions and attitudes of the Burmese – cannot be helpful here.

As for more constructive Burmese voices, one should certainly mention Mon Mon Myat's brave and intellectually honest, yet unconvincing, attempt to defend Suu Kyi's stance. Mon employs the perspective of Max Weber's famous distinction of ethics of convictions and ethics of responsibility.[19] Mon offers several valuable insights about "a cognitive dissonance" between the actions of the politician Suu Kyi and the activist Suu Kyi, as well as about the imagined Suu Kyi as an embodiment of human rights groups' ideals in the West. Mon's theoretical observation on Weber is particularly important. Unfortunately, Mon is blinded by her admiration for Suu Kyi. She has justified Suu Kyi's unwillingness to help the Rohingya citing, quite shockingly, one of the Ten Duties of a King – an ancient moral Buddhist guidance for governance. Additionally, Mon's main argument, that Suu Kyi does not live in a liberal democracy so she cannot do much, is unconvincing at best. Furthermore, Mon's text suffers from a typical (albeit presented in a more sophisticated and intellectually elegant way than usual) Burmese illusion: "the world does not understand us". This perspective has some valour, as universalizing attempts by some groups in the West indeed may irritate (e.g. the allochronism of the many narratives on Myanmar)[20] and demands a response. One may also ask valuable questions as to what extent outsiders may familiarize themselves with such a closed and self-isolating country as Burma (the 'hermit kingdom'!). But overall, the argument "we are so unique so that foreigners/Westerners cannot understand us" (a sentiment expressed in other Asian countries as well, see e.g. Japan's *nihonjinron* or Thailand's *khwampenthai*) is weak. Texts can be translated, intricacies resolved, cultural differences pointed out and discussed. Not everything is lost in translation. We do not live in a compartmentalized world where cultures are within cages with little or no contact with the outside world. With globalization, standardization, the influx of social media and a worldwide dominance of the English language, this is not so. Consequently, one cannot honestly claim that the West was that unfamiliar with Suu Kyi. That is too easy. Although Suu Kyi became an icon without her consent (deification of her person beginning during her first house arrest), once liberated, she actively shaped and sustained her international image. Her words and actions touched a chord because she knew Western cultural patterns well. She knew them because she assimilated them. Her own words concerning Tagore, "the assimilation of foreign elements in Tagore's intellectual apparatus was so complete that they form an integral part of the depth and breadth of his unique talent",[21] can easily be applied to her as well. This is especially so given her fascination with the Indian "synthesis of East and West", and she made good use of it. Suu Kyi wanted to remain both a mother of Burma and a worldwide democracy icon and behaved accordingly. Only the Rohingya crisis annihilated her plans.

Finally, one should also mention the Burmese dissidents, both domestic (the former 'third force') and diaspora, grouped around several (often conflicted) organizations and media outlets. The Burmese dissidents have a complicated relationship towards Suu Kyi. On one hand, they respect her and understand her much better than most of the outside world. On the other, not infrequently they feel a resentment towards her for 'stealing' their revolution and/or failing to bring about real change in Myanmar. This all, however, is balanced by their unwillingness to harm the democratic cause she is personifying. These considerations produce a fascinating, conflicting landscape of texts – sometimes books,[22] more often articles – that will be used in this book. They, however, do not constitute a united approach on Suu Kyi.

All these narratives are valuable to an extent; they point out and explain several aspects of Suu Kyi's behaviour and the reality surrounding her. As such, they must be taken into consideration. However, none provides a comprehensive way to resolve the puzzle around Aung San Suu Kyi. None of them offers a fully satisfactory answer that would explain Suu Kyi's actions both before the 2010s and after. This book has the ambition to fill this gap by using postcolonial theory.

Theoretical and conceptual framework

In the current globalized world ideas cross borders, cultural spheres and influence one another; the interactions and exchanges take place across societies, changing them decisively. This is particularly true in the postcolonial world, where various exchanges between the colonizers and colonized people (and the heritage resulting from these interactions) led to a new, complex identity: fluid and relational. In researching such areas there are no grand theories. One cannot explain a politician's behaviour by such overarching, essentialist categories as liberal universalism, political culture, Asian values, etc. To paraphrase a famous metaphor, a researcher who is left in the dark has too many directions to point their torch.

How can one then explain the behaviour of a politician like Suu Kyi, who at one moment can say that "democracy is the only ideology consistent with freedom"[23] and at the same time calls those who disagree with her "renegades and traitors"[24]; the behaviour of one who was considered to be an embodiment of the best of East and West in the 1990s and 2000s while at same time being criticised for her Westernized behaviour inside Burma (publicly by the regime and quietly by the rest),[25] and who is now accused of being a Burman-Buddhist nationalist.

Here postcolonial theory with its concept of hybridity offers a helping hand. Homi K. Bhabha's "cultural and historical hybridity of the postcolonial world" is our paradigmatic place of departure. For Bhabha, hybridity is something more than just the effect of mixing two cultures – it is a way of negotiating between the boundaries that form identities and cultures. In the researcher's words hybridity is: "an *inter*national culture, based not on the exoticism of multiculturalism or the diversity of cultures, but on the inscription and articulation of culture's hybridity"; called the "third space" that lies "in-between" those two and has "no primordial unity or fixity that even the same signs can be appropriated, translated, rehistoricised and read anew".[26] In other, simpler words, upon the point of contact of two cultures, a third one comes into existence with its own structures, objects and practices. However, it is not a simple result of mixing these two cultures, but a new entity, new quality, a creative yet ambivalent one. Bhabha is acknowledged in postcolonial studies for this observation. His recognition of the third space as an ambivalent space of cultural identity offers a perspective to "overcome the exoticism of cultural diversity in favour of the recognition of an empowering hybridity".[27] This hybridity has the ability to "transverse both cultures and to translate, negotiate and mediate affinity and difference within a dynamic of exchange and inclusion". Consequently, "hybrid strategy opens up a third space of/for rearticulating negotiation and meaning".[28] Hybridity "releases power" that allows "a means of evading the replication of the binary categories of the past and developing new antimonolithic models".[29] It "involves fusion, the creation of a new form, which can then be set against the old form, of which it is partly made up".[30]

Applying hybridity to an individual from a postcolonial country is risky. Hybridity originally described power relations in colonial times; later it was used in postcolonial theories, sociological theories of identity, in studies on multiculturalism and globalization.[31] Yet, it can be creatively used elsewhere: transferred from postcolonial theory to political science and applied to a political agent – Aung San Suu Kyi. After all, political science frequently borrows theories, paradigms, terms and concepts from other sciences for its own good. Hybridity is no different here. In political science this term is used to view interactions between international and local levels of international systems, although it is usually used in a 'undertheorized' way, that is, without conceptual reflection. Hybridity is used in analyses of the space of political interventions and in the critique of binaries of such interventions (international/modern and local/traditional).[32] Most frequently, however, the term is just used descriptively, to name entities that do not fit into established definitions (consider the popularity of terms like 'hybrid regime' or 'hybrid war'). However, hybridity is rarely, if ever, used to analyse individuals in politics; I have not found the expression 'a hybrid politician'. Perhaps this is due to sensitive overtones that may coincide while using it. Applying the concept of hybridity to an individual, especially an individual from Southeast Asia, is risky given the inglorious colonial usage of this word.[33] This is even more so, given the fact that Suu Kyi was mercilessly slandered by the Burmese military regime for her marriage to an Englishman.[34] Hence, using the concept of hybridity here is a risky undertaking. However, in the case of hybridity, the "emancipative potential of negative terms" is materialized. In the 1990s the concept was taken on and subverted to challenge the essentialist model.[35] Consequently, the postcolonial theorists transformed this concept into a "celebrated and privileged kind of superior cultural intelligence owing to the advantage of in-betweeness, the straddling of two cultures and the consequent ability to negotiate the difference".[36] In short, hybridity lost its colonial overtones, at least on the academic level, and became a neutral term which can be effectively applied as it combines antithetical and contradictory features and meanings. Given the fact that hybridization better describes current processes than older terms, such as homogenization, modernization or Westernization,[37] it seems an adequate lens to research such political agents as Aung San Suu Kyi. Let alone the fact of associating hybridity with India in postcolonial studies (Bhabha and many other postcolonial theorists, as well as writers are either Indian or of Indian origin/roots), Suu Kyi with her fascination of India and the Indian fusion of East and West, seems a interesting, nonobvious case study here. There is also one more reason why Suu Kyi is adequate to be researched via hybrid lenses: one connected to social class. Suu Kyi comes from postcolonial Burmese elites, who wanted to be independent yet were "culturally Anglicized"; their elite status was based "on their enlightenment British style".[38] Among other features, they used English in official correspondence and sometimes in private as well (Aung San wrote letters in English to his Burmese friends), they read British classics and sent their children to British schools. Thus, hybridity applies to this upper class of Burmese elites (contrary to the Burmese masses and to the majority of the Tatmadaw soldiers).

Using hybridity, this book claims that Suu Kyi is indeed a product of many worlds, a person where East and West meet, but not exactly the way her pre-2010s admirers had thought. She is not the unifier of East and West and not necessary the ideal one, for hybridity does not have to automatically mean a positive thing. Suu Kyi is a hybrid politician, both Burmese and international at the same time: she is immersed in Burma's tradition of policymaking, especially in the modernized version of her father, and yet she has been influenced by many foreign concepts, both Western and Asian. Hybridity offers a way to resolve the problem of apparent inconsistencies of her agenda. Thanks to this concept, it is possible to understand why Suu Kyi considers herself a democrat (and is considered so in Burma) and yet rules autocratically. Why she can honestly speak about fear and freedom from it, and remain indifferent to more than 700,000 people who escaped her country in total fear. And so on.

Moreover, Aung San Suu Kyi's case shows both the strengths and the limits of hybridity. For two decades (late 1980s – early 2010s) she was able, consciously or not, to switch codes in order to function successfully in politics. She spoke to Burmese people using local idioms and to the world in a language it understood. For a long while, it proved successful and brought her priceless political assets: visibility, recognition and support. For a time, Suu Kyi's hybridity seemed to be a perfect, even if illusionary, answer to both Burma's multiple domestic problems as well as to global challenges. But then came the moment of truth during the Rohingya crisis and Suu Kyi's two worlds began to diverge. She could no longer stay on the fence about this issue. Suu Kyi had to choose and it was a dramatic choice. Throughout her political career she had always had two main assets:

popular support and foreign backing. Now, picking one equalled losing the other. That is why Suu Kyi's story shows the strengths and the limits of hybridity in the world of politics. It proved that such a model of leadership can be effective only to a point. Consequently, applying the hybridity theory allows us to ask questions not only about Suu Kyi as a unique political actor within Myanmar. We can ask about her role in Myanmar's extraordinary political system of 'disciplined democracy', which is stuck midway between democracy and autocracy.

This book's proposed approach is naturally an agency-centred explanation. Agency-centred theories stress the ability of individual agents to (re)construct their worlds. Agents here can be individuals (politicians, decision-makers, activists) or groups (interest groups, lobby groups, clans, protest movements and other). Agency is understood as the capacity of individuals to consciously make their own choices, realize their intentions and act in accordance with their free will (*human agency*). Such theories as 'great man theory' (and its contemporary equivalents, such as 'great leaders of crowds', 'charismatic authority', 'personal legitimization') or different intentionist theories (e.g. rational choice theory; public choice theory; and pluralism) are individualistic. They are based on ideas of the central importance of agents in social systems and/or on the presumption that only the actions/deeds of actors can be researched.[39]

Such aspects as the dominance of personalization of power in Burmese politics (individuals are much more important than institutions), the political transformation carried out by conscious elites and overall weakness of Myanmar's political and economic institutions all influence the agency-centred theoretical choice of this monography. The main reason for choosing agency-centred explanations is, however, different. The reason is the absolute dominance of Suu Kyi's person over all other factors of the Burmese transformation, combined with the intellectual discourse concerning Burma in the world (in both academic and popular writing). As a consequence, Suu Kyi is politically unassignable. The Burmese leader plays "a critical role" in Burmese politics and, "accordingly, those who want to understand Myanmar politics will have to understand her personality, her political philosophy and her role in the political life of the country".[40] The importance of Suu Kyi can be seen in the fact that her political foes, the military generals of Myanmar, tried to carry out the transformation into a legitimized, internationally accepted military-dominated system of governance without her (1988–2011), but failed to do so (their failure was signalled in the international sanctions against Myanmar, spanning from 1997 to 2012). It was only once they realized she was irreplaceable that they co-opted Suu Kyi to the elite and shared power – which they did effectively. They finally succeeded in transforming themselves from international pariahs to accepted leaders (recent soft condemnation after Rohingya expulsion notwithstanding), thanks to co-opting Suu Kyi.

Moving onto a methodological level, this book will apply a hermeneutic approach, based on an attempt to understand social actions.[41] According to Bogdanor's explanation of hermeneutics, "in order to understand the way people behave, we need to understand their motives for doing what they are doing and what they think they are doing, and also to know their world outlook and how they see their place in the world".[42] In other words, the aim is to place Suu Kyi's behaviour and her actions within a specific cultural and socio-cultural context. This follows Gadamer's "horizon of understanding", which is determined by all the socio-cultural environments a person is integrated in. A human being "understands the world as a result of complex interaction of specific horizons of understanding, that are constantly overlapping".[43] This guarantees value-free criterion of social science.[44] This is not a frequently used perspective in political science. Usually discussions over constitutive elements of politics (such as power, order, state, interest, etc.) prevail in a decontextualized, depersonalized sphere. However, a political science that abstracts or neglects the everyday meaning of political-ness and the meaning of intersubjective relations, is a science that deals with anatomized political exhibits. Instead, this book will try to look for the sources and dynamics of political phenomena and processes in interactions between domestic sources of a personality and identity of a political agent, and structured forms of external reality for her or him. That is why it will focus on the cultural schemes of Burmese policymaking and will try to extract a certain logic from their meaning and their orientated activities. The book is an attempt to capture the subjective and objective mechanisms of Burma's "moral universe",[45] of politics that shaped the policymaking of Aung San Suu Kyi, along with her external influences. This interpretative framework is possible, however, only if the Burmese doctrinal, philosophical, cultural, political and social conditions are taken into account. This is an attempt to catch 'the Burma-ness' of meanings and casual connections. These connections originate from a theoretical line that demands knowledge of everyday meanings and symbols that shape the Burmese attitudes towards politics in order to make the intentional acts of a political agent meaningful in social and cultural context. Through the structuralized meaning of everyday practice, the book tries to understand and explain the norms and values of Burmese policymaking as well as the axiological and normative background of their system of motivations and behaviour. As such, this attempt may be called an example of interpretative political science.

Notes

1 "Democracy icon" was the narrative of the majority of Suu Kyi's biographies. Among others, see: Barbara Victor, *The Lady: Aung San Suu Kyi: Nobel Laureate and Burma's Prisoner*, 2nd edition (New York, NY: Faber & Faber, 2002); Peter Popham, *Aung San Suu Kyi. The Lady and the Peacock* (London: Rider, 2011); Popham, *Aung San Suu Kyi. The Lady and the Generals* (London: Rider, 2016); Jesper Bengtsson, *Aung San Suu Kyi. A Biography* (New Delhi: Amaryllis, 2012); Rena Pederson, *The Burma Spring. Aung San Suu Kyi and the New Struggle for the Soul of a Nation* (New York, NY: Pegasus, 2015). These works – Justin Wintle, *Perfect Hostage. Aung San Suu Kyi, Burma and the Generals* (London: Arrows, 2007), Bertil Lintner, *Aung San Suu Kyi and Burma's Unfinished Renaissance* (Clayton VIC: CSAS, Monash University, 1990); Lintner, *Aung San Suu Kyi and Burma's Struggle for Democracy* (Chiang Mai: Silkworm Books, 2011) – stand out as probably the best and most balanced ones, yet for now they remain outdated.

2 "Iconic Obama artist unveils Suu Kyi image", *The Sydney Morning Herald*, 26 September 2009.

3 Alan Clements, *The Voice of Hope. Conversations with Aung San Suu Kyi* (London: Rider, 2008), p. 12.

4 Among so many examples of this most popular narrative, see "Aung San Suu Kyi's cowardly stance on the Rohingya", *The New York Times*, 9 May 2016; "Aung San Suu Kyi Is In Power. So why is she ignoring her Country's Most Vulnerable People?", *Foreign Policy*, 9 June 2016; "Aung San Suu Kyi's silence on the genocide of Rohingya Muslims is tantamount to complicity", *The Independent*, 20 May 2015.

5 "State racism meets neoliberalism", *Jacobin*, January 2018.

6 "The fall of Aung San Suu Kyi, democracy icon", *The Nation*, 6 October 2017.

7 "Aung San Suu Kyi, the ignoble Laureate", *The New Yorker*, 15 September 2017.

8 Ronan Lee, "Politician, not an icon: Aung San Suu Kyi's silence on Myanmar's Muslim Rohingya", *Islam and Christian–Muslim Relations*, vol. 25, no. 3 (2014); "Aung San Suu Kyi is a politician, not a monster", *Foreign Policy*, 14 May 2018; "The realism of Aung San Suu Kyi", *Foreign Policy Blogs*, 5 January 2016.

9 Hans-Bernd Zöllner and Rodion Ebbighausen, *The Daughter. A Political Biography of Aung San Suu Kyi* (Chiang Mai: Silkworm Books, 2018).

10 "What happened to Myanmar's human-rights icon?", *The New Yorker*, 27 September 2017.

11 Suu Kyi was given this dog by her younger son in 2010 and this gift was very personal (Suu Kyi's previous dog died just months after she left her family and engaged in politics in Burma in 1988); Beech in her article shows that Taichito, initially a loving puppy, became a horrible creature. This might be read as a metaphor of Suu Kyi's own transformation.

12 "What happened to Aung San Suu Kyi?", *The Atlantic*, 9 August 2019.

13 "As Aung San Suu Kyi's biographer, I have to say that the only good thing she can do now is resign", *The Independent*, 8 September 2017.

14 Nilanjana Sengupta, *The Female Voice of Myanmar. Khin Myo Chit to Aung San Suu Kyi* (New Delhi: Cambridge University Press, 2015), pp. 315–316.

15 "Aung San Suu Kyi: The myth turns to dust", *Lowy Institute*, 11 September 2017.

16 Andrew Selth, "Be careful what you wish for: The National League for Democracy and government in Myanmar", *Griffith Asia Institute Regional Outlook Paper* no. 56 (2017); "Aung San Suu Kyi's fall from grace", *Lowy Institute*, 8 December 2017.

17 "Aung San Suu Kyi's quiet, puritanical vision for Myanmar", *Nikkei Asia Review*, 29 March 2017.

18 Jessica Harriden, *The Authority of Influence. Women and Power in Burmese History* (Copenhagen: NIAS Press, 2012), p. 227.

19 Mon Mon Myat, "Is politics Aung San Suu Kyi's vocation?", *Palgrave Communications*, vol.5, no.50 (2019).

20 All these narratives of Burma as "a country stuck in time" are precisely what Fabian described as superimposing a Western worldview onto non-Western cultures. Johannes Fabian, *Time and the Other. How Anthropology Makes Its Object* (New York, NY: Colombia University Press, 2014), p. 80.

21 Aung San Suu Kyi, "Intellectual life in Burma and India under colonialism," in: Aung San Suu Kyi, *Freedom from Fear and Other Writings*, ed. M. Aris, 3rd edition (London: Penguin Books, 2010), p. 115.

22 Aung Zaw, *The Face of Resistance* (Chiang Mai: Mekong Press, 2013).

23 Words of her father, quoted by her in "Speech to a mass rally at the Shwedagon Pagoda", in: *Freedom from Fear and Other Writings*, p. 194.

24 *Daw Aung San Suu Kyi's Speech on 27–5–1999*, Online Burma Library (OBL).

25 Kyaw Yin Hlaing, "Daw Aung San Suu Kyi: A Burmese dissident democrat", in: *Burma or Myanmar? The Struggle for National Identity*, ed. L. Dittmer (Singapore: World Scientific, 2010), p. 126.

26 Homi K. Bhabha, *Location of Culture* (London and New York, NY: Routledge, 2004), pp. 31, 38, 55–56.

27 "Homi Bhabha's concept of hybridity", *Literary Theory*, 8 April 2016.
28 Cristina-Georgiana Voicu, *Exploring Cultural Identities in Jean Rhys' Fiction* (Berlin: de Gruyter, 2014), p. 28.
29 Bill Ashcroft, Gareth Griffiths, and Helen Tiffin, *The Post-Colonial Studies Readers* (London and New York, NY: Routledge, 2006), p. 137.
30 Robert Young, *Colonial Desire. Hybridity in Theory, Culture and Race* (London and New York, NY: Routledge, 2005), p. 23.
31 Ashcroft, Griffiths, Tiffin, *The Post-Colonial Studies*, pp. 135–138.
32 Paul Jackson and Peter Albrecht, "Power, politics and hybridity," in: *Hybridity on the Ground in Peacebuilding and Development: Critical Conversations*, eds. J. Wallis, L. Kent, and M. Forsyth (Canberra: ANU Press, 2018), pp. 37–39.
33 In colonial discourse hybridity was an abuse for those of mixed breed; it became associated with racist and eugenic thought, Young, *Colonial Desire*, pp. 1–27, 133–157.
34 The outright racist remarks targeted at her in mid 1990s will be described later on.
35 Nikos Papastergiadis, *Multi-Cultural Identities and the Politics of Anti-Racism* (London: Zed Books, 1997), p. 258.
36 Ankie Hoogvelt, *Globalization and the Postcolonial World: The New Political Economy of Development* (Baltimore, MD: Johns Hopkins University Press, 1997), p. 158.
37 Jan Nedervenn Pieterse, "Globalisation as hybridisation", *International Sociology*, 1 June 1994.
38 Manuel Sarkisyanz, *The Buddhist Background of Burmese Revolution* (New York, NY: Springer, 1965), pp. 9, 130, 165.
39 Stuart McAnulla, "Structure and agency", in: *Theory and Methods in Political Science*, eds. D. March and G. Stoker (London: Palgrave Macmillan, 2002), pp. 273–276; Walter Carlsnaes, "The agency-structure problem in foreign policy analysis", *International Studies Quarterly*, vol. 36, no. 3 (1992), p. 245; Derek Laydler, *Understanding Social Theory* (London: Sage, 1994), p. 22; Chris Barker, *Cultural Studies: Theory and Practice* (London, Sage: 2005), p. 448.
40 Kyaw Yin Hlaing, "Aung San Suu Kyi of Myanmar: A review of the lady's biographies", *Contemporary Southeast Asia: A Journal of International and Strategic Affairs*, vol. 29, no. 2 (2007), p. 374.
41 Max Weber, *Economy and Society* (Los Angeles, CA: University of California Press, 1978), p. 4.
42 *The Blackwell Encyclopedia of Political Science*, ed. V. Bogdanor (Blackwell: Oxford, 1999), p. 153; Franziska Blum, *Teaching Democracy. The Program and Practice of Aung San Suu Kyi's Concept of People's Education* (Berlin: Regiospectra, 2011), p. 13.
43 Quoted in: Blum, *Teaching Democracy*, p. 15.
44 Weber, *Economy and Society*, p. 4.
45 Matthew J. Walton, *Politics in the Moral Universe: Burmese Buddhist Political Thought*, unpublished PhD thesis (Seattle, WA: University of Washington, 2012), pp. 2–11.

1

BECOMING A HYBRID POLITICIAN

What makes Aung San Suu Kyi a hybrid politician is a complex fusion of over-lapping political perspectives, both Burmese and foreign. Naturally, the Burmese component is stronger. Suu Kyi was influenced by the moral, Buddhist under-pinnings of policymaking (politicians are judged by morality more than by competence), by the Ashokan model, the personalization of power, the importance of unity and the eclectic, utilitarian assimilation of foreign elements. However, this does not mean that the external ideas that shape her policymaking can be neglec-ted. Suu Kyi at various stages of her life, but particularly before entering politics, inhaled Christian influences, the 'non-violence' ideology personified by Gandhi, Martin Luther King and Nelson Mandela, Western democratic ideas and Indian syncretic cosmopolitanism.

The Burmese background

Aung San Suu Kyi once wrote that "to be Burmese is to be Buddhist",[1] and Buddhism is certainly the most important feature of Burmese identity, historically providing the idioms, structure and concepts for Burmese policymaking. The atti-tude of doctrinal Buddhism towards politics is clear: politics is an inevitable activity, yet of secondary importance.[2] That is why in Buddhist texts political engagement is often depicted as the antithesis of enlightenment-seeking. However, this does not mean that Buddhism is "unpolitical or anti-political".[3] Politics is not central to Buddhism, yet it matters; political aspects are clearly visible in canonical and post-canonical texts. The fundamental goal of politics is to guarantee stability, order and peace with a strong accent on preventing poverty ("only when your stomach is full can you keep the precepts") and limiting the evil tendencies of mankind. From this understanding, sets of normative imperatives for a ruler originate: she or he should be moral, care for the people and rule in an enlightened manner. Otherwise there would be natural disasters, people would transgress and, ultimately, society would collapse. It is this tradition that prompted Suu Kyi to write: "the root of a nation's misfortunes has to be sought in the moral failings of the government".[4]

Emperor Ashoka (304–232 BC) represents the archetype of this behaviour, though it is often conveniently forgotten that Ashoka started his enlightened governance after causing the death of around 100,000 people. His lesson, however, is not lost on many Buddhist rulers who have applied what can be called 'the Ashokan model': carrying out 'necessary' yet immoral actions first, followed by more moral and enlightened rule.[5] Hence, the tradition of Burmese 'warrior kings' who made imperial conquests first and later turned (or hoped to turn) to piety. It is worth bearing in mind this practice of the Ashokan model of behaviour when interpreting the Tatmadaw's massacre of the '8888' (8 August 1988) revolution or even Suu Kyi's reaction to the Rohingya crisis. The Ashokan model, as well as other multiple ways to bypass the inconvenient Buddhist moral precepts in governance, both doctrinal[6] and practical,[7] was born out of the tension between Buddhist ideals and the hard realities of politics.[8] The tradition of 'modifying' such politically inconvenient Buddhist rules as prohibition of killing by saying that "in certain cases one may destroy life"[9] or by claiming that the defence of *dhamma* overrides the laws of *kamma*, [10] although not central to Buddhism, nevertheless survived into the twenty-first century.

From the basis of Buddhism originates the Burmese tradition of policymaking. It is founded on consideration of politics as a field of moral actions under Buddhist laws.[11] This deeply religious background of politics in Myanmar produces a reality where the moral perception of politics still dominates, leading to the personification of power (institutions and laws are secondary to individuals and loyalty is personalized), the sacralization of the leader and condemnation of the opponents and everlasting calls for unity (the central value in Burmese political thought) understood as a moral ability to move beyond one's selfishness.[12]

On a more social level, policymaking in Burma was and still is state-centred, where the general population is disinterested and/or excluded from this sphere of life. Although this elitist approach has been challenged by more inclusive voices,[13] including that of Aung San Suu Kyi, it still remains the dominant approach, albeit on a lesser scale than before.

The traditional political paradigm of Burma emphasizes the imperfection of human nature: people are prone to transgression and enter into conflict with others which produces a never-ending cycle of violence. Only a strong political authority can be a remedy to that, as it can keep the imperfect nature of people in check.[14] This is the authoritarian, antidemocratic tradition (the people cannot be the ultimate source of sovereignty because the people are immoral)[15] that has dominated in the history of Burma.

The alternative, which may optimistically be called a feeble democratic tradition in Burma, does not argue about people's desire-driven nature, but stresses their capacity to overcome it and live ethical lives; here, the purpose of politics is, then, to establish circumstances that encourage the moral behaviour of the people.[16] This is a more inclusive approach that may – but does not have to – lead to the estab-lishment of a democratic system. One may ascribe to this tradition the ambitious yet failed democratic reforms proposed by Hpo Hlaing and other modernizers (U Kaung, Kyaw Htun) in the mid-nineteenth century; Nu's erratic democratic gov-ernance in the 1950s and the unfulfilled universalism of the "Buddhist modern-ists"[17] in the mid-twentieth century. This is a tradition where one could place Aung San Suu Kyi, though not necessarily her father.

Aung San, the father of Suu Kyi and the founder of modern Burma, is the pivotal figure for both Suu Kyi and Myanmar. Following several political, military and ideological twists during World War II, Aung San secured Burma's indepen-dence and, although assassinated shortly before it became a reality, became a Bur-mese hero. Until 1988 all Burmese governments built their legitimacy upon him and so did Suu Kyi when entering politics. It was all too easy given the fact that Aung San was a realist pragmatist, with a quite flexible and eclectic political agenda.[18] In the Burmese context, Aung San represented "a syncretic mixture of Burmese tradition and 'modern' global ideas".[19]

If Suu Kyi had not been Aung San's daughter she would not be in politics, as was the case with Sirimavo Bandaranaike, Indira Gandhi, Benazir Bhutto, Sheikh Hasina Wajed, Khaleda Zia Rahman, Corazon C. Aquino, Megawati Sukarnoputri and Park Geun-hye; the "infectious charisma that came from being 'widows-of-him' or 'daughters-of-him'"[20] is well-researched in literature. From this standpoint, Suu Kyi with her "karmic credentials"[21] that came from her perfect lineage is just a Burmese equivalent of an Asian phenomenon. But in the case of Suu Kyi, there is more at stake. Her obsession with her father (visible in so many aspects)[22] turns the power struggle in Myanmar into 'family quest' for regaining the power from the hands of military usurpers.[23] Finally, and most importantly, Aung San, with his eclecticism, his ideological flexibility, his skilful usage of Buddhist rhetoric, his Leninist style of party governance and many other aspects, remains the ultimate model of leadership for Suu Kyi.

Aung San, who employed several foreign ideologies to suit his policies, followed a local tradition of assimilating foreign ideas. In Southeast Asia there exists a cen-turies-long tradition of accepting, assimilating and transforming foreign ideas in a way that with time one can barely recognize the original versions.[24] This tradition dates back to at least the Indianization, while in more modern history it became very visible during the colonial times. Responding to the challenge, modernizing movements in Southeast Asia did not consider Westernization as the only guaran-tee of success (as it was in the case of Atatürk's Turkey for example), but they assumed ideological eclecticism instead. They strived to emulate the sources of the West's successes – 'external' (technical or technological) modernization without compromising the identity of the country and without undergoing a deep social change. Mindon's modernization with its Buddhism and monarchical power at the centre accompanied by technological modernization in the background is the best example.[25] This attitude, similar to Japan's Meiji reforms or to China's *zhong ti, xi yong*, in Southeast Asia succeeded only in Thailand (then known as Siam). In

Burma, despite the brave yet unfinished reforms in the mid-nineteenth century, it failed. It left, however, an important legacy on Burmese policymaking. Since then, almost all Burmese political leaders have considered Western-born ideologies as the means to their goal of regaining independence first and rebuilding the country's greatness later. Ideologies, concepts and political systems taken from the West changed, though the eclecticism remained constant: they chose parts and rejected the rest. Western ideas are not considered autotelic values. Eclectic usage of these ideas functions as a way of modernizing a country. This attitude was true for Aung San as well as to his direct successors: Nu ("the Buddhist socialism") and Ne Win ("the Burmese way to socialism"), who both tried to assimilate the then fashionable, socialist ideas. Post-1988 Tatmadaw generals did the same with the most popular global idea of the last half-century: democracy. Hence, 'the disciplined democracy' was born. This is the intellectual tradition where one should locate ideas formative for Suu Kyi.

The reason why Burmese reforms failed, both in the nineteenth and twentieth centuries, offers perhaps a clue as to why Suu Kyi is unsuccessful in governance now. According to widespread opinion in Burma, the British colonized the country because they were stronger (they had guns, better weapons) not because they had more just social institutions. From then on, the Burmese elites were looking to the West in search of sources of power and influence. This was connected to the idea of copying the 'good things' from the West (science, technology) and discarding the rest (a concept they called 'preserving traditional values') – just like Mongkut and Chulalongkorn successfully did in Siam.[26] And it was and still is not about establishing a more just social system or empowering the individual or masses. The people do not matter. The leader does. The aim is to empower the leader: king, adipati, prime-minister, chairman of the military council, president or state counsellor.[27] This is where the personalization of power in Burma shows itself: the Burmese elites (in the very tradition of Mahā-Sammata – moral leaders make a good system, nothing else matters) do not transform institutions (as institutions are secondary to individuals) and consequently cannot transform a country. The same applies to Suu Kyi. She has spoken a lot about empowerment of an individual (all her "revolution of the spirit" ideas). Yet her policies are about her (what she can do for the country, how she can reform it, etc.), not about the people, not about the system. The contradiction between Suu Kyi's words and actions is clearly seen in the fact that she did not empower any member of her party. And if one listens to the National League for Democracy (NLD), one may come to the conclusion that the biggest problem in Myanmar as of 2019 is the lack of amendment to chapter 3, no 59 (f) of the Constitution (prohibiting her from becoming president because of her children's foreign citizenship). Many more examples of these self-centric policies of Suu Kyi will be presented later.

The international dimension

The Burmese dimension is naturally the most important for Suu Kyi. Yet, one should not marginalize or neglect the international one. Suu Kyi in her texts and speeches invoked and quoted such authors as David Hume, John Locke, Karl Popper, Mahatma Gandhi, Abraham Lincoln, Nelson Mandela, Martin Luther King, Václav Havel, Berthold Brecht, George Orwell, Natan Sharansky, Edith Bone, Rabindranath Tagore, Sulak Sivaraksa and many others. This should not come as a surprise, for there are many sources of Suu Kyi's inspiration. The years she spent in India, the UK, the USA, Japan and Bhutan intellectually influenced her in a significant way.

In her childhood Suu Kyi attended Christian schools in Rangoon and in Delhi which together with her Christian maternal grandfather opened her to some Christian influence. She will later say "saints are the sinners who go on trying",[28] quote the biblical "perfect love casts out fear"[29] and write personal letters to her husband saying that the trust of her people "is the biggest cross" she would have to bear.[30] In freshly postcolonial India, where Suu Kyi went next (1960–1964) as a teenager, she studied in a college and mastered the English language, even though with a touch of prissy Victorianism. There she came across Gandhism and its non-violent means; something which would have a long-lasting and formative effect on her – non-violence would become one of the cornerstones of her political agenda. But there was more than Gandhism for her in India. She absorbed the postcolonial cosmopolitan intellectual atmosphere of India and would later present it as a model for Burma, envying India's ability to achieve "the intellectual impulse that sought a harmonious fusion of East and West".[31] Then she moved to study at Oxford University (1964–1967), living at the Gore-Booth's family home in Chelsea during study breaks and after graduating. Here, she was almost treated as an extra daughter by Sir Paul (former British Ambassador to Burma) and his wife Patricia, becoming almost like them and certainly inspiring to be so. This, together with her later marriage (1972–1999) to a British man, Michael Aris (whom, incidentally, she had met at the Gore-Booths), would shape her profoundly. Suu Kyi, a child of post-colonial elites, who mastered English in the impeccable way worthy of Eton alumni and developed an aristocratic style of Englishness, would then enter the British elites and inhale the core Anglo-Saxon ideas of parliamentarianism, rights-based democracy, rule of law, checks and balances, empowerment of the people, and so on. She would assimilate as well many aspects of Western culture, both high and popular.[32] It was at Oxford, too, that she became inspired by Nelson Mandela's struggle in South Africa, especially by the political role of international sanctions. A stay in New York (1969–1970) and work for the United Nations opened Suu Kyi to Henry David Thoreau's ideas of civil disobedience, best fulfilled by Martin Luther King. His struggle for civil rights would become a model for her 1989 movement; she would quote his famous words ("injustice anywhere is injustice everywhere")[33] and try to copy his methods. Her almost yearly stay in Bhutan (1972) exposed her to the importance of traditional identity based on religion in keeping the country united. Finally, a research stay in Japan (1985–1986), where she followed the footsteps of her father, allowed her to personally confirm the pros and cons of this 1980s' Asian success story.

The world Suu Kyi lived in before 1988 had undergone profound political, cultural and social changes: decolonization reshaped the global order; the USA underwent countercultural revolution; Western Europe redefined itself in a more inclusive way; East Asian 'tigers' started to catch up with the developed countries; China initiated its ground-breaking reforms; the first serious cracks in the Eastern Block appeared and the issues of international justice and responsibility of the international community began to be addressed more seriously. When Suu Kyi entered politics in 1988 the West was no longer afraid of communism as its main ideological rival and after decades of economic growth was entering a period of optimism. The third wave of democratization was on the way and soon would spectacularly reshape Eastern Europe and contribute to the USSR's fall. In 1988 change was already in the air.[34] The subsequent events in the collapsing Eastern Block and the end of South Africa's apartheid contributed further to a triumphant intellectual mood, where democracy seemed the only successful ideology world-wide. Democratic change and progress seemed behind every corner.[35] The strong conviction of being on the right side of history empowered Suu Kyi and helped her in her first steps in politics, yet with time it also became a burden.

Before politics

Before Suu Kyi entered politics, she was a housewife and an aspiring academic. Her academic texts are quite good from the point of view of literary studies[36] and more controversial from the point of view of political science.[37] What is important in these texts is the fact that her overriding theme was not to seek universal aspects binding East and West; despite her admiration for Tagore, she was not a humanist philosopher following in his footsteps. As one critical of Suu Kyi, a former British Ambassador commented:

> she is no great intellectual, and only managed a modest 3rd class degree at Oxford. This intellectual inferiority has stayed with her. She is terrified of being out-argued, which is why she has declined any BBC Hard Talk interview (...) She avoids debate whenever she can. She is in her element when offered the world stage – her address to both Houses of Parliament in the UK and her two BBC Reith Lectures lacked any substance and in parts were sheer bunkum.[38]

Although his remark about Suu Kyi's Oxford degree is a bit petty – history knows many great intellectuals with low grades at school and even more good politicians who were poor political science students – he has a point. Suu Kyi is not a pro-found intellectual and when she tries to act as one, the result is shallow ("there is no hope without endeavour"),[39] infantile ("the person who sees only the worldly materials, has only one eye but the person who tries to achieve both worldly and spiritual goals has both eyes")[40] or worthy of Mao Zedong's "Little Red Book" ("we have to know the right from wrong)".[41] Unsurprisingly, one Burma watcher later concluded that "some of her speeches have the intellectual depth of a Chinese fortune cookie".[42]

Indeed, Suu Kyi's strength lies not in intellectualism but in her eclectic combination of ideas. In her texts one can see an overarching attempt to understand how to successfully adjust Burma to the modern (Western) world and how to blend Burmese Buddhist ideas with Western concepts.[43] Hence she was critical of Burma's heritage not being able to create a "synthesis of East and West", between "the true synthesis of traditional and modern, Burmese and Western"; according to her, the "old ways should be adapted, pruned, revitalized or in some cases even discarded altogether".[44] The reason why the Burmese were unable to do so, and consequently Burma lagged behind the world, was the lack of leadership. Her father started the work but was assassinated. So, she as the successor of Aung San, felt she was destined to lead the people of Burma – to combine the good elements of their tradition with the requirements of the modern world (democracy), so that Burma may finally realize its full potential. The time to fulfil her self-proclaimed destiny came in 1988.

Suu Kyi returned to Burma on 2 April 1988 after 28 years abroad to take care of her ill mother. Quite unexpectedly, she found herself in the eye of the storm. A popular revolt against 26 years of army rule was raging on the streets. Initially, Suu Kyi did not intend to step into politics but eventually she got carried away and took the lead ... or so the narrative goes.

There are many different versions: from "accidental politician"[45] to the call of duty of a national hero's daughter.[46] Common here, quite conveniently for Suu Kyi, is the notion of being somehow forced to enter politics by circumstances; although she did not plan it, she could not have stayed on the sidelines. The current state of knowledge does not allow rejection of this version out of hand. Yet there are reasons to suspect that Suu Kyi had planned on entering politics much earlier.

Politics was always around the corner for Suu Kyi. Her childhood passed in the shadow of her deceased father, the memory of whom was cultivated by her mother.[47] She grew up among the Burmese establishment and must have overheard more than a few conversations led by her politically conscious mother. During her teenage years she took part in Khin Kyi's — then Burma's Ambassador to India – many meetings, both formally and less so. Suu Kyi chose to study political science in Delhi and then again in Oxford, though one may suspect that these decisions were not entirely of her own making – a suspicion further enhanced by her poor grades and failed attempts to change political science into forestry and English literature. During her studies politics was not her calling: she was politically inactive. After graduating she had no heart in assisting Hugh Tinker and Frank Trager, then top political scientists, on Burma. There is no record of her political engagement during her work for the UN in New York. The same can be said about her marriage (marrying a British man was not the best entry into Burmese politics). So, there is solid evidence of her disinterest in politics before 1988.

But there are also traces that disturb this narrative. The first one is Suu Kyi's letter to Michael Aris from the early 1970s, where Suu Kyi wrote "should my people need me, you would help me to do my duty by them"; not a random message, given Aris's comment that "she constantly reminded me that one day she would have to return to Burma".[48] This is not only an unorthodox way of saying to your fiancée that you have second thoughts (a suspicion reinforced by Suu Kyi's displeasure that her husband disclosed this letter in 1991).[49] The second trace is Kyi Maung's interview from 1996 where he surprisingly revealed that Suu Kyi in 1987 sounded him out about an involvement in politics (but he refused to help).[50] Other clues are more circumstantial. Such as Suu Kyi being questioned upon her trips to Burma before 1988 as to whether she had political ambitions by the secret service (according to her own account),[51] by former general Kyaw Zaw[52] and by librarian Myint Swe.[53] Some biographers, too, point to her stay in Japan in the mid-1980s as the turning point in her political awakening.[54] But this is still too little, especially given the counterevidence, such as family friend Peter Carey's testimony: he ridiculed suggestions about Suu Kyi's political plans ("I didn't get the sense that here was somebody plotting in an old Oxford house, like Lenin in Zurich, to get back to Burma in a great political role").[55] Given the current state of knowledge one may not formulate any conclusive statements about Suu Kyi's political plans prior to 1988: one may only ask questions and raise doubts.

What is certain is that in the 1980s Suu Kyi was looking for her place in the world. Her life until then, though not average, did not give her satisfaction: she found herself a mere appendix to her husband and felt professionally unfulfilled. Given her strong conviction of whose daughter she was – which sometimes expressed itself in an unusual way[56] and later led to a sense of mission[57] – politics was certainly an option. A hypothesis may be the following: Suu Kyi was considering entering politics in the 1980s (perhaps earlier) but she waited for a good moment. Before 1988 there was no space for entering politics: the political scene of Burma was cemented by the Tatmadaw – the *ana* of the military had been unquestioned. Besides, her children were too young: she, as Aris hinted, might have imagined "that if a day or reckoning were to come, it would happen later in life, when our children were grown up. But fate and history never seem to work in orderly ways".[58] When Suu Kyi found herself in Burma in April 1988 it might have been earlier than she wanted and planned.

Notes

1 Suu Kyi, "Intellectual life", p. 83.
2 Matthew J. Moore, *Buddhism and Political Theory* (New York, NY: Oxford University Press, 2016), pp. 2–11.
3 Max Weber, *The Religion of India* (Glencoe: The Free Press, 1958), p. 206.
4 Aung San Suu Kyi, "In quest of democracy", p. 171.
5 Stanley Tambiah, "The Buddhist conception of kingship and its historical manifestations: A reply to Spiro", *The Journal of Asian Studies*, vol. 37, no. 4 (1978), p. 807.
6 E.g. *Hārita-jātaka* or *Suvaṇṇakakkaṭa-jātaka*.

7 They temporarily ordained themselves as monks to improve their *kamma* or resolved to the ultimate justification: that their merit acquired via moral acts (such as buildings of pagodas) would outweigh their other immoral action
8 Walton, *Politics in the Moral Universe*, p. 89.
9 *Hārita-jātaka* (no. 431), in: *The Jataka*, Vol. III, Sacred Text.com
10 "Sitagu Sayadaw and justifiable evils in Buddhism", *New Mandala*, 13 November 2017.
11 Walton, *Politics in the Moral Universe*, p. 2–14.
12 Ibid. pp. 2–14, 70–124; Maung Maung Gyi, *Burmese Political Values. The Socio-Political Roots of Authoritarianism* (New York, NY: Praeger, 1983), pp. 17–75, 94–125; Gustaaf Houtman, *Mental Culture in Burmese Crisis Politics: Aung San Suu Kyi and the National League for Democracy* (Tokyo: ILCAA, 1999), pp. 161–180; David Steinberg, *Burma. The State of Myanmar* (Washington, DC: Georgetown University Press, 2001), pp. 38–42.
13 Walton, *Politics in the Moral Universe*, pp. 70–71.
14 Matthew J. Walton, *Buddhism, Politics and Political Thought in Myanmar* (Cambridge: Cambridge University Press, 2017), pp. 96–105.
15 William J. Koenig, *The Burmese Polity, 1752–1819. Politics, Administration, and Social Organization in the Early Kon-baung Period* (Ann Arbor, MI: The University of Michigan, 1990), p. 71.
16 Walton, *Politics in the Moral Universe*, pp. 18, 67, 81, 83, 107.
17 Jordan Winfield, *Buddhism and the State in Burma: English-Language Discourses from 1823 to 1962*, unpublished PhD thesis (University of Melbourne, 2017), pp. 81–213.
18 Stephen McCarthy, *The Political Theory of Tyranny in Singapore and Burma: Aristotle and the Rhetoric of Benevolent Despotism* (New York, NY: Routledge, 2006), pp. 154–185.
19 Zöllner and Ebbighausen, *The Daughter*, p. 51.
20 Arnold Ludwig, *King of the Mountain. The Nature of Political Leadership* (Lexington, KY: University Press, 2002), p. 22.
21 Harriden, *Authority of Influence*, pp. 210–211.
22 Ma Than E, "The flowering of the spirit", in: *Freedom from Fear*, p. 280. Suu Kyi once said that Aung San was her "first and best love", *Desert Islands Disc Aung San Suu Kyi*, BBC, 1 February 2013.
23 As former British Ambassador Derek Tonkin commented, she believes she was born to rule, email correspondence, 9 September 2019.
24 See e.g. Craig J. Reynolds, "A New Look at Old Southeast Asia", *The Journal of Asian Studies*, vol. 54, no. 2 (1995), pp. 419–446.
25 Thant Myint-U, *The Making of Modern Burma* (Cambridge: Cambridge University Press, 2007) pp. 24–185.
26 Thongchai Winichakul, *Siam Mapped. A History of a Geo-Body of a Nation* (Honolulu: University of Hawaii Press, 1997), pp. 4–5, 169.
27 Conversation with Anna Zongollowicz, Paris, 19 September 2019.
28 Suu Kyi, "Freedom from fear", in: *Freedom from Fear and Other Writings*, p. 183.
29 Clements, *The Voice of Hope*, pp. 44 and 99.
30 Aung San Suu Kyi, "A letter to Michael Aris", in: *Freedom from Fear and Other Writings*, p. 218.
31 Suu Kyi, "Intellectual life", pp. 133–134.
32 A good example of Suu Kyi's hybridity is her choice of items she would take on a desert island, *Desert Island, Aung San Suu Kyi*. Another example of her hybrid heritage may be her favourite literature heroes, Sengupta, *The Female Voice of Myanmar*, pp. 255–256.
33 "Speech on Sunday, 4 February, 1996", in: *Daw Suu's 25 Dialogues with the People 1995–1996*, ed. H.-B. Zöllner (Hamburg and Yangon: Abera Verlag, 2014), p. 358.
34 Best remarked on a year later by Fukuyama. Francis Fukuyama, "The end of history?" *The National Interest*, vol. 16 (1989), pp. 3–18.
35 Perhaps the fact that Burma, unlike Eastern Europe, did not democratise and fell behind "the third wave of democratization" contributed in a way to a greater interest in Burma in the West. Maybe this bigger interest was driven by question: why it did not work out there?

36 E.g. her pieces, "Literature and nationalism in Burma" and "Intellectual life", in: *Freedom from Fear and Other Writings*, pp. 82–167.
37 Robert H. Taylor, *The State in Myanmar* (Singapore: Singapore University Press, 2009), pp. 411–413.
38 Derek Tonkin, email correspondence, 9 September 2019.
39 "The lady abroad", *Time*, 1 June 2012.
40 *Aung San Suu Kyi's Speech, Sunday, 10 March 1996 (no. 22)*, in: *Daw Suu's 25 Dialogues with the People 1995–1996*, transl. Ko Ko Thet, Frankie Tun, ed. H.-B. Zöllner (Hamburg and Yangon: Abera Verlag, 2014), p. 490.
41 *Aung San Suu Kyi's Speech, Saturday, 2 March 1996 (no. 20)*, in: Ibid., p. 465. To compare with Mao's profound thought: "We should never pretend to know what we do not know".
42 Quoted in: "Aung San Suu Kyi's Fall", *McLean's* 7 January 2014,
43 Zöllner and Ebbighausen, *The Daughter*, p. 68.
44 Suu Kyi, "Intellectual life", pp. 108, 112, 115, 121 and 133–135.
45 "Rangoon Journal; A daughter of Burma, but can she be a symbol?", *The New York Times*, 11 January1989.
46 Aung San Suu Kyi, "Speech to a mass rally at the Shwedagon Pagoda", in: *Freedom from Fear*, p. 193.
47 The role of Suu Kyi's mother, Khin Kyi, in making Suu Kyi a politician is crucial yet overlooked: it was Khin Kyi who installed the values of discipline into her daughter and it was via Khin Kyi that Suu Kyi learned about her father, "The mother who was overlooked," *The Irrawaddy*, 3 October 2013; Zöllner and Ebbighausen, *The Daughter*, pp. 60–62.
48 Michael Aris, "Introduction", in: *Freedom from Fear*, p. xix.
49 Victor, *The Lady*, p. 125.
50 Clements, *The Voice of Hope*, p. 236.
51 Aung San Suu Kyi, "In the eye of the revolution", in: *Freedom from Fear*, p. 206.
52 Popham, *The Lady and the Peacock*, p. 230.
53 Ibid., p. 414; Wintle, *Perfect Hostage*, p. 214.
54 Popham, *The Lady and the Peacock*, pp. 238–241.
55 Quoted in: "Dark victory in Burma," *Vogue Magazine*, Oct. 1995, Online Burma Library.
56 If Michael Aung-Thwin is to be trusted, Suu Kyi tried to show his 7-year-old daughter how famous Aung San was by showing her a Burmese coin with his face on it, "Interview with Professor Michael Aung-Thwin", *New Mandala*, 28 November 2007.
57 Maung Maung, *The 1988 Uprising in Burma*, Monograph no. 49 (New Haven, CT: Yale SE Asian Studies, 1999), pp. 270–273. Martin Morland, British Ambassador to Burma said Suu Kyi already "had a sense of mission" when she married Aris, quoted in Pederson, *Burma Spring*, p. 163.
58 Aris, "Introduction", in: *Freedom from Fear*, p. xx.

2

THE KAIROS MOMENT

Kairos, Zeus' youngest son, is a little known yet important figure in Greek mythology. He is the god of used opportunities and wasted chances. When Kairos appears on someone's path, the passer-by has only moments to catch him. But if Kairos escapes, there is no hope to get him. Once in Burma, Suu Kyi realized – consciously or not – that this was her 'Kairos moment': the short-term political window of opportunity.

The 'Kairos moment' did not materialize instantly upon her arrival on 2 April 1988. Sources say (and there is no reason to disbelieve them), that initially all Suu Kyi did was take care of her ill mother; first at a hospital and then, from 8 July, at home. The anti-regime protests had already started and Suu Kyi was paying attention to them from the sidelines, but the turning point probably came on 23 July. Ne Win, at the hurriedly called Congress of the BSPP, realizing that the protests had significantly weakened the position of the army, unexpectedly resigned from his position and called for a referendum on reintroducing a multi-party system. He most likely made a calculated concession but, if so, he miscalculated badly. By resigning, Ne Win not only united the protestors (a short-term euphoria followed – nothing delights people more than a dictator's fall) but he also created a political vacuum. Most importantly, however, he showed weakness. And in Burmese political tradition, a sign of a ruler's weakness automatically leads to his de-legitimization and to the emergence of *minlaungs* – contenders to the throne.

"I can still remember watching with Suu the scene (of Ne Win's resignation) in the congress as it was shown on state television" – recalled her husband –

> She, like the whole country, was electrified ... . I think it was at this moment more than any other that Suu made up her mind to step forward. However, the idea had gradually taken shape in her mind during the previous fifteen weeks.[1]

Prior to this moment, the political scene in Burma had been constricted, so any thoughts Suu Kyi may have had to enter politics were merely in the sphere of fantasy. Now the impossible became possible.

A cautious beginner

We do not know for certain why Suu Kyi decided to enter politics. A sense of mission mixed with a search for her own place in life and seizing the opportune moment seem to be the most probable explanations.[2] Whatever the reason, once Suu Kyi made the decision, her steps became rational and calculated moves to increase her political options. Contrary to the popular belief that Suu Kyi – seeing mass protests against the military regime – took the lead and became the unquestioned leader of the democratic opposition (she herself contributed to this image),[3] she initially waited and weighed her options. Between the probable decision of entering politics (23 July 1988) and her breakthrough speech at Shwedagon Pagoda (26 August 1988), she waited and refused to join the protests. This was despite the fact that many people placed high hopes on her. The protestors, who demonstrated on the street holding pictures of Aung San, were looking for a leader. In accordance with 'karmic' logic, Aung San's children were the obvious first choice. When Suu Kyi's brother Aung San Oo proved to be a hopeless option, protestors turned to Suu Kyi. Political pilgrims began flocking to her house at University Road 54. Lawyers, doctors, students, journalists, retired politicians and random protesters started calling her house and persuading her to join the protests. Soon Suu Kyi's house became "the main centre of political activity in the country".[4]

Yet Suu Kyi was cautious: "she was no fool, she waited and studied".[5] Initially she did not back the protestors other than "morally",[6] which frustrated some protesting students. Suu Kyi declared that she wanted to remain neutral; to mediate between the regime and the protesters.[7] That is why her first political action was a letter sent on 15 August to the military regime where she proposed to set up a People's Consultative Committee in accordance with the 1974 Constitution.[8] The letter suggested mediations between the regime and protesters. Such an action proves that Suu Kyi entered politics wisely through positioning herself as a mediator between the army and demonstrating students. Unfortunately, the regime was not interested in maintaining a dialogue and her request was initially ignored.[9] So, too, was her request for a private meeting with Ne Win and, to make matters worse, she was informally warned by the regime not to engage in politics.[10] Only then, in an attempt to force the generals to negotiate, did Suu Kyi turn to opposition. It was a rational decision: if the regime rejected her proposals, the only chance to remain in the political game was to jump on the bandwagon with the protests.

Initially Suu Kyi did this without burning bridges. Before her first public speech, she secretly met justice minister Tin Aung Htein and via him asked Ne Win for approval on her planned first public speech (making speeches was officially illegal due to the martial law), ensuring the dictator that she had "no political aspirations" or "hidden agenda". Tin Aung Htein advised her not to mention Ne Win in public and not to criticize him. When Suu Kyi agreed, martial law was lifted the day before her speech.[11] This fact sheds light on her method of political action. It shows, too, that from the very beginning she was playing behind-the-scenes games with the regime instead of becoming an all-out dissident.

Suu Kyi's maiden speech took place on 24 August 1988 in front of the General Hospital: she was precise and to the point. She confirmed rumours about her political involvement, expressed her hope of transition to a democratic system and invited everyone to listen to her new speech at Shwedagon Pagoda two days later. This was a good move: she invoked interest and curiosity among the public. But she also pushed the limits of her unwritten agreement with the regime. During her talks with Tin Aung Htein, Suu Kyi had informed him about one speech only – near the hospital – not a new one, let alone a speech at the Shwedagon which, with its profound politico-religious symbolism, was in an entirely different category. Ne Win might have felt that Suu Kyi had broken the rules. On the other hand, Suu Kyi had to show the regime that she needed to be reckoned with. The army responded to it with its boorish style by producing racist anti-Suu Kyi leaflets, which explored her political weak point: marriage to a foreigner.[12] Although the regime agents were caught (a terrible incompetence of Military Intelligence!) before they distributed their brochures on 26 August, that very fact showed the way Khin Nyunt's secret service worked. This was the first warning. A warning that the regime would fire back and not hesitate to use underhand tactics. By then, however, it was much more important for Suu Kyi to give a good speech. Apart from the short hospital introduction, she had had no public experience and there were doubts whether her Burmese would be good enough after almost three decades outside of Burma.[13] Yet this did not discourage the crowds that gathered at the bottom of Shwedagon. Around half a million curious people arrived to see Aung San's daughter.[14] Under this 'show-style' first major appearance, under her father's painted picture and Dobama's fighting peacock flag, she burst onto the national political stage.

The Shwedagon speech

At Shwedagon, Suu Kyi made her first and perhaps most important rally speech. Speaking spontaneously without notes, in fluent Burmese, she convincingly put her point across. Suu Kyi presented impressive rhetoric skills: she started her speech by greeting the monks, then asked for a minute of silence in memory of students killed and smoothly rejected accusations of not being patriotic enough due to her living abroad and marrying a foreigner.[15] Her greatest moment was playing the 'Aung San' card. Initially when Suu Kyi entered politics she had only her name, but she used this asset in a politically brilliant way. She evoked her father's words about different kinds of politics and noting that her father had rejected 'power politics', so did she. So why did she change her mind to pursue a political path? "The answer is that the present crisis is the concern of the entire nation. I could not as my father's daughter remain indifferent to all that was going on. This national crisis could in fact be called the second struggle for national independence".[16] In other words, Suu Kyi did not reject politics per se, but only one kind of politics – power politics – which her father apparently had dismissed too. Considering Aung San's actions (not words) – this was Suu Kyi's eristic at its finest.[17] It allowed Suu Kyi to smoothly justify her previous absence in politics (suggesting the regime was conducting dirty politics) and her current involvement (by claiming to follow Aung San's good politics). This eristic argument explained and justified Suu Kyi's entry into politics: she was forced to step into politics by dire political circumstances to finish her father's job. The "second national independence" argument was far-fetched at best – Aung San founded the Tatmadaw and the analogy between the British rule and the rule of the army was "spurious"[18] – but by this convenient interpretation of Aung San's heritage, Suu Kyi had stolen the army's legitimacy. She delegitimized the Tatmadaw's rule and placed herself as the rightful 'heir' to the throne. Although there had certainly been personal reasons for Suu Kyi's attitude, what matters here is that Suu Kyi had skilfully used her father in her political career, de facto monopolizing the memory of Aung San. Initially Aung San was the only card Suu Kyi had while entering politics, but she made the best use of this asset making it her trump card in Burmese politics. This is how a "second struggle for national independence" became Suu Kyi's political *raison d'être*. Now the time came to fulfil her theoretical thoughts. Burma had been unable to match the good elements of its tradition with Western ideas, and lagged behind the world. Aung San had realized this and tried to fix it, but did not manage to. His successors failed too. Now it was Suu Kyi's task to do it. She believed that the means to achieve "a synthesis of East and West"[19] is through democracy. This is what makes Suu Kyi a hybrid politician. She borrowed "democracy" (alongside with "discipline", "unity", "sacrifice" etc.)[20] from her father's speeches, but poured her own meaning into these concepts. From then on, she presented democracy in her unique, eclectic way, which combines populism, sloganeering, moral phraseology, a shortage of details and a deep conviction that only democracy allows economic development as well as an utopian belief that democracy would heal all the problems of Burma. Such an idea of democracy would become enormously popular as it exemplified everything the military government was not.[21] Democracy understood in that way would become a unifying slogan. The Shwedagon speech was Suu Kyi's first victorious battle in a political struggle to secure legitimacy built on Aung San. By playing with the public's emotions, juggling facts and interpreting history in accordance with her political needs, Suu Kyi proved that she was a natural born politician.

Moreover, she was a politician who, being conscious of the negative social connotations of this profession, from the very beginning tried to manoeuvre herself into a position above politics: that of a national leader forced to step in due to extraordinary circumstances. Later, she developed this line when telling the press that "a life in politics holds no attraction for me. At the moment I serve as a kind of unifying force because of my father's name and because I am not interested in jostling for any kind of position".[22] These words had little to do with reality. In August/September 1988, Suu Kyi was only one of three (or four, if Nu is counted) major opposition figures, along with Tin Oo and Aung Gyi, but she was hardly the unifying force. However, these words must be read as a statement of intent rather than as an analysis of a real political situation. They prove that, from the very beginning, Suu Kyi politically understood that words create worlds.

The rest of the Shwedagon speech is less exhilarating, but equally meaningful. Emphasizing "unity and discipline" she deplored "dissension" between the people and the army and reminded them that her father founded the army. The Tatmadaw should have been "a force having the honour and respect of the people", otherwise the army would have been built in vain. That is why not only did she feel a "strong attachment for the armed forces" (this is the first time Suu Kyi declared her love to the army in public!), but she also appealed to the people "not to lose their affection for the army".[23] These seemingly unintelligible words – in light of recent massacres enacted by the army – should not come as a surprise. They prove Suu Kyi's correct political assessment: she must have been conscious that her success depended not only on popular support but on influencing army ranks as well. Most probably, contrary to her declarations about the need for unity, she gambled on a split within the army, hoping for the defiance of ordinary soldiers against the commandership. It seems that she was following de Talleyrand's remarks of: "speech was given to man to conceal his thoughts". To achieve her goal, she needed to remind soldiers who the founder of the army was; to make them understand that Aung San's successors misused his ideas for their own, personal purposes.

If, most likely, hope for disunity within the Tatmadaw was Suu Kyi's hidden agenda, then escalating political demands was her public policy. This is clearly seen at the end of the Shwedagon speech and in her subsequent interviews. Suu Kyi rejected the idea of both Ne Win's and Maung Maung's promised referendum about multiparty democracy.[24] But this was just the beginning … an interim government was required to "put the country back on an even keel".[25] This was a clear attempt to push further than forcing more concessions from the Maung Maung government.[26] It was a bid to make it surrender to public pressure and dissolve. This was a bridge too far: Suu Kyi would soon realize that she was powerless to achieve this. So far, however, she was triumphant. The Shwedagon speech was her major success. In her (almost) debut speech, she had won the hearts and minds of the people and transformed herself from a random child of a famous father into a serious political contender.

Approaching climax

The time was good for Suu Kyi, but not for Burma. The initially joyful revolution was turning into an anarchy, with revenge becoming prevalent ("beheadings became an almost daily occurrence") – Suu Kyi tried to prevent lynchings, but was not successful.[27] This shows she did not control the opposition movement. Nobody did – the lack of central leadership was the 8888 revolution's biggest weakness. Aung Gyi, Tin Oo, Suu Kyi and Nu had no vision or plan; instead they quarrelled for leadership. The reformist regime under Maung Maung was ready to make concessions, but only up to a certain point. This was the bone of contention. The regime agreed to organize general elections within three months, but the opposition, backed by mass protests raging on the streets, demanded an interim government (Nu even announced his government, but others, including Suu Kyi, disagreed with him). Mistrust ran high. The regime established an electoral commission, yet this was rejected by the opposition – nullifying the chance for compromise. Maung Maung in his later memoirs criticised those politicians who "roused excited people to frenzy" and added "fuel to fire", most likely having Suu Kyi in mind.[28] Seen from this point of view, because of their escalating demands the opposition lost its chance to strike a deal with the reformists within the regime when it was on the table. However, forcing concessions on the regime had proved to be a winning strategy till this point, so they possibly felt that they had good reasons to continue to do so.

The opposition had the street's support, but not that of the army. Despite some defections, the core of the Tatmadaw remained loyal: "any high ranking army officer who had taken an armed infantry unit into the capital and declared his support for the uprising, would have become a national hero immediately, and the tables would have been turned".[29] But none did. There are reasons to believe Suu Kyi understood the key importance of the army well. On 12 September, she explicitly stated that "the role of the army in Burma in crucial".[30] A comparison of her statements from 15 August till 13 September shows her growing criticism of the armed forces and diminishing hope for achieving a satisfactory settlement. She moved from refraining from criticism (15 August), by reminding who founded the army and why (26 August), to warning "my father said the army should keep out of politics and I support that view totally" (29 August) and dotting the "i" by saying that "Aung San gave many warnings against the army turning into a tyrannical force of oppression" (13 September).[31] For comparison, during her Shwedagon speech, she quoted her father's single warning about the army going astray. Now this had been replaced with the message that Aung San had given 'many warnings' about it. It was almost an open call to soldiers to rebel against their leaders. Suu Kyi was clearly gambling on a split within the army. Finally, on 13 September, she crossed the Rubicon by declaring that the "creation of a neutral" interim government could only happen "if Ne Win were exiled first" from Burma.[32]

This not only shows how far Suu Kyi had come within just one month – from negotiating with the regime to calling for expulsion of the former dictator. More importantly, if so far Suu Kyi had behaved wisely and consciously, now she made her first major political mistake. Theoretically speaking, in developing countries, where power, privileges and survival of the regime are intertwined, preserving the regime becomes a paramount necessity. When losing power often means losing not only privileges or property, but even one's freedom or life, the stakes of the political game rise dramatically. Suu Kyi, a hybrid politician socialized in a Western democratic political culture, may not have understood this sentiment adequately.

The events were reaching their climax. On 13 September, the triumvirate of Aung–Suu–Tin rejected the regime electoral commission and on the next day they demanded an interim government, later setting 19 September as the date of its appointment. Meanwhile, incidents on the streets intensified, with attacks on state institutions (e.g. bank, town hall), riots and an aborted attempt to lay siege to army headquarters; in short "the situation was getting out of hand".[33] Whether the chaos and the degeneration of the protest movement was autogenous or Tatmadaw-inspired (the latter interpretation was propagated by Suu Kyi)[34] is not that important here. Until the very end (even on the day of the coup), negotiations took place between the regime's reformists and the opposition, but the Tatmadaw's coup on 18 September turned the tables. The army mercilessly restored its power.

Could Aung San Suu Kyi have done more? Did she have a chance to take over power? Contrary to her many declarations from that period, she was quite politically weak at that time: she neither united the movement nor controlled it. Having little assets, she skilfully used the major one: her descent and added personal charisma. Not having the army's support (Suu Kyi tried to divide the army in vain – it was the ranks' loyalty that contributed to the Tatmadaw's victory), she used the escalation of demands – a reasonable tactic in these circumstances. On reflection, she could have called for an uprising, but it is probable that she would have ended up just like Nu in 1969: i.e. marginalized. So, peaceful escalation was her best option, albeit insufficient. Perhaps she could have been a little bit more conciliatory towards the reformists within the regime and could have resorted to behind-the-scenes deals with Maung Maung and other soft liners. But they had ignored her once and could have sidelined her in the future. All in all, her political debut performance was acceptable, despite its negative final outcome. It has to be remembered that barely a month and half before, she had been a political nobody. Now, she had skilfully used the window of opportunity created by extraordinary circumstances to enter politics. And after more than 20 years of searching for her own place in life, she found her calling: to finish the job that (she thought) her father set out to do.

Notes

1 Aris, "Introduction", in: *Freedom from Fear*, p. xx.
2 Clements, *The Voice of Hope*, p. 165; Maung Maung, *The 1988 Uprising*, pp. 270–271.
3 Aung San Suu Kyi, "In the eye of the revolution", in: *Freedom from Fear*, p. 206.
4 Aris, "Introduction", p. xx.
5 Maung Maung, *The 1988 Uprising*, p. 273.
6 Clements, *The Voice of Hope*, p. 135.
7 Zöllner, *The Beast and the Beauty*, p. 34.
8 Aung San Suu Kyi, "The first initiative", in: *Freedom from Fear*, p. 191.
9 Bertil Lintner, *Outrage. Burma's Struggle for Democracy* (London: White Lotus, 1990), p. 113.
10 Aung Zaw, *The Face of Resistance*, p. 12; Maung Maung, *The 1988 Uprising*, pp. 273–274.
11 Popham, *The Lady and the Peacock*, p. 51. Crediting Suu Kyi for lifting the martial law may be overestimated.

12 Lintner, *Outrage*, p. 121.
13 According to some sources she remastered her native language upon returning back home, email communication with Derek Tonkin, 9 September 2019.
14 Lintner, *Outrage*, p. 115.
15 Aung San Suu Kyi, "Speech to a mass rally at the Shwedagon Pagoda", in: *Freedom from Fear*, p. 193.
16 Ibid., p. 193.
17 Aung San rejected power politics in words, not in actions: he was a Machiavellian politician for whom the goal (Burma's independence) justified any means. Suu Kyi must have known that, but she manipulated his legacy to serve her political goals or was blinded by her love towards her father.
18 Taylor, *The State in Myanmar*, p. 404.
19 Suu Kyi, "Intellectual life", in: *Freedom from Fear*, pp. 108–135.
20 Zöllner and Ebbighausen, *The Daughter*, p. 71.
21 Zöllner, *The Beauty and the Beast*, pp. 32–34.
22 Aung San Suu Kyi, "The objectives", in: *Freedom from Fear*, p. 201.
23 Suu Kyi, "Speech to a mass rally", p. 195.
24 Ibid., p. 197.
25 Suu Kyi, "The objectives", p. 201.
26 Maung Maung was a distinguished Burmese intellectual and a lawyer who supported the military regime. Once Ne Win's direct successor, Sein Lwin, a hardliner with much blood on his hands, resigned on 12 August, Maung Maung was nominated the president on 19 August as the moderate voice of the regime (his nomination signified change the tactics from stick to carrot). Widely considered a puppet for his weak position within the regime, Maung Maung nevertheless tried to reach a compromise between the army and the protestors.
27 Lintner, *Outrage*, p. 121.
28 Maung Maung, *The 1988 Uprising*, pp. 87, 187.
29 Lintner, *Outrage*, p. 127.
30 Suu Kyi, "In the eye of the revolution", p. 205.
31 Suu Kyi, "The objectives", p. 202; Suu Kyi, "In the eye of the revolution", p. 205.
32 Quoted in: Michael W. Charney, *A History of Modern Burma* (Cambridge: Cambridge University Press, 2009), p. 158.
33 Lintner, *Outrage*, p. 128.
34 Suu Kyi, "In the eye of the revolution", p. 204.

3

THE LIONESS

The post-coup period proved decisive for Aung San Suu Kyi's political life. By 18 September 1988, Suu Kyi had become recognizable. However, she was still not a national leader, just one of several *minlaungs*. Only after the coup, Suu Kyi's time had come.

Party politicking

Having staged a coup and massacred protestors, the generals announced their intentions to restore law and order (hence the name of the junta: State Law and Order Restoration Council, or SLORC). They proclaimed their hope to secure the well-being of the country and – in a response to domestic and international criticism – declared their intentions to hold democratic elections. Internal security coupled with regime survival became a predominant issue for the junta. Consequently, repressions against student leaders soon followed, though initially the SLORC left the most famous dissidents, Suu Kyi included, alone. Just after the coup Suu Kyi behaved in a conciliatory way too. Instead of criticizing and condemning the coup, she tried to resume negotiations. Her first move was to write a "politely worded" request for dialogue to general Saw Maung, the nominal chief of the SLORC, receiving a "vague promise of talks" in return.[1] Only when she was de facto ignored did she condemn the massacre and send letters to Amnesty International, the United Nations and foreign ambassadors with requests for help.[2] These actions mark the end of the 'conciliatory' period and the beginning of her balancing tactics against the generals. But all bridges were not yet burned.

At the same time, the junta allowed for the formation of political parties (21 September) and reiterated its will to hold free and fair elections (23 September). In the limited political space in post-coup Burma, this gave Suu Kyi and other dissidents room for manoeuvre and a reason not to be too confrontational towards the junta. From then onwards, the opposition faced an irreconcilable, structural predicament: the military was both the political contender and the organizer of multiparty elections that were a means to achieve regime change. Initially, given lack of better options, they decided to accept the conditions dictated by the SLORC. For Suu Kyi it required a modification of previous declarations. Barely a month before Suu Kyi had declared her disinterest in party life,[3] now she changed her mind and on 24 September, along with Aung Gyi and Tin Oo, co-founded the National Democratic United League (NDUL), renamed the National League for Democracy (NLD) three days later; Aung Gyi became the chairman, Tin Oo his deputy while Suu Kyi took up the position of secretary general. This showed Suu Kyi's real political position at that time.

From the very beginning the NLD was not a properly organized political party but rather a beneficiary of the "spontaneous mass movement for democracy", with chaotic organization, a lack of control over regional branches and no ideological blueprint.[4] These issues, however, were not necessarily disadvantages. The NLD soon became a mass party that capitalized on social protest against the military establishment. If energy and zeal were its assets, then its inability to formulate constructive propositions was the NLD's biggest failure. Simply put, the NLD lacked (and probably still lacks) ideas on how to rebuild Burma. The NLD's first programme, accepted during the founding meeting, was full of platitudes ("importance of free enterprise"), melodramatic assessments ("misfortune verging on the tragic") and universally accurate postulates ("we must seek solution to the problems") without any specifics.[5] Very little changed after a year of functioning when the NLD announced its manifesto. Indeed, the NLD from the very beginning was "a broad coalition" of people disenchanted with Ne Win, deeply "divided by factionalism",[6] which was so bad that "the party could have split into different groups".[7] The founding of the party took place at Aung Gyi's s house after "heated discussions" between various factions.[8] Of these, there were at least three major ones, corresponding with the leading triumvirate: Aung Gyi's faction (mostly his business associates, many with a military past, e.g. Kyi Maung); Tin Oo's 'ex-commander group' (former military men such as U Lwin or Aung Shwe); and Suu Kyi's intelligentsia wing (students and intellectuals such as Win Tin, Myint Myint Khi, Aung Lwin, Khin Maung Swe, Tin Myo Win, Maung Thaw Ka and others). Each faction had different interests and strategies.[9] The majority of the NLD's Central Committee (CC) and its Executive Committee (CEC) consisted of persons from Aung Gyi and Tin Oo's factions.[10] Distrust and tensions between civilians and ex-military men, and between young and old members of the party, ran high. The first major clash commenced between Aung Gyi and Suu Kyi as early as late November 1988, barely two months after the NLD's founding. Various reasons for this altercation were cited: from different organizational and leadership styles, social background and life choices to disagreements about political strategy and direction of actions. Mutual personal dislike, however, seems the major one. The conflict boiled under the surface and finally erupted on 25 November when Aung Gyi accused several members of the CC of being crypto communists and demanded their expulsion. Suu Kyi fired back: on 3 December she called for extraordinary voting and won this dramatic contention.[11] A war of words followed and after his defeat Aung Gyi was either expelled from the party or resigned by himself.[12] Suu Kyi emerged victorious from this debut power struggle within the party (and, if Aung Gyi's accusations were true, she executed her first successful purge). She won thanks to her newly formed alliance with Tin Oo, who despite being a former general like Aung Gyi, backed her, not him.[13] In return, Tin Oo seized chairmanship of the party (Suu Kyi became the vice), which set the NLD's functioning mode for the next two decades, with Tin Oo as the nominal leader and Suu Kyi as the de facto one – a symbol of the party. Despite initial tensions between Tin Oo and Suu Kyi, with time Tin Oo accepted her de facto leadership (and his real function as her first deputy), believing that only Aung San's daughter could secure victory. Other party members followed suit. Among them was Kyi Maung, another former officer (an ex colonel), who remembered 'the first national liberation'. Now he believed in 'the second one', despite his initial reservations about Suu Kyi. Kyi Maung was the only Aung Gyi supporter who stayed in the party by switching sides during the dramatic vote on 3 December 1988. He mastered the most important skill in a politician's life: knowing the right moment to betray – joining the Suu–Tin camp and thus becoming one of the most important party leaders. Other significant members of the ex-commander's group were Aung Shwe (former Ambassador to Australia, Egypt and France) and U Lwin (the NLD's treasurer and former deputy prime minister and finance minister under Burma Socialist Programme Party or BSPP). All those ex-military men supported Suu Kyi, whose de facto leadership was secured in spring 1989.

Yet, interfactional tensions remained high. The divisions ran along the lines of age (students vs. elder members) and previous membership in the army. In the first situation, Suu Kyi backed the students, who gained control of her daily schedule and cut many people from access to her, creating resentments that led some members to quit.[14] The more serious factional tension was, however, between the intellectuals and ex-commanders. The former, backed by students, envisioned a more assertive policy towards the regime and neither liked nor trusted the latter for their past role in the military government, suspecting them of playing both sides by informing the SLORC of the party's intentions and actions. In turn, the ex-commanders were unwilling and unable to proceed to all-out confrontation with their ex-mother institution and understood that successful transition required a modus operandi with the military. Suu Kyi was initially balancing these elements within the party, understanding that the party was in a 'double bind': the NLD depended on the government for organizing some kind of general framework in which a democracy could be achieved; on the other hand, the party could not afford to disappoint the people who supported it and demanded change.[15]

Eventually, around spring/summer of 1989, when relations with the SLORC turned sour, Suu Kyi distanced herself from the ex-commanders and sided with the radical wing which ensured their dominance within the party.[16] Suu Kyi allied herself with people like Win Tin, a veteran journalist.[17] During the Ne Win period, Win Tin was the voice of what is called the 'legal opposition' in autocratic countries. It was allegedly Win Tin who introduced Suu Kyi to Henry David Thoreau's civil disobedience ideas – which fitted very well with her hybrid identity – and, since December 1988, it was he who had masterminded the NLD's confrontational tactics towards the regime.[18] As Suu Kyi has conceded, she finally realised, probably in early 1989, that the generals were not going to negotiate, and she embarked on a long journey to force them to make concessions. If she couldn't make a deal with them, she needed to challenge them. And so she started her 'lioness' tactics.

Non-violence

When Suu Kyi co-founded the NLD, she had one major political asset: lineage. Now she started working hard to gain another: popular support. She became an accessible politician.[19] Her hybrid background helped her understand a novelty in Burma: that a voter met in person is more likely to support you on the ballot. She understood, too, that Rangoon was not enough: in rural countries, one wins elections in the countryside. Hence, she made another out-of-the box move: she started her campaign trail out there, in provincial Burma.

Suu Kyi started campaigning on 30 October 1988. She visited regional NLD members, opened new branches of the party and held public meetings with local people. Everywhere she went, she was given a superstar welcome, with flowers, perfumes and standing ovations. People rushed to see Aung San's daughter and were not disappointed. She became "the continuation of a legend"; postcolonial Burma's myth was that if Aung San had not been killed, everything would have been perfect, so now people began to believe "that the story could be replayed, this time with a happy ending".[20] It was even easier given the fact that she resembled her father physically and emulated his behaviour, way of speaking and PR methods – for many, she was his reincarnation. A beautiful one at that: during the campaign Suu Kyi developed her unique style of dress, with flowers in her hair and traditional clothes becoming the trademarks of her public appearances. But it was not only public relations – she had something to say; a stark contrast to the dreadful speeches made by the generals. During the campaign of 1988/1989, she spoke more than a thousand times, quoting her father; introducing little known concepts of democracy or human rights in an attractive way; emphasizing the importance of unity, discipline and responsibility; and warning about factionalism and militarism.[21] Suu Kyi often mentioned more trivial matters such as the importance of reading books or not shouting at one's children.[22] Apparently, being personally affected by some Burmese vices,[23] she embarked "on a movement or crusade to transform the 'Burmese mentality'" since, according to Suu Kyi, it was "rooted in an authoritarian past" that made dictatorship possible. Conversely, by changing the hierarchical patterns of Burmese culture, she hoped to give dawn to democracy.[24] For people who had been forced to listen to authorities for decades, she and her message represented something new and fresh. Step by step her prestige grew; day by day she became the most popular politician in the country. She sensed the universal need for change in Burma and made good use of it: for so many she became the one who could lead the country out of turmoil.

In widening her supporter-base, Suu Kyi made another brilliant, unexpected move in early 1989: she reached out to ethnic minorities by touring Shan state (February) and Kachin state (April). By wearing ethnic clothes, she won their hearts and minds. From then on, ethnic minority people would place their hopes on Suu Kyi: these illusions would last long, very long. Unfortunately, the ethnic minorities did not know that apparently in private Suu Kyi remarked that she looked silly in ethnic clothes.[25] They did not read her international interviews where she admitted she had little idea about ethnic minorities[26]; did not know about the NLD's programme on ethnic issues, which kept the privileged status of Bamars; and overlooked the NLD's hegemonic approach towards smaller ethnic parties.[27] Most importantly, ethnic minorities did not listen carefully to Suu Kyi's speeches, where she clearly expressed ideas that could be summarized in one sentence: democracy first and then she would consider their demands.[28] All what mattered was that Suu Kyi became the first Bamar politician in decades who had seriously noticed them and approached them. For them, her actions spoke louder than thousands of words. Thanks to this unexpected move, Suu Kyi was becoming a truly national leader.

And one recognized internationally. Suu Kyi with her hybrid heritage, quickly understood, as probably the only Burmese politician who did at that time, the power of international media. She knew how to handle Western journalists. Either genuinely or out of calculation,[29] she charmed them with her class, erudition and upper-class 'Englishness'.

Initially sceptic journalists, within just a few months, 'fell in love' with Suu Kyi.[30] Contrary to most other dissidents, not to mention military leaders, she spoke impeccable English and made use of shared cultural codes. That is why, when Suu Kyi spoke about democracy, human rights and non-violence, she seemed to share their value system (at least they thought so). This is how a great intellectual romance between the Western media and Suu Kyi began. For more than two decades (too) many journalists had listened to her as to an oracle and acted accordingly as her unconscious, unpaid PR. Suu Kyi became their connection between Burma and the world. It proved priceless for her political career.

Initially the regime turned a blind eye to the fact that the NLD's public gatherings breached the provisions of martial law (and other SLORC declarations). Perhaps it was the magic of her name or maybe the generals underestimated her, hoping that her popularity would eventually wane. Whatever reason, the generals initially did not disperse the NLD's gatherings. They even liberalized conditions of martial law, yet they were deaf to her calls for cancelling Order 2/88 prohibiting public gatherings. In accordance with this law her meetings were, technically speaking, illegal – only the SLORC's goodwill enabled them to continue. With her growing popularity, this tolerance began to shrink: the generals started perceiving her as a threat and became more assertive. By the end of 1988, first warnings were issued, and minor repressions followed: disturbance of meetings, arrests of NLD members, prohibition of the NLD 'fighting peacock' signs and negative PR targeted personally at Suu Kyi. To that Suu Kyi responded brilliantly, by introducing novel (or forgotten) tactics into Burmese political life: non-violence.

This was hybrid policy par excellence, one which encapsulated Suu Kyi's own hybrid heritage. It was foreign-inspired, yet mixed with local traditions (particularly of the monks U Ottama and U Wisara). It was appealing to the world and acceptable to the Burmese. For a moment, it made a difference: this was Suu Kyi's way to escape from the SLORC's trap. The junta promised elections but did not allow an electoral campaign to be conducted. The generals wanted to control the process and were unwilling to share power. That is why they kept the provisions of martial law such as curfew or prohibition of public gatherings which, if respected, would turn an electoral campaign into a series of intellectual discussions confined to private houses and party offices. Suu Kyi, an actor much weaker politically, had to play along with the rules set by the military while, at the same time she had to challenge the structural advantages of the SLORC, manoeuvre herself a political space and somehow force generals to give concessions. A call for arms was ruled out: if Suu Kyi had called for mass protests or started an uprising, then her movement would have been easily crushed and the regime would find it easy to justify such an action. Non-violence seemed a much better option, at least temporarily. By switching the field of political contention into a moral sphere and presenting her political agenda as stemming from ethical convictions, she made a virtue out of necessity. Suu Kyi was able to take "a high moral ground",[31] positioning herself as the much more *moral* candidate and putting the military onto the defensive.

By non-violence she firmly but peacefully defied the SLORC orders. She bypassed regime limitations (prohibition of gatherings of more than five people) by ignoring them. She toured the country, attracting 10–15,000-strong crowds, which gathered to hear her speak in defiance of the SLORC's prohibitions and threats. The reason she could carry this out, of course, was that she was Aung San's daughter. She had both "the courage of her conviction and her connections".[32] That was her asset: she competently used the cards she had. By calling upon party members and the public to disobey the SLORC regulations, she questioned the legitimacy and disparaged the power of the military government.[33] Additionally, she pacified confrontational elements within the NLD ranks[34] and boosted her profile both home and abroad. For all these reasons, non-violence was a rational, calculated decision; it was the best of the available options. Unsurprisingly, she confessed a few years later: "I was attracted to the way of non-violence, but not on moral grounds, as some believe. Only on practical, political grounds".[35] By non-violence Suu Kyi turned her political weakness into strength.

Her demonstration of political power came during a painful personal moment: her mother's funeral. Khin Kyi died peacefully in her bed on 27 December 1988. We will probably never learn whether there was a mother's 'invisible hand' in influencing Suu Kyi's decision to enter politics. What is certain is that Khin Kyi had an enormous impact on her daughter, both intellectually and politically. In

1988, Suu Kyi must have consulted her mother during her first steps into politics. Despite Khin Kyi's terminal illness, she remained conscious and her experience, political choices and strong yet difficult bond with her daughter in all probability affected Suu. Whatever the influence (or lack of it), Suu Kyi's mother was now gone.

Politically, Khin Kyi's funeral was potentially trouble; the spectre of U Thant's funeral haunted both the regime and the people.[36] For once, however, both sides managed to cooperate and behaved in a proper way. The regime provided for a state funeral and built a mausoleum, while Suu Kyi successfully appealed to mourners for restraint: more than 100,000 people marched in respect, without causing serious anti-governmental incidents. Moreover, the SLORC leaders came in person to the house at University Road 54 to express their sympathies to Suu Kyi.[37]

Towards confrontation

The funeral led to a series of unintended consequences. Suu Kyi had demonstrated her strength: political maturity, the ability to control the masses and support from foreign diplomats. By 1989 Suu Kyi had matured politically, ceased to be an 'accidental politician', developed personal charisma and no small amount of political skills.[38] After 'lineage', she added public support as the second structural source of her personal political power. And she knew how to use her popularity for her political purposes: to strengthen both her external position (vis-à-vis SLORC) and her internal one (vis-à-vis other challengers within the opposition). She was able to silence party contesters, who from then on did not dare to criticise her in public.[39] Wresting with the generals in this shadow boxing match, she had to find a middle ground between the radicalization in her own ranks (revenge was the emotion of the day among students and many intellectuals) and the tiny window of opportunity left by the SLORC. For a long time, she was able to walk this tightrope.

The regime, however, was continuously learning too, and adjusted its behaviour accordingly.

In 1989 negative PR against Suu Kyi intensified, more arrests of opposition members followed, a ban on information about the NLD's events was introduced and Suu Kyi's campaigns were obstructed more heavily. This was particularly the case in the Irrawaddy Delta, where Suu Kyi had personal issues with regional commander, General Myint Aung. She embarked on three trips there (January, March and April 1989) that ended with the 'Danubyu incident', which almost cost Suu Kyi her life. The 5 April, a long day of nervous contests with soldiers obstructing her campaign, ended with a nerve-wracking struggle with a certain Captain Myint U. Suu Kyi ignored his orders and threats and moved on, straight into the line of soldiers in firing positions. The Captain started counting down and when he was just about to give the final order to shoot and kill her, his orders were revoked by a senior officer, a Major, who in the last moment came out of the crowd and nullified Myint U's orders. Suu Kyi heard about this later on: by that moment, she had already passed the line of "shaking" soldiers, who were pointing their guns at her, and won this thrilling duel.[40]

Suu Kyi proved her extraordinary bravely. She was afraid of nothing, even death, and by defying the soldiers demonstrated her determination to fulfil her goals. It was her triumph. The 'Danubyu incident' made Suu Kyi a legend, and became central in Suu Kyi's celebrity cult.

Politically, however, her uncompromising stance was a mistake. First, she was jointly responsible for causing this situation to develop. She kept coming back to the Delta, clearly testing her opponents' patience and further antagonizing her foe, General Myint Aung. If sources (Win Thein, Ma Thanegi) are to be trusted, during this memorable day she missed several chances of face-saving solutions, provoking Captain Myint U to actions that might have had fatal consequences. Had she been stronger politically, that might have made sense. However, given the fact that she was weaker, these can be seen as risky, foolhardy and inadequate tactics.

Second, both sides lost control. Among the mutual emotions, ambitions, resentments and grudges, chaos reigned supreme, which nearly led to tragedy. It was only by the actions of the Major that bloodshed was prevented. This does not negate Suu Kyi's bravery – it was extraordinary – but it does change the political assessment of this incident. The behaviour of the Major, who had accompanied the NLD all along and showed up at this moment of crisis, proves the existence of the 'invisible hand' of the regime. Seen from a wider perspective, the SLORC might have been in the defensive, unsure of how to react to Suu Kyi's massive public support, but it had not lost control over the developments: the generals observed the NLD discreetly, infiltrated it and still had the advantage. They controlled the political process and, at the end of the day, Suu Kyi needed to strike a deal with the Tatmadaw if she wanted to come to power. Naturally, the military was unwilling to share power with anyone. However, the art of the deal was how to convince them to do so. And that was possible only if the army felt that their interests and their security were protected. Strictly speaking, Suu Kyi had to manoeuvre herself into a position strong enough to be reckoned with – which she did spectacularly – and, at the same time, she had to assure the generals that she was not a threat to them. In other words, public and foreign support were only the means to a goal, not a goal in themselves. To secure her victory, she needed a deal with the Tatmadaw. After Danubyu, however, agreeing terms with the Tatmadaw became much more difficult.

To make matters worse, immediately after coming back home to Rangoon she went straight to the British Embassy to inform the world about what happened (via the BBC). By doing so, she added insult to injury. She should have defused the incident instead of publicly humiliating a politically stronger opponent. Suu Kyi did otherwise and consequently she won a battle but lost the war. If Nicollò Machiavelli was correct – according to him a successful politician was to be "a fox to discover the snares and a lion to terrify the wolves" – then Suu Kyi had proven to be a lioness, but not necessarily a fox.

Right is not might

Throughout the first half of 1989, Suu Kyi without respite toured the country and hypnotized the crowds. The opposition had gained political maturity and developed a leader who could address fundamental issues. Her movement was unifying "all segments of Burmese society".[41] If the regime thought they would be able to manipulate the divided political scene and play off one party against another, those hopes were dashed by early 1989.

As Suu Kyi's popularity reached its zenith and she became the paramount leader of a united opposition, the political reality became clear-cut. On one side there was the army, without legitimacy but with a structural advantage and the ultimate argument of physical power. On the other, there was the much weaker opposition movement, albeit with mass social support. The army had 'might', the opposition was (morally) right.

The sides should have struck a deal. It was in their mutual interests. The Tatmadaw should have been conscious that ruling without legitimacy would be challenging. The generals could have invited Suu Kyi to govern. Once in power, she would have then had to reckon with their institutional advantage and might have lost popular support while governing. The NLD for its part should have known that some kind of cooperation with the military was necessary to administer the country. Suu Kyi should have hampered some party members' revanchism as she understood that, institutionally, the Tatmadaw was irreplaceable if she was to run a country. Moreover, the SLORC and the NLD were not that different: many party members were former military men. Until June 1989, there was no hostility between the two sides: their dislike, resentment and competition were still far from hatred. They knew their limits in mutual criticism. They should have come to terms.

It was not to be.

The SLORC–NLD contest became a zero-sum game. The Tatmadaw defined its role as that of a referee who made authoritative and respected choices during a crisis. The NLD, empowered by mass public support, did not recognize this self-imagined role of the army – the party saw itself filling it. It was a recipe for disaster. And this meant one thing only: the prevention of confrontation was possible only if one side accepted the preconditions of the other. Since no one was willing or able to do so, "confrontation was unavoidable".[42]

Various cultural reasons have been cited as causes of the unfolding drama: weak mechanisms of conflict solving in Burmese culture; a finite understanding of power; the personalization of power; lack of outlet for opposition; or the moralization of Burmese politics.[43] These are all valuable yet insufficient explanations. Politicians, regardless of geography and cultural differences, have a tendency to act pragmatically. Patterns of culture influence policymakers but do not determine their actions. Why, then, did it not work out in Burma?

Both sides are to blame, though their faults are different. On the side of the Tatmadaw, it was hubris; on Suu Kyi's, it was trying to run before she could walk.

The generals assumed that since they possessed the ultimate argument, that of physical power, they would win anyway, so they did not have to reckon with Suu Kyi. History proved them … right, though Burma paid a high price for their decision. The country lost two decades to political stalemate, which resulted in economic malaise. The Tatmadaw lost on this too (albeit less so). Had the generals accommodated Suu Kyi, in the eyes of the world they might have turned out to be legitimate leaders as early as 1989 (and being legitimate was important for them for prestigious reasons). They could have struck better deals with the outside world than they actually did.

The Tatmadaw did not wish to share power, while the NLD was unwilling to continue playing along to the rules set by the junta. This was the NLD's ultimate political mistake. In mid-1989, the NLD already achieved considerable popular support that was impossible for the generals to ignore. Now political expediency demanded seeking a settlement with the regime. Only a deal with the army would have allowed the NLD a chance, albeit slim, to come to power.

Within the NLD there were people who understood this reality. Chan Aye (a CEC member) in a report to party CC proposed an attempt to come to terms with the junta. Kyi Maung was of similar mind: "what we must have is a democratically elected government. If in exchange we have to guarantee the generals' security or their wealth, never mind: we must give them anything they want".[44] If this is true, these words prove that they understood that army officials controlled the political process.

The NLD's plan for coming to power was to win elections and form a government. This necessitated a type of cooperation, even if technical, with the military. It was the Tatmadaw that ruled and administrated the country, held all institutions, including the coercive apparatus, and organized elections. A confrontational course, advertised by the NLD's radical wing, meant one scenario. In it, the NLD criticised the army and demanded political reckoning with it. In the NLD's imagined scenario, the army would endure it all, allowing elections to happen and give power away to its opponents. The army would then renounce its almost 30-year political and economic dominance, privileged social position and uncountable sinecures, and possibly face lustration and accountability for its past crimes. What a perspective!

To use a football (soccer) metaphor, the NLD's team was a better one, one supported by almost all fans; but the army was both the opposing team and the referee at the same time. In such conditions, it would be extremely challenging to win. The NLD's only chance was to buy (bribe) the referee. Unfortunately, after initial hesitation Suu Kyi finally succumbed to Win Tin and the students,[45] believing that she could defeat the generals in a fair way ("right is might").

Suu Kyi's idealism and inexperience in politics are usually cited as the reasons for her ill-advised decision.[46] While not totally disagreeing with these interpretations, I propose another explanation. This time, Suu Kyi's hybridity was her disadvantage. After decades of living in the West, she firmly believed in democracy as a non-alternative system,[47] and in doing so she was the hero of her times. The revolution in the Philippines had succeeded three years prior, Eastern Europe's transformation was just around the corner soon to be followed by the USSR's fall and the end of apartheid. Freedom was in the air, but not automatically and not everywhere.

The point of no return

Until late May 1989, the regime had been on the defensive, unable to answer Suu Kyi's non-violent tactics successfully. When it finally found a way, the military empire struck back in late May/early June 1989. On 31 May, the regime announced a new electoral law, which forbade those personally associated with foreigners (read: Suu Kyi) to contest elections. In early June, the SLORC declared that martial law would not be lifted after the elections and that elected representatives would draw up a Constitution that would be endorsed by popular referendum. Only then would a transfer of power be possible.[48] In other words, the army unexpectedly changed the nature of the coming elections, from parliamentary ones to that of a constituent assembly. By doing so, the Tatmadaw demonstrated its power as the referee who could change the rules of the current game as and when they pleased. Moreover, in mid- and late-June, the junta made several shows of force. It introduced a ban on printing anti-SLORC materials; changed the international name of the country from Burma to Myanmar; and started an anti-NLD and anti-Suu Kyi media campaign.

The NLD answered rhetorically. The party condemned the decision concerning elections; threatened to boycott them; declared it would not respect restrictions; rejected the name Myanmar and announced a list of new national holidays. Suu Kyi declared that she was not interested in 'pseudodemocracy' (read: rejected playing along to the rules of the regime).[49] Again, she tried to divide the army. She returned to her tactics of hoping for a split within the army and, starting in July, she once more started personally criticising Ne Win; quite harshly and sometimes even *ad personam*. [50] Her behaviour was either shockingly brave or very foolish.

The SLORC fired back with Saw Maung's 'personal appeal' to stop breaking laws; rejecting talks with the NLD; intensifying personal attacks on Suu Kyi in the press; and by arresting the most radical NLD members, including Win Tin (on 4 July).[51] After the aborted attempt to celebrate the anniversary of the demolition of the Student Union Building (7 July), on the next day Suu Kyi crossed the red line (8 July): she announced the civil disobedience movement.

Quoting Gandhi and Martin Luther King, Suu Kyi declared her goal as to "defy as of duty every order and authority not agreed by the majority".[52] Suu Kyi hoped to force concessions from the SLORC by paralyzing the functioning of the state. Unfortunately, at the end of the day, most civil servants, publishers and especially soldiers complied with the regime.[53] The country did not go into a mass strike. Consequently, "holding the 'moral high-ground' worked for Gandhi and Mandela (her models), but whereas the political and social context was favourable for them, for her, it was not".[54] Myanmar's regime – although disliked and with time hated – was homemade, their own, Burmese; not colonial (like the British Raj) or racially different (like in South Africa). Autocratic SLORC was unbound by democratic rules, which had further enabled Martin Luther King's victory in the USA. The generals were tyrants pure and simple and could turn the tables at any time. As Suu Kyi's foe, General Myint Aung declared, "You can forget about democracy. Even if you have an elected government, we will stage a coup again".[55] Unfortunately for her, Suu Kyi, a hybrid politician, was too internationalized in 1989 to understand the political reality in Myanmar. Furthermore, she pacified those who tried to make her see reason: when in July 1989, military veterans from the 'ex-commanders' faction in the NLD objected to Suu Kyi's civil disobedience tactics, she did not mince her words, asking them "if they were followers of Aung San or Ne Win". As one observer noted with disgust, "she was basically asking all these ex-military commanders if they were cowards. She should not have talked to older people like that. We could only conclude that she was very westernized".[56] This remark is telling, for it shows one thing: hybridity was both Suu Kyi's asset and weakness. It was the former because she used non-violence, out-of-the box (initially) ground-breaking tactics; she popularized breakthrough ideas (democracy, human rights); and by reaching to Western media she built her international profile. Without being a hybrid politician, she would not have achieved all that. Her hybridity helped her make a difference. On the other hand, it hindered her too. Both her ex-military party comrades and the members of the ruling military establishment considered her too Occidentalized.[57] The regime used this tool; starting to portray her as an outsider, insufficiently Burmese or Buddhist enough, or even as a foreigner, targeting her marriage to an Englishman especially.[58] She was able to stylishly rebuff these accusations, in fluent Burmese, by ridiculing them.[59] She, too, neutralized accusations of foreignness visually by wearing Burmese clothes and renewing the Burmese female tradition of putting flowers in her hair.[60] Still, not all were convinced. An anecdote from the 2000s tells a story of Suu Kyi who during an interview apparently lost "self-control and started doing things, which she, as a Burmese woman, should not do": she was "very upset when she saw a picture of Ne Win hanging on the wall, loudly expressed her displeasure and ultimately sprang up on a table to take the picture down".[61]

These problems prove one theoretical observation: hybrid politicians are often considered too Westernized by their own compatriots, while being considered 'quintessentially local' by the West (in Suu Kyi's case: "foreigner" vs. "Suu Burmese"). Much more importantly here, however, was something different. Politically, Suu Kyi might have been too internationalized to understand that at the end of the day, in this part of the world in the late 1980s and early 1990s (and long after), Mao Zedong's formula was continuously adequate: power still grew out of the barrel of a gun. Consequently, she misread the political conditions and lost the political confrontation.

The die was cast on 19 July, Martyr's Day. Both sides planned their own commemorations, with Suu Kyi intending to stage a march of her supporters to the Mausoleum. The army prepared itself for riots and more bloodshed, bringing soldiers with live ammunition into the city, putting new restrictions in place and introducing a curfew. In short, establishing "a martial law within martial law".[62] Suu Kyi initially confirmed her march only to cancel it later at 6 AM and calling for a boycott of the regime's ceremony instead. Thanks to this concession nobody was killed and the anniversary went by tensely, yet peacefully. Suu Kyi explained her stance as unwillingness to bring her people "into the killing field" and called the SLORC a "fascist regime" (this label ultimately infuriated the generals).[63] These harsh statements were clearly aimed at hiding the inconvenient truth: her decision was a political concession. While morally praiseworthy (she avoided a bloodbath), politically it showed the limitations of her confrontational tactics. If she was ready to exchange blows with the regime, she should have been expecting the army to behave the way they did – predicting the Tatmadaw's reaction was not that difficult. Instead, Suu Kyi toughened her rhetoric and started a war of nerves, only to reach a point of no return and pull out in the last moment. Consequently, she won morally and lost politically.

On the next day, the regime confined her to house arrest.

Notes

1 Wintle, *Perfect Hostage*, p. 284.
2 Burma Press Summary (BPS), vol. II, no. 9, 1988; Aung San Suu Kyi, "Two letters to Amnesty International", in: *Freedom from Fear*, p. 208.
3 Suu Kyi, "In the eye of the revolution", p. 207; Suu Kyi, "The objectives", p. 202.
4 Lintner, *Aung San Suu Kyi and Burma's Struggle*, p. 66.
5 Quoted in: ibid. p. 66.
6 Taylor, *The State in Myanmar*, p. 406.
7 Kyaw Yin Hlaing, "Aung San Suu Kyi of Myanmar," p. 366.
8 Zöllner, *The Beast and the Beauty*, p. 87.
9 Taylor, *The State in Myanmar*, pp. 405–406; Kyaw Yin Hlaing, "Aung San Suu Kyi of Myanmar", pp. 365–366; Aung San Suu Kyi, *Letters from Burma* (London: Penguin, 1997), pp. 149–157.
10 Taylor, *The State in Myanmar*, p. 406.
11 *Burma's Communist Party's Conspiracy to Take over State Power*, SLORC press conference, 5 August 1989, Online Burma Library (OBL).
12 BPS, vol. III, no. 2, February 1989.
13 Ibid.
14 Kyaw Yin Hlaing, "Aung San Suu Kyi of Myanmar", pp. 365–366.
15 Zöllner, *The Beast and the Beauty*, pp. 101–102.
16 Kyaw Yin Hlaing, "Aung San Suu Kyi of Myanmar", p. 365.
17 Suu Kyi, *Letters from Burma*, p. 79.
18 *Burma Communist Party's Conspiracy*; Taylor, *The State in Myanmar*, p. 408.
19 Wintle, *Perfect Hostage*, p. 290.
20 Thant Myint-U, *The Hidden History of Burma. Race, Capitalism, and the Crisis of Democracy in the 21th Century* (New York, NY: Norton, 2020), pp. 40–41.
21 Suu Kyi, "The role of the citizen in the struggle for democracy", in: *Freedom from Fear*, pp. 212–213; Suu Kyi, "The need for solidarity among ethnic groups", in: ibid., p. 223; Lintner, *Aung San Suu Kyi and Burma's Struggle*, p. 71; Sengupta, *The Female Voice of Myanmar*, pp. 192–198
22 Suu Kyi, "The need for solidarity", p. 219.
23 Popham, *The Lady and the Peacock*, p. 141.

24 Taylor, *The State in Myanmar*, pp. 410–413.
25 Popham, *The Lady and The Peacock*, pp. 109 and 138.
26 Clements, *The Voice of Hope*, p. 197.
27 Kyaw Yin Hlaing, "Aung San Suu Kyi of Myanmar", p. 263.
28 E.g. Suu Kyi, "The need for solidarity", p. 223.
29 A passage in one of her "Letters from Burma" (no. 36) indicates her dislike towards journalists; Suu Kyi, *Letters from Burma*, pp. 143–145.
30 Quoted in: Pederson, *Burma Spring*, p. 189.
31 E.g. her words in: "Opposition leader is confined by Burmese rulers", *The New York Times*, 21 July 1989; Clements, *The Voice of Hope*, p. 31; "Suu Kyi's choice", *Al Jazeera*, 23 January 2012.
32 Ma Than E, "The flowering of the spirit", p. 287.
33 Taylor, *The State in Myanmar*, p. 408.
34 Kyaw Yin Hlaing, "Aung San Suu Kyi of Myanmar", pp. 263–264.
35 "Suu Kyi's choice". Even earlier, she did not reject using violence under "certain circumstances," calling it "an occupational hazard" of policy making in general, Clements, *Voice of Hope*, pp. 153, 208.
36 The funeral of the deceased former UN secretary general U Thant in early December 1974 turned into a grotesque, and ultimately macabre, political event. After the Ne Win regime refused Thant – their political opponent – a state funeral, students snatched the coffin and organized anti-regime rallies over the coffin at the campus. When a compromise was reached with the regime (a funeral near Shwedagon), another more radical group of students snatched the coffin again. This led to the army storming into campus, fighting with students and resulting in a third snatch of the coffin. In bloody riots that accompanied the funeral dozens of people were killed or injured and a few thousand were arrested.
37 Lintner, *Outrage*, pp. 169–171.
38 "With her martyred father as her card of entry into politics she has developed a solid and almost magical reputation of her own in 18 months", Martin Morland, "Valedictory dispatch to Douglas Hurd," 26 April 1990, Confidential, "Internal affairs" FCO, The National Archive, Kew.
39 Kyaw Yin Hlaing, "Aung San Suu Kyi of Myanmar", p. 264.
40 Clements, *Voice of Hope*, pp. 52–53; "The lady who frightens generals", *The Sunday Times*, 14 July 1996; Victor, *The Lady*, p. 88; Wintle, *Perfect Hostage*, pp. 311–314; Popham, *The Lady and the Peacock*, pp. 123–127.
41 Lintner, *Aung San Suu Kyi and Burma's Struggle*, p. 71.
42 Zöllner, *The Beast and the Beauty*, pp. 108–117.
43 Ibid., pp. 106–118; Steinberg, *Burma. The State of Myanmar*, p. 39; Houtman, *Mental Culture*, p. 214; Walton, *Politics in the Moral Universe*, p. 164.
44 Quoted in: Popham, *The Lady and the Peacock*, pp. 146–151.
45 Ibid., p. 151.
46 Michael Aung-Thwin and Maitrii Aung-Thwin, *A History of Myanmar Since Ancient Times* (London: Reaktion Books, 2012), p. 265.
47 Suu Kyi, "The need for solidarity", pp. 220–221.
48 BPS, vol. III, no. 6, June 1989; Derek Tonkin, *The Conundrum of the 1990 Elections in Myanmar/Burma*, 2 October 2010, Myanmar Network.
49 Amnesty International (AI), *Myanmar (Burma) Prisoners of Conscience a Chronicle of Developments since September 1988*, 15 November 1989, p. 56.
50 Ibid., p. 53–59; "Speeches by Daw Aung San Suu Kyi", *Burma Alert*, vol. 2, no. 10 (1991); BPS, vol. III, no. 7, July 1989; Aung San Suu Kyi, "The people want freedom", in: *Freedom from Fear*, p. 225; "As tensions increase, Burmese fear another military crackdown", *The New York Times*, 18 July 1989.
51 PBS, Vol. III, No. 7, July 1989; AI, *Myanmar (Burma) Prisoners*, pp. 56–58.
52 *BCP's Conspiracy*; Houtman, *Mental Culture*, p. 46.

53 "since 1988 not a single senior military figure has either defected to the NLD or joined the party on retirement – to this day," Derek Tonkin, email correspondence, 15 January 2020.

54 Aung-Thwin and Aung-Thwin, *A History of Myanmar*, p. 265.

55 "The waiting game", *Asiaweek*, 10 February 1989.

56 Kyaw Yin Hlaing, "San Suu Kyi of Myanmar", pp. 365–367.

57 Taylor, *The State in Myanmar*, p. 412.

58 "Rangoon Journal"; "2,000 Burmese protest attack on opposition chief," *The New York Times* 24 June 1989; Clements, *The Voice of Hope*, p. 68; "A rich country gone wrong".

59 Aung San Suu Kyi, "The people want freedom", in: *Freedom from Fear*, p. 225; Clements, *Voice of Hope*, p. 68.

60 Zöllner, *The Beast and the Beauty*, p. 303.

61 Kyaw Yin Hlaing, "Daw Aung San Suu Kyi: A Burmese dissident democrat", in: *Burma or Myanmar? The Struggle for National Identity*, ed. L. Dittmer (Singapore: World Scientific, 2010), p. 126.

62 Zöllner, *The Beast and the Beauty,* p. 133.

63 "Opposition leader is confined by Burmese rulers", AI, *Myanmar (Burma) Prisoners*, p. 65; PBS, Vol. III, No. 7, July 1989; "Excerpts from interview", *VOA*, 21 October 2010.

4

THE NON-LEVEL PLAYING FIELD

The confinement of Suu Kyi to house arrest set the political scene for the next two decades. In this competition between the strong (army) and the weak (Suu Kyi), she had two trump cards: popular support and foreign backing. This proved to be too little to enable her to come to power, but was enough to prevent her being marginalized. The Tatmadaw was politically winning; however, it could not fully defeat Suu Kyi. She was losing, but never lost. Consequently, this situation led to a prolonged political deadlock.

The Inya Lake lady

Suu Kyi's first house arrest (1989–1995) is well documented. She spoke about it eagerly just after being released and afterwards. She was confined to her house, separated (with short intervals) from her family and almost cut off from the world (radio being her only contact with it). She exercised, read books, played the piano, sold furniture and meditated.

Politically, the house arrest started with her first (and only) hunger strike undertaken to protect arrested students – her party members. It ended with a compromise (being de facto Suu Kyi's surrender on honourable terms), negotiated by her husband, Michael Aris, with the junta.[1] The episode is interesting from both feminist and postcolonial perspectives (the generals made a deal with a white, Anglo-Saxon, male professor), yet it remains a random one. Aris never again played an active role in Suu Kyi's political life, only a passive (yet dramatic) one.

The period 1989–1995 marked the junta's cruel and successful repressions, which significantly diminished the NLD's power and intimidated society. Not all party members had (partial) immunity for being the Tatmadaw founder's daughter. Tin Oo, after initial house arrest, was sentenced to hard labour; Maung Thaw Ka to a life sentence, where he soon died. A similar fate awaited other imprisoned

NLD leaders: Kyi Saung, Boh Set Yaung, Hla Than, Tin Maung Win, Maung Ko, Leo Nichols and many others. Throughout the country NLD members and other activists were chased, locked up and sentenced to prison and labour camps or to battlefields as porters (the list of human rights violations by the regime is long and depressing). The junta enforced obedience (restored 'law and order', according to their vocabulary). The society was terrorized and silenced.[2]

A decimated NLD came round from the junta's blows thanks to Kyi Maung, who rebuilt the party. The NLD was allowed to continue their electoral campaign, albeit in a much more restricted manner. Although the campaign continued without Suu Kyi (who was barred from contesting on grounds of her marriage with a foreigner),[3] she was symbolically omnipresent, with her face becoming the mark of the NLD and the reason for its success.[4] The junta's clumsy criticism of Suu Kyi even increased her popularity amongst society. To the regime's shock and disbelief, the NLD won the 27 May 1990 elections by a landslide, securing 392 out of 492 (485 contested) mandates in Pyitthu Hluttaw (80 per cent of the seats in Hluttaw and 59 per cent of all votes). It was effectively a referendum on the Tatmadaw's rule.

In this time full of anxiety and emotions, the essential issue was overlooked: What kind of elections were they? Was the Hluttaw to become a parliament or a constituent assembly? All parties, including the pro-regime NUP, their candidates and the gross majority of voters (if not all), believed these were parliamentary elections designated to form a government.[5] The regime interpreted it otherwise. On 27 July Khin Nyunt announced Declaration no. 1/1990 informing, or reminding, that the elected Hluttaw representatives will have "the responsibility to draw up the constitution".[6] Was it the SLORC's unwillingness to swallow defeat or its inability to communicate the nature of the elections earlier on? A list of contradictory statements made by Saw Maung suggests he might have been unaware of what kind of elections his junta was organizing. Khin Nyunt's speeches, on the other hand, were consistent on the interpretation of the constituent assembly from June 1989 onwards. The SLORC was either internally split over this issue or changed the designation of the elections in favour of a constituent assembly without being able to communicate it properly.[7]

Whatever the answer, politically speaking it does not matter much, as the transfer of power could have happened only on the army's conditions – for that the NLD needed a modus operandi together with the Tatmadaw.[8] It never achieved it, instead capitalizing on the notion of 'stolen' elections both at home and abroad. Suu Kyi herself, despite her initial statements,[9] contributed significantly to convincing the world of this interpretation.[10] The NLD won this PR battle decisively, pushing the junta onto a deep ideological defensive by depriving it of domestic and international legitimacy. Unfortunately, it was not enough to bring the NLD to power.

To evoke the football metaphor once again, Myanmar was the non-level playing field, where the Tatmadaw was both a player and a referee at the same time. Team NLD, despite having its best player (Suu Kyi) sent off, scored a magnificent goal after a combined attack. Unfortunately, the referee whistled offside – to the rage of frustrated fans. It did not really matter whether it was an offside or not (no VAR available); the match continued and the NLD had to live with the referee.

The NLD was torn over what to do. Apparently, just after their victory, Kyi Maung asked an astonished French press correspondent "what the Party should do", revealing "no game plan at all".[11] One may comment that ad hoc actions are typical features of Burmese politics, while lack of forward planning is its plague. Kyi Maung chose wisely: a conciliatory approach, arguing against pushing the SLORC into a corner.[12] This was the only real (although dreadful) option, as it might have convinced the SLORC to let the NLD write the Constitution. If appeased, the SLORC – which feared that the NLD might declare an interim government and "start another crisis like that of 1988"[13] – would perhaps transfer power in the (very distant) future. Apparently, the ex-commander faction within the NLD was ready to accept the military's governance of the country for a year until the Constitution was ready, and then expected the NLD to form a government.[14] Others, however, did not want to wait. Torn by factional struggle between the ex-commanders' faction (which believed they could strike a deal with the SLORC) and the radical faction (which thought otherwise), the NLD was seriously split. After a stormy meeting at Rangoon's Gandhi Hall on 29 July, the moderate approach was rejected in favour of a demand to hand over legislative power to the victorious party. The party even set up a deadline for the SLORC: September 1990. The Gandhi Hall Declaration had devastating consequences: the NLD was too weak to secure its demands and had no plan 'B',[15] while the SLORC saw the declaration as "an ultimatum, even an attempted coup".[16] It gave the SLORC the pretext to settle affairs their own way: to jail NLD members and write the Constitution by themselves. The Tatmadaw arrested Kyi Maung and other CEC members, thus breaking the backbone of the party and leaving leadership to "third rung leaders" under Aung Shwe, a former general.[17] Without Suu Kyi, Tin Oo or even Kyi Maung, the NLD did not function well.[18] Shaken by deep internal divisions and deprived of real leaders, the NLD became an easy target for the SLORC; it made "mince-meat of the divided party".[19] Weak and intimidated, the new leadership of the NLD was forced to accept Declaration 1/1990, participate in SLORC's scheme of a National Convention and even expel Suu Kyi from the party. By 1991 the NLD had effectively been neutralized.

When Suu Kyi was released, she aptly summarized her party's dilemmas:

> There are some who would argue that if I had not criticised them, they would have spoken to me. But they would not even consider speaking to U Aung Shwe, who has never criticised them and who has tried his best to be cooperative.[20]

Elsewhere she complained about the regime's rigidity:

> the SLORC has to understand that flexibility is not the same as weakness. And rigidity doesn't mean strength ... 'give and take' means 'I give a little, I take a little; you give a little, you take a little.' It doesn't mean 'you give and I take'.[21]

She was correct: the generals believed they did not have to listen to anyone and did not need to share power with anybody. Once the SLORC decided to stay longer in governance, it postponed any prospects of transferring power. It formed the National Convention in 1992, cancelling most of NLD's mandates (the party now had 107 delegates out of 702 representatives in total). The NLD, after stormy interparty discussions, accepted this scheme and took part in the (rare) proceedings, which proved to be a farce. The army dictated the basic principles of the project without considering any other propositions. After 1992, SLORC's new leader Than Shwe sought to establish a Tatmadaw-controlled political system, where any civilian government would be checked and balanced by the army, leaving little room for independent governmental actions.[22]

Thus, Suu Kyi made a good point when she identified the essence of the NLD's predicament: the generals' uncompromising attitude. It is, of course, easy to be wise after an event – her situation was indeed unenviable – but she was partially to blame for the deadlock. She did not understand the (unfair) political rules of the game: she criticised the junta when she should have negotiated with them and under Aung Shwe's weak lead it was too little, too late for mending fences. Contrary to what some say, an attempt at rebellion, marching to release Suu Kyi and taking over power immediately after the 1990 elections,[23] was not an option: the army had shot down the movement in 1988 and they would have done so again in 1990.[24] And, although the alternative – accepting the rules of the SLORC – was psychologically, politically and personally next to impossible for the NLD, it remained the only, albeit small, way of coming into power.

Having neutralized the NLD, the SLORC won this battle, yet not completely. The generals were unable to marginalize Suu Kyi. However hard they tried to diminish Suu Kyi's importance, to ignore her, or to make people forget about her – they failed. Two structural reasons allowed Suu Kyi to remain in the political game: public support and foreign backing.

Although the Tatmadaw effectively terrorized the people, the army had never been successful in completely silencing society. Locked in her house at University Road 54, Suu Kyi became the personalization of social aims and hopes. In a way, the generals inadvertently contributed to her popularity (for locking her up saved her from making political mistakes). The Burmese praised, sacralized and elevated Suu Kyi to a position above politics, the people's hero: a female *bodhisattva*, a benevolent *nat*.[25] It was a grassroots personality cult and, as such, a fascinating case study. What matters here most importantly, however, is something different. Although Suu Kyi spoke unequivocally against a personalized approach to politics many times,[26] she achieved her position thanks to her personal features (lineage, charisma and perceived correct moral choices in politics). Most importantly, she owed her survival in Burmese politics to these very personalized mechanisms.

The second structural source of Suu Kyi's political position was foreign backing. The early 1990s saw the beginning of Suu Kyi's popularity in the West. She had worked hard to win the support of the West during her entry into politics in 1988/1989. However, it was only once she was locked in house arrest that she became widely recognized outside Burma. For her stance and proclaimed ideas, she received a deluge of awards, the most important being the Nobel Peace Prize in 1991. This admiration had its serious political implications. With time it translated into the West's political support of Suu Kyi and this, in turn, made it much more difficult to marginalize her.

Although domestic adoration and international recognition came to her without her personal contribution, as she was under house arrest, being a skilful politician she was able to make use of it. Since the early 1990s, local and foreign support had become her two assets in the struggle against the military. Otherwise doomed to be sidelined, with this kind of aid she was able to remain in the game.

These two structural factors forced the generals in 1994 to accept (unsuccessful) mediators (Bill Richardson and Rewata Dhamma) and to conduct backstage (even if bogus)[27] negotiations with her (she had two personal meetings with Khin Nyunt and one with Than Shwe, but these attempts came to nothing as both sides were entrenched in their own positions). These factors finally led to her release on 10 July 1995. There are two major interpretations as to why the generals released her: the SLORC's self-conviction of having full control of the political situation and Japanese backstage lobbying.

Right versus might yet again

Once released, Suu Kyi was laconic and conciliatory in her statements. She met Kyi Maung, Tin Oo and Aung Shwe and restarted political activity. Quite contrary to international expectations – her release hit the world headlines and sparked hope of quick reconciliation – Suu Kyi downplayed the importance of the event; probably understanding her release was the regime's show of strength, not a gesture of willingness to compromise.

Suu Kyi had to somehow force the generals to the negotiating table. In a way, the mountain came to the prophet: when news about Suu Kyi's release reached the town, people gathered at the gate of her house to greet her. She climbed to the top of the gate and spoke to them over it. She repeated the action on the next day, and then again every day. Finally, after a month, she decided to hold weekly rallies, with people gathering at the front of her house and Suu Kyi (together with Tin Oo and Kyi Maung) speaking to them from over the gate. This is how one of 1990s' most unusual political performances came into being.

Gate rallies were an out-of-the box, brilliant political move that increased Suu Kyi's political profile while circumventing existing regulations forbidding public gatherings. It allowed the NLD to reach out to their supporters (bypassing censorship), simultaneously sending signals to the regime. It boosted Suu Kyi's international profile too, as her rallies became political events, if not a tourist attraction. Most importantly, the gate gatherings made Suu Kyi even more popular in society. Suu Kyi enjoyed this communication. She replied to letters, talked to people, laughed, used wordplay, joked and lightly, though clearly, ridiculed the regime; and, by "educating the people", was able to present her various ideas on political, social and economic issues that could be summarized in one sentence: "democracy first".[28]

Compared with what she had preached before her house arrest, her ideas underwent significant Buddhisation. Previously only randomly present in her speeches, Buddhism now became one of her hallmarks.[29] She described her first house arrest as a time of spiritual strengthening and there is no reason to doubt it. At the same time, it is hard to miss the fact that, upon being released from house arrest, Suu Kyi found the regime legitimizing itself through religion. The SLORC abandoned Ne Win's complicated – yet rather distanced – relationship with clergy and instead embraced very traditional means of legitimacy, such as building pagodas and supporting monasteries. Suu Kyi had to somehow politically balance this newly found religiosity of the generals and counter their negative PR campaign, which portrayed Suu Kyi as a Westernized renegade. Presenting herself as the purer Buddhist, who was religious in public, used Buddhist terms extensively, visited monasteries (Thamanya and others), fed monks and listened to their advice (and wrote about all this) was a good option.[30] In other words, Suu Kyi's turn towards Buddhism was probably both a genuine, personal change of heart as well as a politically convenient move.

Thanks to this all, Suu Kyi politically stitched herself back together. She rebuilt her party, becharmed Madeleine Albright (then US Ambassador to the UN) and used her political celebrity status to appeal to the world to help her force the uncompromising generals to make concessions. Since her post-release calls for talks and compromise with the junta were effectively ignored, Suu Kyi resorted to what amounted to a 'nuclear option' in Burmese conditions. Feeling that she had the West's backing and misled by South Africa's example, she called for "no aid, trade or investment"[31] – supporting sanctions on Myanmar.[32] Despite partial successes (tourism boycott, withdrawal of many global companies, the Unocal case), sanctions failed to bring down the regime for two structural reasons: first, sanctions were not universal and only applied fully by Western countries which meant trade, including an illegal one with Asian partners, especially China, continued and, second, because of the inward-looking nature of the Tatmadaw.[33] Sanctions irritated the generals, as they questioned their legitimacy, but could not overthrow them; at the same time, sanctions hurt some parts of society (though the primary reason for the Burmese people's plight was the regime's own mismanagement of their country). Suu Kyi either underestimated the social price or calculated it as a necessary cost.[34] Although she had clear political interest in introducing and keeping sanctions – they helped her remain in the political game – it would be unjust to accuse her of consciously supporting harmful policies (for 'her' people) for her own political gains. Rather, her 'regime change first' strategy deluded her (and her Western supporters) that regime change was possible. According to them, political change had to anticipate deeply needed economic and social reforms, allegedly unworkable under the SLORC/SPDC. Unfortunately even then, in the 1990s, although not impossible, regime change was improbable.[35] Perhaps Suu Kyi's hybridity was partially to blame too. As a hybrid politician Suu Kyi unconsciously overestimated the importance of the Western world. She overlooked the emergence of new Asian powers, especially China, but also Thailand, Singapore and Malaysia. Engagement with these countries saved the junta both politically and economically (emerging local Asian capitalism, unnoticeable from both Inya Lake and the West, gave the generals the means for survival). To Suu Kyi's disadvantage, the West proved to have limited clout here.

Back then, in the mid-1990s, things seemed to look differently. Thanks to her gate rallies and foreign support, Suu Kyi established an illusion of an "alternative power centre".[36] Suu Kyi felt strong enough to challenge the regime, which remained unwilling to compromise; Suu Kyi again wanted to force them to the negotiating table. Thus, she started testing the limits of her allotted political space (she repeated this in 2002/2003).[37] Consequently, a new phase of confrontation commenced from late 1995. This lasted until 2000, when Suu Kyi was put back under house arrest.

This period was characterized by a series of political skirmishes between the NLD and the regime against the background of Myanmar's weakening economic situation and building international pressure. In November 1995, the NLD deputies walked out of the National Convention, paralysing its proceedings, in protest against the SLORC's proposals of a Constitution. Starting March 1996, the NLD threatened to convene a parliament (more vocally from mid-1998) and on 17 September 1998 the party called together its own 'shadow parliament', which symbolically nullified all junta decisions made from 18 September 1988 onwards.

The regime responded to Suu Kyi's above-mentioned policies by harassing the NLD members, obstructing its events, briefly arresting dissidents and – at times – physically assaulting some of them. Censorship intensified as well as did threats and brutal *ad personam* attacks on Suu Kyi in the press. Gate rallies became obstructed and finally terminated in September 1996. Nationwide repressions targeting party members followed, with many jailed yet again. Suu Kyi was kept confined to Yangon and not allowed to travel outside of the city. She tried to break free in four publicized stand-offs in the summer of 1998. These ended in two draws (negotiated compromises) and two defeats on Suu Kyi's part. In 2000 Suu Kyi again attempted to travel outside of Yangon. She failed once again and was put back in *de facto* (though not de jure) house arrest in September 2000.

These political tugs-of-war were just another act of the Burmese power play: might versus right. The army had power but no authority, whereas Suu Kyi had authority but no power. She wanted to force the generals to make concessions and in order to do so she conducted a policy of high moral ground: her "politics of *metta*".[38] As she put it in one speech, "we have no power, we have no weapons. We also don't have much money ... . What are our foundations? It is *Metta*".[39] Given "the unequal distribution of physical power, Suu Kyi could only act symbolically" through this "mix of principles and pragmatic considerations".[40] The aim of her benevolent rhetoric was to present the public with an opposition which was morally superior. This was based on a hope – desperate if genuine, hypocritical if not – that by moral example the opposition would be able to soften the generals and convince them to relinquish their power. In essence, this was "a non-violent threat to the generals' legitimacy".[41] Thus, it was not as idealistic and naïve as it might have looked (especially when combined with international sanctions – rather hard political measures), but it failed nevertheless, as it did not force the generals to compromise.

Politically, the regime had the upper hand again, but Suu Kyi did not think of surrendering. Although the regime was winning in the political realm, it could not defeat her fully and so could not enforce its vision of the country. Suu Kyi was in a losing position, but she never lost. Being unable to win yet being too strong to lose, Suu Kyi had to trust that time was on her side. The generals believed the same. Consequently, the sides entrenched their positions and stalemate continued. Some had had enough.

"Renegades and traitors"

After leaving house arrest, Suu Kyi's de facto leadership in the NLD remained unquestionable. However, as the confrontation with the SPDC (State Peace and Development Council, SLORC's new 1997 name) intensified with little tangible results for the NLD, some important NLD members and other Suu Kyi supporters started questioning her policies.

First, there was a group of disillusioned party members who objected to Suu Kyi's unilateral way of decision-making and who favoured a compromise with the regime – partial participation in power was better than none, they claimed. Headed by Than Tun and Thein Kyi, MPs and former political prisoners, the interparty opposition group tried to prevent the National Convention walkout and even later demanded a more realistic approach. Suu Kyi shouted at them and carried out an open ballot – favouring her, as only few people dared to oppose her openly – and won; in January 1997 they were expelled from the party for "disobeying policy" and "creating disunity".[42]

Soon, more serious splits followed. Ma Thanegi, Suu Kyi's personal assistant, was the first major figure to defect due to disagreements over the sanctions policy and attitude towards SLORC (and apparently over personal issues as well). Even more significantly, though much more murky, was Suu Kyi's split with Kyi Maung, one of her closest colleagues (she had named him her "guide, mentor and friend").[43] Even so, by the end of 1997 they parted ways as the result of differences in their approach towards SLORC (Kyi Maung allegedly favoured a more moderate stance) and apparently over personal disagreements. Kyi Maung resigned, never revealing the reasons of their split, and neither did Suu Kyi, who downplayed his role, stating that Kyi Maung had never been her "key adviser".[44] In April 1999, another group from the opposition party – 28 MPs strong and headed by Tin Tun Maung, a CEC member – called for talks with the regime without Suu Kyi. She retaliated by labelling them "lackeys", accusing them of "colluding" with the junta and suspending them from the party.[45] Soon after, on 27 May 1999, she gave one of her harshest speeches:

> It is very important for our members to be extra loyal. If we are disloyal at times of difficulties we become faithless persons. According to democratic principles, everyone has the right to have their own beliefs, to think independently and to have freedom of expression. But if one acts disloyally in exercising those rights, one is a renegade, a traitor (…). At a time when great loyalty is needed, don't make excuses for disloyalty.[46]

And indeed, there was no place for disloyalty within the NLD: all intraparty opponents were expelled or silenced (and marginalized). Later, this spread to all democratic movements, both inside Myanmar and outside. The unique political situation of Myanmar, where all opposition to the regime remained on the shoulders of one person, gave rise "to a cultural practice that no one in the movement must challenge Daw Suu and her policies"; criticising her or doing things she would not approve of became "a taboo for pro-democracy activists".[47]

Inside the NLD, Suu Kyi held the party together with an authoritarian grip, not tolerating any criticism, quelling antagonists, eliminating factionalism and making the party an appendix to herself. As one onlooker commented: "The party defers to her on all things big and small; her view is to be ascertained prior to any decision" and the CEC members are "incapable of the least action without Daw Suu".[48] This, in fact, worked in her personal favour in the 2000s when, locked in house arrest, she left the party leadership to a loyal yet incompetent 'old guard'. They resembled "inept caretakers" and did "little more than keeping the party alive on a drip", not being able to function effectively without her.[49] As Wikileaks revealed in 2010, by the late 2000s the politically weak party was headed by a "sclerotic leadership of the elderly NLD 'Uncles'", which "frustrated" active members. The party was "strictly hierarchical", where "new ideas are not solicited or encouraged from younger members, and the Uncles regularly expel members they believe are 'too active'". According to these sources, "the Uncles spend endless hours discussing their entitlements from the 1990 elections and abstract policy which they are in no position to enact": they hoped the UN would intervene and the USD would "invade" to place them in positions of power. At the same time, they showed "little concern for the social and economic plight of most Burmese".[50] Unsurprisingly, by the late 2000s the NLD was labelled "a haphazard congregation under the guidance of a charismatic leader rather than a properly institutionalized political party" being in "critical state".[51]

The family issue

All the controversies surrounding Suu Kyi were overshadowed by the single most tragic aspect of her political struggle: her family drama. In itself worthy of a Shakespearian play, it is an invidious thing to present objectively; hence only a political analysis will be offered here.

When Suu Kyi entered politics, she put it before family. Yet, she most probably believed that she would be able to reconcile her public activities with family life.

Once her confrontation with the regime escalated however, this proved to be impossible. Her family became the target of SLORC's attacks. Her sons' Burmese passports were withheld while visas for them and for Aris started to become a source of political manipulation. By separating her from her family, the generals hoped to break her: force her to concessions or, better still, to relinquish political activity.

Her marriage, an important element of her hybrid heritage, was her asset internationally: Aris' tireless lobbying convinced many to her cause (and allegedly, it was important in securing her Nobel Prize). Their enforced separations won her universal sympathy. In Myanmar however, her marriage was a burden. It exposed her to xenophobic sentiments among the ruling establishment and beyond. Understanding – let alone accepting – Suu Kyi's hybrid Burmese-ness was too much for the generals. They hoped to arouse similar resentments within society, stopping at nothing to make this Suu Kyi's political weak point. After 1995 an avalanche of brutal, heinous anti-Suu Kyi PR campaigns commenced: she was regularly slandered, vilified and calumniated in regime media outlets as a "traitor", "renegade", "puppet", "lackey", "race destroyer", "destructionist", "obstructionist", "ogress", "prostitute", "witch" and so on.[52]

Suu Kyi responded by neutralizing the impact of her marriage to an Englishman. She constantly distanced herself from her husband in her interviews; emphasized that Myanmar was more important to her than her family; downplayed the personal costs of her political struggle by presenting the separation from her family as irrelevant in comparison with the suffering of other Burmese. She considered divorcing Aris due to political reasons (but dropped it); during her house arrest, she refrained from correspondence with him and even did not once allow him to stay at her home. Since the mid-1990s, she forbade him from speaking to the media; finally, when Aris was dying of cancer in 1999, Suu Kyi decided not to bid him farewell, fearing that once she left Myanmar the generals would not allow her to come back.[53]

Her choices must have had enormous personal costs. When judged from a purely political perspective however, her actions were a winning strategy of minimizing the damage of a politically incorrect marriage by sacrificing it to her political cause. By doing so, Suu Kyi countered the regime's propaganda, washed away the error of her youth in the eyes of many Burmese people and proved that she indeed put her country first. At a high personal cost, she turned her political weakness into an asset.

Latterly, in the late 2000s and 2010s, she followed this by building up her position as "mother of Myanmar", who symbolically sacrifices her own needs for the good of her new children: the Burmese people.[54] This fitted nicely into the social archetype of proper behaviour: quitting material comforts for a spiritual quest.[55] And this, together with her feminine dress and emphatically Burmese image compensating her hybridity, was how she bypassed gender limitations and other traps set for women in Myanmar politics. She successfully navigated herself into a position of a socially acceptable female authority figure.[56]

The celebrity

By 1989 Suu Kyi had become recognizable to the outside world. House arrest only added to her publicity. A combination of factors – non-violence, her charisma, popularity, media skills and tragic family story, plus the brutality and PR incompetence of SLORC – guaranteed such international fame. The dividing line became crystal clear: a courageous, pretty, tragic woman against a bunch of Third World despots. Consequently, the political struggle in Myanmar became inseparably linked with Suu Kyi, who dominated the picture for outside world.

In the early 1990s, a growing Suu Kyi-centred lobbying movement made its first gestures and signs of support; starting with an honorary degree at Oxford's St Hugh's College (1990), via the Thorolf Rafto Prize (1990), up to the Sakharov Prize (1990) and, ultimately, the Nobel Peace Prize (1991). The latter was particularly important, as it contributed significantly to a dominant yet false vision of Suu Kyi being a dissident fighting for human rights. Many, if not most, of her supporters and lobbyists unconsciously encouraged such a narrative. By her influential writing, using language, metaphors and ideals widely understandable outside of Burma, she was able to convince half the world, the Nobel Committee included,[57] that her political struggle for power in Burma represented higher, humanistic values; that it was a quest for good.[58] Politically, it was a masterpiece of PR and it secured Suu Kyi's political interests for two decades. As for Myanmar, the results were more mixed. The first ever Nobel Prize for a Burmese influenced Myanmar politics, though probably not the way the Committee intended and hoped. The Prize strengthened Suu Kyi's position. From then on, the proverbially stubborn[59] Suu Kyi believed that time was on her side, which made her even more inflexible. If she had come to terms with the logic of a non-level playing field earlier, Myanmar might not have lost two decades of underdevelopment. On the other hand, global admiration perhaps saved Suu Kyi from marginalization projected onto her by the junta.

After the Nobel honour, a deluge of awards, prizes and honorary degrees followed. Suu Kyi's publicity was not limited to the circle of elites – movies, novels, albums, plays and posters are the pop culture tributes to Suu Kyi. Interestingly, her popularity outside Myanmar, just like inside the country, was a grassroots phenomenon.[60]

The mainstream narrative of Suu Kyi, as a story of a beautiful woman fighting peacefully against a bunch of generals at a high personal cost, was so suggestively Hollywoodish that it transformed her story from its political ground into a morality tale, a fairy tale. Suu Kyi became Burma's Gandhi, Burma's Jean of Arc, an icon, a saint, an epitome of the universal battle of good and evil. That made her a factor in Western countries' policies towards Myanmar, which is more she could have ever dreamed of in 1988.

But there was a flip side of her global popularity. These ways of portraying Suu Kyi depoliticized her.[61] Being locked in house arrest, she could not only make no bad moves or mistakes, but she also ceased being seen as a serious politician. It stripped her of her 'politicalness'. Instead it placed her in the realm of celebrity, alongside movie stars, singers and other showbusiness individuals. She was unconsciously expected to behave accordingly, to give a moral example. This celebrification spoke more about the hopes that foreigners projected onto Aung San Suu Kyi, than about herself.

The phenomenon of Suu Kyi's iconic status has been analysed in several ways, by communication theory and iconic presentations[62] as well as by feminist theory.[63] While agreeing with these approaches, I would like to propose another way of looking at it: through hybridity and postcolonial theory. Suu Kyi's deification would not be possible if she did not possess the ability to speak to the world in a language it understands. Being a hybrid politician, Suu Kyi knew how to win the hearts and minds of the West and beyond: she wrote passionate articles about non-violence, the compatibility of democracy with Buddhism and brought down the house with calls for freedom from fear. Her political ideas were intelligent, eclectic; they were a justification of her struggle, which mixed local and international legitimization with wit, a sense of humour and literary talent. Although her hybrid political philosophy was not the most important aspect of her global publicity – this role certainly went to her dramatic personal story – Suu Kyi's political ideas certainly played their part, even if a subsidiary one. For, in the 1990s and 2000s, it seemed that Suu Kyi was a perfect, non-Western propagator of democracy, human rights, rule of law and other Western-cum-universal values. When we dig into her political ideas, however, we may find that although Suu Kyi and the West had been speaking the same language and saying identical things for more than two decades, they had something very different in mind. Take democracy for example. Suu Kyi's vision of democracy does have a Western rights-based component. Yet it plays a secondary role only. Her idea of democracy is built not on external mechanisms or institutions, like in the West, but on very Burmese, Buddhists fundamentals (one should start the improvement of the world from one's own transformation). It is based on the internal, inward-based moral qualities of an individual, who is an agent of societal change. Establishing democracy understood in this way necessitates a disciplinarian approach based on unity, responsibilities and sacrifices. Consequently, if one then disagrees or disunites, then one is not moral enough. That is why Suu Kyi spoke rarely and vaguely about concrete ways of democratic governance (institutions, mechanisms, etc.) and more about individual responsibility and the necessity of choosing a leader morally most equipped for governing.

We may easily dismiss these ideas as hypocrisy – a smokescreen for the power-hungry and so on. But this would be unjust. There is something much deeper at stake here. We should not condemn Suu Kyi for not respecting our values, because she has been fighting for her vision of democracy all along. Democracy, as other Western-cum-universal values, became so blurred and eclectic in the postcolonial world, so much of a hybrid, that it came to be an entity in itself. When Suu Kyi wrote that "there will be as many kinds of democracies as there are nations ... each democratic country will have its own individual characteristics"[64] she described this phenomenon quite well.

The unsuccessful Renaissance Man

The 2000–2002 informal second house arrest of Suu Kyi is important for a single reason. Unlike her other arrests, this one ended thanks to external mediation. The United Nations, after a series of depressingly unsuccessful attempts to influence the situation in Myanmar, seemed to achieve a breakthrough thanks to its special envoy, Malaysian diplomat Razali Ismail.

Razali decidedly hit it off with Suu Kyi, whose hybridity he additionally clearly enjoyed.[65] He was acceptable as an envoy for the generals too. Perhaps unsurprisingly then, it turned out that Razali's company won the bid to produce e-passports for Myanmar. When criticised for this clear conflict of interests, the undaunted diplomat retorted: "I am a Renaissance Man who is able to do different things at the same time".[66]

His backstage diplomacy, several unpublicized meetings with Suu Kyi and the generals, and between the generals and Suu Kyi, led to some conciliatory gestures from both sides, and eventually to Suu Kyi's release on 6 May 2002. The unwritten and unspecified deal was feeble from the very beginning and produced only a short-lived political thaw. Both sides were unwilling to grant serious concessions. The SPDC, now much more firmly in control of the country, demanded acceptance of its constitutional scheme and saw the NLD's role as auxiliary. This is because by the early 2000s the generals were strengthened by profits from the Yadana gas field project[67] and regional trade, and hence no longer feared an overthrow. They allowed Suu Kyi to travel and eagerly showed her developmental projects (bridges, roads and dams), but were unwilling to seriously share power with her. Suu Kyi decisively rejected their plans to be a politically powerless figurehead and demanded that they hand back power to the NLD in accordance with the 1990 elections. In short, the regime wanted Suu Kyi to be a figurant, who approves of the governmental line; she wanted them to share power. Thus, she made 'a calculated risk': in order to force them to the negotiating table, she again embarked on a nationwide tour in the hope of strengthening her own political position by public pressure.[68] Again it proved to be a vicious cycle: while her popularity reached new highs, prospects of a deal with the regime drew further away as the junta saw her actions as undermining the SPDC's legitimacy.

Initially the SPDC tolerated her activities, albeit with difficulties starting in Autumn 2002. Tensions built during Suu Kyi's Shan State trip in November. Her December Rakhine tour was even more nerve-wracking (it ended with a bizarre fire engine incident in Mrauk-U) – with Suu Kyi heralding support for maintaining international sanctions and the junta's accusations of breaking their unwritten agreement. Incidents intensified during Suu Kyi's next trip – to Chin State (April 2003). By then, it became clear that the unwritten Suu Kyi–SPDC deal had collapsed.

Suu Kyi's triumphant tour put the regime back on the defensive – with dire consequences. Razali negotiated with Khin Nyunt, leader of the "pragmatic"[69] faction within the regime, which consisted of influential military intelligence personnel as well as a few trained professionals within the army (Hla Min, Thein Swe, Win Aung). Being more understanding of international issues, this faction favoured striking a deal with Suu Kyi (on the regime's conditions, naturally) due to the poor international standing of Myanmar.[70] The opposed 'hard-line' faction (Maung Aye, Soe Win, Kyi Aung) did not care at all. Neither did they feel the need or the will to share any power and did not mind Myanmar's isolation. Their attitude was encapsulated in Soe Win's January 2003 statement: "the SLORC/SPDC not only won't talk to the NLD but also would never hand over power to the NLD".[71] Senior General Than Shwe, who started SLORC/SPDC chairmanship in 1992 and initially was *primus inter pares*, became the paramount leader by the late 1990s. He did so by playing one faction off against another, steadily limiting the importance of regional generals and increasing his personal power. Meanwhile, Khin Nyunt's faction, weakened by Ne Win's imprisonment and then death in 2002, regained some strength thanks to an unwritten deal with Suu Kyi. They later lost their influence again due to Suu Kyi's 2002/2003 tour. By May 2003 paramount leader Than Shwe apparently was convinced by hard-liners that enough was enough.

Consequently, Suu Kyi's last tour, to Mandalay, Sagaing and Kachin, was beset with various incidents. It ended with the dramatic, bloody 'Depayin massacre' on 30 May 2003, which almost cost Suu Kyi her life: her convoy was attacked by a violent pro-regime mob that killed more than a dozen (the number 70 is frequently quoted) NLD members in an extremely brutal way. Suu Kyi most probably survived thanks to her driver (who broke away from the siege) and also to the assassins' incompetence (they did not block all the escape routes).[72] However, despite this being a plausible explanation for what happened there, the mystery of Depayin remains unsolved.

Whatever the outcome of the junta's interfactional struggle, after Depayin Suu Kyi was arrested, put into Insein prison, then hospital and finally under house arrest, where she remained until 2010. It was there that she was taken care of by two aids and a physician, and lived a disciplined, half-hermit styled life. Politically speaking, the 2002–2003 thaw ended amid widespread international condemnation. Soon after Khin Nyunt's fall (see below), a hopeless Razali, who had previously built his position on close relations with him, resigned in January 2006. A similar failure awaited his successor, Ibrahim Gambari, as well as other UN officials who tried to mediate in Burmese affairs (Ban Ki-moon, Vijay Nambiar) or attempted to improve Myanmar's dramatic human rights record (Paulo Sérgio Pinherio, Tomas Ojea Quintana). Myanmar became a "political graveyard" of international negotiators.[73]

In the mid-2000s, political stalemate in Myanmar persisted. Nothing helped. Behind-the-scenes negotiations, international mediations, pressure and incentives and even the assassination attempt on Suu Kyi's life at Depayin did not resolve the impasse. The two sides entrenched their positions and Myanmar paid the price, losing year after year.

Notes

1 Aris, "Introduction", in: *Freedom from Fear*, pp. xxiii–xxv.
2 Christina Fink, *Living Silence in Burma. Surviving Under Military Regime* (Chiang Mai: Silkworm Books, 2009), pp. 70–73.
3 "Burmese ban top opposition candidate", *The New York Times*, 18 January 1990.
4 "The vote on 27 May was essentially a personal vote for Aung San Suu Kyi", Julian Hartland-Swann, "Democracy Burmese style – the great illusion?" dispatch, Confidential, FAB 014/6, 1 August 1990 "Internal affairs" FCO, The National Archive, Kew.
5 Tonkin, "The 1990 elections in Myanmar", p. 47.
6 *State LORC Declaration No. 1/90 of July 27, 1990*, OBL.
7 For the latter interpretation and for impressive collection of contemporary sources, see: Derek Tonkin, "The 1990 elections in Myanmar: Broken promises or a failure of communication?," *Contemporary Southeast Asia*, vol. 29, no. 1 (April 2007), pp. 33–54 and other articles by this author.
8 "It is certain, therefore, that a transfer of power, if and when it comes, will only be conceded on conditions which guarantee the Army's interests and continuing political role", David H. Colvin, comment of "Democracy Burmese style – the great illusion?" dispatch, Confidential, FAB 014/6, 1 August 1990 "Internal affairs" FCO, The National Archive, Kew.
9 "Whoever is elected will first have to draw up a constitution that will have to be adopted before the transfer of power" (1 July 1989), Suu Kyi, "The people want freedom", p. 225.
10 Suu Kyi, *Letters from Burma*, pp. 123 and 149 (*Letters* no. 31 and 37). Suu Kyi's interpretation was accepted globally.
11 Quoted in: Tonkin, "The 1990 elections", pp. 47–48.
12 Ibid., p. 49. Kyi Maung told the British Ambassador just after the elections that "they were prepared to be generous and flexible", and "would not at that point put forward any conditions", Julian Hartland-Swann, "Burmese elections: NLD intentions", Confidential Dispatch 30 May 1990, FAB 014/1, "Internal affairs" FCO, The National Archive, Kew.
13 Ye Htut, *Myanmar's Political Transition and Lost Opportunities (2010–2016)* (Singapore: ISEAS, 2019), p. 7.
14 Kyaw Yin Hlaing, "The state of pro-democracy movement", p. 97.
15 Ibid. p. 99.
16 Derek Tonkin, email correspondence, 4 March 2019.
17 Lintner, *Aung San Suu Kyi and Burma's Struggle*, p. 129.
18 As the British Ambassador informed, after Kyi Maung's arrest the party was "in a state of shock", Julian Hartland-Swann to David Colvin, "The NLD after the arrests", 22 September 1990, FAB 014/1, "Internal affairs", FCO, The National Archive, Kew.
19 Derek Tonkin, email correspondence, 20 March 2019.
20 Clements, *The Voice of Hope*, p. 185.
21 Suu Kyi, "The need for dialogue," p. 251.
22 Ye Htut, *Myanmar's Political Transition*, pp. 8–9.
23 Lintner, *Aung San Suu Kyi and Burma's Struggle*, p. 130.
24 "If the people take to the streets again, the SLORC will again mow them down," Hartland-Swann, "Democracy Burmese style – the great illusion?".
25 Houtman, *Mental Culture*, pp. 328 and 382. A *bodhisattva* is an individual on the path to becoming a buddha; *nats* are local, worshipped spirits – a folk religion in Burma.
26 Clements, *The Voice of Hope*, p. 81; Suu Kyi, "The need for dialogue", in: *Freedom from Fear*, p. 249; *Daw Suu's 25 Dialogues with the People*, pp. 95, 175 and 323.
27 Ye Htut, *Myanmar's Political Transition*, p. 14.
28 Blum, *Teaching Democracy*, pp. 31–48; Suu Kyi, *Letters from Burma*, p. 192. Most of her speeches were published in: *Daw Suu's 25 Dialogues with the People*, pp. 18–543.

29 Lintner, *Aung San Suu Kyi and Burma's Struggle*, pp. 96–98.
30 Clements, *The Voice of Hope*, pp. 48, 55, 119, 144, 189; Suu Kyi, *Letters from Burma*, pp 3–19, 161; Lintner, *Aung San Suu Kyi and Burma's Struggle*, pp. 96–98; Houtman, *Mental Culture*, p. 294.
31 "Aung San Suu Kyi", *Prospect*, 20 July 2001.
32 Clements, *The Voice of Hope*, pp. 25 and 218; Suu Kyi, *Letters from Burma*, pp. 87–89; "Suu Kyi urges Britons to boycott Burma", *The Independent*, 17 March 1996. She called for sanctions already in 1989, "Aung San Suu Kyi calls for trade boycott", *Bangkok Post*, 4 June 1989.
33 Thant Myint-U, *The River of Lost Footsteps. A Personal History of Burma* (New York, NY: FSG, 2007), pp. 342–346.
34 Clements, *The Voice of Hope*, pp. 193, 207; Suu Kyi, "The people want freedom", p. 226; "A conversation with Daw Aung San Suu Kyi", *The New York Times*, 30 September 2012; Pederson, *Burma Spring*, p. 190.
35 Thant Myint-U, *The Hidden History of Burma*, p. 61.
36 Zöllner, *The Beast and the Beauty*, pp. 245–246.
37 David Steinberg, "Aung San Suu Kyi and U.S. policy toward Burma/Myanmar", *Journal of Current Southeast Asian Affairs*, no. 3 (2010), pp. 35–59.
38 McCarthy, *The Political Theory of Tyranny*, pp. 168–169.
39 *Statement by Daw Aung San Suu Kyi at the Closing Ceremony of the 9th NLD Party Congress*, 29 September 1997, OBL.
40 Zöllner, *The Beast and the Beauty*, pp. 269–274.
41 McCarthy, *The Political Theory of Tyranny*, pp. 171–172.
42 "How things look inside the NLD", *Asiaweek*, 16 July 1999; "Burma caught in a state of limbo", *The Nation*, 28 April 1998.
43 Levy, "Aung San Suu Kyi"; Suu Kyi, *Letters from Burma*, pp. 71–75 and 188–191.
44 Lintner, *Aung San Suu Kyi and Burma's Struggle*, p. 90; Levy, "Aung San Suu Kyi".
45 "Aung San Suu Kyi", *Prospect*, 20 July 2001; "How things look inside the NLD".
46 *Daw Aung San Suu Kyi's Speech on 27–5-1999*, OBL.
47 Kyaw Yin Hlaing, "The state of the pro-democracy movement", p. 98.
48 Ibid., p. 97.
49 Ibid.
50 *Continuing the Pursuit of Democracy in Burma*. Confidential. 08RANGOON557_a 14 July 2008, Wikileaks.Org The "Uncles" were members of the former military faction, which gradually lost its influence within the party. This suited Suu Kyi as nobody challenged her leadership, but was fatal to the military faction, which then no longer existed in the NLD, Derek Tonkin, personal correspondence 15 January 2020.
51 Kyaw Yin Hlaing, "The state of the pro-democracy movement", p. 97.
52 BPS, vol. IX, no. 7, July 1995; BPS, vol. X, no. 6, June 1996; BPS, vol. X, no. 7, July 1996; BPS, vol. X, no. 10, October 1996; *Myanmar Alin*, 30 June 1996, BNN; *Myanmar Alin*, 12 July 1999; *The New Light of Myanmar*, 9 May 1997, BNN; *The New Light of Myanmar*, 21 July 1996, BNN; *The New Light of Myanmar*, 19 August 1996, BNN; "Myanmar news release", vol. 10, no. 17, 29 July, BNN; *Kyemon*, 14 October 1996, BNN; Houtman, *Mental Culture*, pp. 27–43, 86, 277–280.
53 Clements, *The Voice of Hope*, pp. 139–147; BPS, vol. IV, no. 7, July 1990; BPS, vol. VI, no. 5, May 1992; Victor, *The Lady*, pp. 82–141; "Dark victory"; Wintle, *Perfect Hostage*, p. 366.
54 Harriden, *The Authority of Influence*, pp. 225–227.
55 Thant Myint-U, *The Hidden History of Burma*, pp. 42–43.
56 Sengupta, *The Female Voice of Myanmar*, pp. 241–243, 323–325.
57 Francis Sejersted, "The 1991 Nobel Prize for Peace", in: *Freedom from Fear*, pp. 228–234.
58 See e.g. Aung San Suu Kyi, "Please use your liberty to promote ours", *The New York Times*, 4 February 1997; Aung San Suu Kyi, "Freedom from fear"; "In quest for democracy"; "Towards a true refugee", all in: *Freedom from Fear*, pp. 167–186; 239–249.

59 Even she admitted it: 'I suppose I do have a stubborn streak in me'. "Aung San Suu Kyi in the UK", *The Telegraph*, 19 June 2012.

60 Houtman, *Mental Culture*, p. 3; Thant Myint-U, *The River of Lost Footsteps*, p. 143.

61 Lisa Brooten, "The feminization of democracy under siege: The media, "the Lady" of Burma, and U.S. foreign policy", *NWSA Journal*, vol. 17, no.3 (2005), pp. 134–156.

62 Zöllner, *The Beast and the Beauty*, pp. 195–229 and 277–359.

63 Brooten, "The feminization of democracy", pp. 134–156.

64 Suu Kyi, "Empowerment for a culture of peace and development', in: *Freedom from Fear*, pp. 268–269.

65 "Meetings with Aung San Suu Kyi", *The Irrawaddy*, 15 April 2007.

66 "Razali Ismail, Renaissance Man", *The Wall Street Journal*, 16 June 2003.

67 The Yadana gas field project, a joint-venture between Burmese, US, French and Thai companies, is the extraction of offshore gas that started in mid-1990s. It was notorious for human rights abuses (e.g. forced labour). The revenues from Yadana allowed the generals to survive (the project was exempted from the Western sanctions).

68 "Aung San Suu Kyi takes calculated risk in shifting stance against junta", *AFP*, 24 April 2003.

69 Terms hardliners/moderates (pragmatists) should be used with (serious) reservations, Kyaw Yin Hlaing "Political impasse in Myanmar," pp. 23–26.

70 "Read this, you dinosaurs!", *Asiaweek*, 18 February 2000; Charney, *A History of Modern Burma*, p. 181; Ye Htut, *Myanmar's Political Transition*, pp. 18–19.

71 "Who is who in junta's line-up", *The Irrawaddy*, 26 August 2003.

72 *Preliminary Report of the Ad Hoc Commission on Depayin Massacre*, 4 June 2003, OBL; *Situation of Human Rights in Myanmar – Report Submitted by the Special Rapporteur*, UN General Assembly, E/CN.4/2004/33, 1 May 2004; Popham, *The Lady and the Peacock*, p. 361.

73 Aung Zaw, *The Face of Resistance*, p. 113.

5

THE ROADMAP

After the Depayin massacre Myanmar entered a dark period of despair, symbolized by Suu Kyi's third and final house arrest, lasting from 2003 until 2010. It was during this time, though, that a specific Burmese political transition was planned and implemented. The SPDC–NLD political stalemate finally prompted the generals to carry on the transition without Suu Kyi: she was bound to be forgotten.

Aung San Suu Kyi amnesia

Following Depayin, the regime cracked down on NLD members, placing Suu Kyi, Tin Oo and U Lwin under house arrest and jailing many others, shutting down the NLD offices and again effectively decapitating the party. International outrage commenced, followed by new US sanctions. The SPDC responded by a cabinet reshuffle: nominating Khin Nyunt as prime minister (the position previously held by Than Shwe) to reduce international pressure. For Khin Nyunt it was a demotion (in the process he lost his Secretary post, having previously been Secretary no. 1 in the SPDC), which confirmed his weakening position. He nevertheless hoped to restore his standing by conducting a successful foreign policy: improving relations with the West.[1] Five days after nomination he announced a roadmap to democracy, which consisted of seven points: resumption and conclusion of the National Convention; drafting a constitution; holding a referendum on it and then parliamentary elections; convening the Hluttaw (parliament) and electing a democratic government.[2] The reason for a roadmap was to ensure the Tatmadaw's control over the political process in Myanmar, while the lack of a timetable allowed the regime to keep watch over the pace of implementation.

During his prime ministerial tenure, Khin Nyunt apparently negotiated with Suu Kyi in secrecy for the return of the NLD to the National Convention. According to Suu Kyi, they were "almost there": the deal was negotiated by Khin Nyunt's envoys Kyaw Win, Tin Hlaing, Than Htun and Suu Kyi, but was allegedly rejected – to Suu Kyi's anger – by Than Shwe.[3] If true, it may mean one thing. It is probable that, in the mid-2000s, Suu Kyi had already come to realise that she would not be able to force the generals to accept handing power to the NLD; instead she would have to come to terms with them, on their conditions. In other words, Suu Kyi might have belatedly understood the rules of Myanmar's non-level playing field. Yet the other side was uninterested. Suu Kyi complained that "anything short of capitulation was seen as confrontation"[4] by the regime. And she was correct. The SPDC thought it could live without her, all disadvantages (lack of domestic legitimacy, external condemnation) notwithstanding. Several explanations of the Tatmadaw's uncompromising stance are cited in literature,[5] yet the most plausible seems to be the legacy of political confrontation in the 1990s/early 2000s. The generals were too arrogant to relinquish power, but also the NLD lacked the persuasive power to convince them. Instead of mending fences, the NLD acted on the contrary: they kept delegitimizing the generals, both domestically and internationally. As well as calls for sanctions, a model example of the NLD burning bridges are its leaders' interviews and speeches where they openly accused the generals of "fear".[6] You do not tell international media and citizens that your (stronger) enemies-cum-potential dialogue partners, who furthermore happen to be soldiers, are cowards, even if it is true (perhaps especially if it is). The NLD's stance was psychologically and morally understandable – the generals were despots with blood on their hands, they terrorized and repressed society and wronged many NLD members. Yet they were firmly in control and, as the Machiavellian saying goes, "who holds power does not have to apologise to anyone". The NLD's rhetoric and actions made them fear that losing power equalled retribution. This, combined with no dialogue at all, produced a lack of clarity about goals as each side kept telling the other what it wanted, which led intransigence on both sides. It ended with 'reciprocal obstinacy': both sides were unwilling to compromise and this turned the political contest into a zero-sum game. Consequently, perhaps the biggest problem in Myanmar's personalized policymaking, was a total lack of trust.[7]

The lack of trust was combined with another most important fatal consequence of the Tatmadaw–NLD confrontation that had been ongoing since 1988: the NLD's unwillingness to play along with the rules set by the generals. Several of Suu Kyi's conciliatory gestures, both in 1995 and in 2002, amounted to next to nothing given her rejection of the military non-level playing field. The generals could only have allowed her to rule under their own conditions, yet in the long run she wanted to replace them. These were irreconcilable standpoints. Once Than Shwe and other SPDC leaders realized Suu Kyi would not abide by the Tatmadaw rules, they decided to carry on without her.

Failure to convince Than Shwe to try and make yet another settlement with Suu Kyi foreshadowed the end of Khin Nyunt's political career. After an unsuccessful attempt to bring the NLD onto the re-conveyed National Convention and equally fruitless attempts to reconcile with the USA (where Suu Kyi herself became a factor in Washington's foreign policy in the 2000s),[8] Khin Nyunt was purged along with his MI (Directorate of Defence Services Intelligence) on 19 October 2004.[9] The roadmap was halted for a while; as were any ideas of partially sharing power. What could be called 'Aung San Suu Kyi amnesia' set in among the regime [10]. The SPDC wanted to marginalize her and make society and the world forget about her. Because of governmental reasons (regime survival), Than Shwe's (and other generals') personal animosity towards Suu Kyi, gender biases and her hybrid Burmese-ness, so different from their own xenophobic nationalism, the ruling generals clearly disliked Suu Kyi as a political opponent.[11]

Whatever the reason, their 'Suu Kyi amnesia' plan did not quite work; an episode on 22 September 2007, when demonstrating monks marched to her house to greet her, proved the ineffectiveness of this policy. However, the rulings of the SPDC remained seriously unquestioned in the 2000s. Myanmar entered a dark period of despair, oblivion, exclusion and prolonged poverty on one hand, with the Tatmadaw's unlimited power, symbolized by their new capital, Naypyidaw, on the other.[12]

The 2007 mass protests of monks motivated, or rather hastened, Than Shwe's implementation of a long-term exit plan. In September 2007 he rejuvenated the National Convention. A new constitutional project quickly formed. It was almost the same to the one first proposed by the Tatmadaw in 1993 which was rejected by the NLD. Now, after a decade and a half of stalemate, which had cost Myanmar dearly, "Than Shwe pushed through what he and the other generals had always had in mind"; he engineered "a very specific transition, to a more diffused and popularly acceptable structure".[13] A transformation from direct military rule to "something else": a "sui generis case",[14] a Burmese "shibboleth of democracy".[15] It is debatable whether Than Shwe indeed "was the mastermind of Myanmar's transition to democracy"[16] (however badly that sounds) or whether the post-2011 changes went further than he intended.[17] The latter is certainly the interpretation preferred by Suu Kyi.[18]

The proposed constitution was put to a referendum on 10 May 2008, despite the fact that Myanmar had been hit by Cyclone Nargis on 2 May 2008 – the worst natural disaster in Myanmar history. It devastated the Irrawaddy Delta, killing more than 130,000 people, and produced international outcry for the junta's inability to conduct a humanitarian assistance campaign and their initial unwillingness to accept foreign help.

The rigged vote (officially 92 per cent voted 'yes') legitimized the 2008 Constitution – the most military-dominated constitution in the world![19] – which introduced 'disciplined democracy' to Myanmar. By giving the army 25 per cent of allocated seats in the National Assembly (a blocking minority, as any amendment of the Constitution requires the consent of more than 75 per cent of MPs, according to Chapter IV, section 109b); three ministries – defence, border affairs and home affairs (Chapter V, section 232 b and ii); one vice president seat (Chapter III, section 60 b and c); administrative autonomy (section 343, a and b) and majority in the NDSC (National Defence and Security Council, Chapter V, section 201), the Constitution ensured the Tatmadaw dominated the political system of Myanmar.

In name, it was a presidential system. It entrusted the President with substantial power, including power to declare emergency in consultation with the NDSC. Just in case, it also made certain that the President could not be Suu Kyi, as the Constitution prohibited any formal foreign liaisons of family members (Chapter III, section 59, f). An emergency could be declared in case of endangering the Three National Causes (non-disintegration of the Union, non-disintegration of national solidarity and perpetuation of sovereignty), where all powers would transfer to the commander-in-chief of the Tatmadaw (Chapter XI, sections 409–422). Hence, in reality, the system ensured the Tatmadaw's dominance regardless of who was in power, military or otherwise. In the best scenario for the Tatmadaw (that is, a military-backed government), it provided a cover up of factual military rule; in the worst (a military-opposed government), it checked and balanced every civilian government decision. The military legally sanctioned its privileged position in Myanmar politics, as the ultimate political referee, one 'above politics'. In a way, this Constitution is a political masterpiece for protecting the army's self-interest.

Having legitimized its rule by a constitution, the army prepared for another step on the roadmap: general elections. Unfortunately for the generals, Suu Kyi's house arrest term was set to expire a year before the elections, which could complicate this orchestrated political show. Something needed to be done with her. Fortunately, a solution came out of the blue, or rather out of the lake. John Yettaw, an American with a challenging mental condition, swam (twice) to Suu Kyi's house – in a scene worthy of a Monty Python sketch – which gave the junta a pretext to extend Suu Kyi's house arrest,[20] meaning she would be freed only after the planned elections.

However, the Yettaw incident had some unintended consequences: talks commenced between the junta and the USA leading to some tentative signs of thaw in their relations. Unfortunately, the election issue stood in the way of reconciliation. The junta steamrolled their roadmap plan, which left the NLD with an fundamental dilemma. The party could either participate in the elections, gaining a chance to take part in the real political process but bidding farewell to any remaining hopes of resurrecting the results of the 1990 elections. Or they could boycott the 2010 elections and risk political marginalization. In was a simple choice: finally accepting the non-level playing field or carrying on with dreams to force the junta to concessions.

There was no unanimity in the party. A faction led by Khin Maung Swe and Than Nyein (both long-term NLD members, MPs from 1990 and former political prisoners) preferred the former, whereas the radical faction under Win Tin (released from harsh imprisonment after 19 years) demanded the latter (sticking to the 2009 'Shwegondine Declaration'). It seems the moderates held the majority, clandestinely being backed by Aung Shwe, but it meant next to nothing because Suu Kyi decided on a boycott ("Six Points"). In her typical way of handling party affairs, Suu Kyi enforced decision making by acclamation, not a secret ballot, which ensured nobody dared to oppose her will. Once again she proved skilful in keeping full control over the NLD, even from house arrest.

The NLD announced their boycott of the 2010 elections and was delegalized. Khin Maung Swe, together with his supporters, quit the party and founded a new one: the National Democratic Force (NDF). Furious with the "traitors", Suu Kyi called the faction "incompatible with democratic process".[21] But she won, not them. The NDF contested the unfair elections on 7 November 2010 and received only slightly over 2 per cent of the votes, ceasing to matter politically. Although there were assertions that the junta had deprived the NDF of victory in some of Yangon's important constituencies by falsifying the results of the absentee ballot, in reality this would have not changed the outcome much. The Union Solidarity and Development Party (USDP), a political wing of the army, would have won anyway, perhaps having less than 76 per cent votes but enough to have majority in the parliament.[22] The generals did not have to invoke Stalin's formula ("the people who count the votes decide everything"), for they themselves had established such a non-level playing field that defeating them became next to impossible.

Suu Kyi was released from her final house arrest a week later (13 November 2010) and was welcomed by cheering crowds. Despite that, on the international stage it was popular at that time to paint her as a marginalized political figure who had lost.[23] Nevertheless, paraphrasing Mark Twain, the reports of Suu Kyi's political death proved to be grossly exaggerated.

A new hope

The 2008 constitution established a Tatmadaw-dominated political system. In accordance with their roadmap, a 'civilianization' process followed. On 30 March 2011, the junta dissolved itself and the generals took off their uniforms to take up posts in the newly civilian administration. But not all.

To universal surprise, Than Shwe did not become President, as was widely expected, even by the Tatmadaw. Instead he retired and made sure his deputy, Maung Aye, did the same. For the presidency he chose his trusted subordinate, Thein Sein. This was the second surprise as Thein Sein, a colourless bureaucrat, ranked only fourth in the junta behind *thura* Shwe Mann (no. 3), who was widely considered the most probable successor. Shwe Mann, however, was only appeased with the post of Speakership of Pyithu Hluttaw (the lower house of the parliament), leaving him second in the newly civilianized hierarchy. By doing so, Than Shwe behaved as if following an autocrat's textbook: placing an ambitious contender behind a loyal bureaucrat, so that they checked one another, leaving Than Shwe to settle their disputes. And – just in case – Than Shwe nominated Min Aung Hlaing, another loyal protégée, as the Tatmadaw's commander-in-chief. With his men occupying top posts and balancing one another, and with Suu Kyi seemingly outmanoeuvred, Than Shwe could safely retire.[24]

For this reason most commentators harboured few illusions. The civilianization process seemed a sham transformation: "an old wine in the new bottle".[25] There was some progress. Yet that was too little to convince the sceptics. Thus, when Thein Sein concededly announced his will to reform, few believed him. The first half of 2011 went by the old way, with tensions between the government and Suu Kyi dominating the scene. She was initially unwilling to give the new administration the benefit of the doubt, criticising the government in interviews with foreign media, keeping her position on sanctions and the 1990 elections and irritating the USDP with remarks about a Second (or, to be exact, a Third) Panglong.[26] The government in turn warned, that she and the NLD would "meet their tragic ends" if they "keep going the wrong way", later reminding her that the NLD was technically an illegal party.[27] It really seemed history would repeat itself again, with yet another Suu Kyi–Tatmadaw confrontation just around the corner.

And yet something would change. The first signs of new winds came with the nomination of U Myint, Suu Kyi's friend, as presidential advisor in April 2011. Then the approach towards Suu Kyi softened. She (along with the NLD) took part in official Martyr Day's commemorations (19 July 2011) for the first time in years. She met with the regime's liaison Aung Kyi twice (25 July 2011 and 12 August 2011) and was allowed to travel to Bago for a political excursion.

A breakthrough came on 19 August 2011 when Suu Kyi met with Thein Sein in Naypyidaw and attended a government-organized economic forum, stealing the show.[28] All this, quite shockingly, was covered by the Burmese media.[29] In a country where Suu Kyi's name had been forbidden for two decades, a picture of Thein Sein and Suu Kyi standing behind a portrait of Aung San (in civilian dress) – who had also been marginalized – spoke louder than a thousand words. It univocally meant that Suu Kyi amnesia (and Aung San amnesia as well) was over. Words were important too, though. Suu Kyi declared that the meeting "went well", Thein Sein wanted "real change", and was "somebody who could be trusted".[30]

What pre-dated this breakthrough event was behind-the-scenes diplomacy between Thein Sein's administration and Suu Kyi. According to Ye Htut, Thein Sein made a decision to reach out to Suu Kyi during a meeting in July 2011 with his soon-to-be crucial ministers Soe Thane and Aung Min as well as some members of the Myanmar Egress organization. He subsequently sent Aung Kyi, a "relations minister", who had served as liaison between the junta and Suu Kyi in 2007–2009, to contact her. Contrary to previous cases, when Aung Kyi's mission was for show only, this time it was real: Aung Kyi was to bring Suu Kyi on board. Suu Kyi demanded amendments to the election and party registration laws (in order to restore the NLD), the opening of the NLD offices in the countryside and public acknowledgement that the NLD had won the 1990 elections and the SLORC had failed to transfer power. Thein Sein, after consulting Shwe Mann and Khin Aung Myint (Speaker of Amyotha Hluttaw, or upper house of the parliament), agreed, thus paving the way for the 19 August 2011 breakthrough meeting.[31] Apparently, the meeting was unconfirmed until the very last moment as many NLD members did not want Suu Kyi to go to Naypyidaw, it was organized at the last minute.[32] Once she got to the capital she "decided on the basis, it is said, of an ad hoc agreement reached with Thein Sein", to enter the political system.[33] If so, this confirms the everlasting importance of ad hockery in Burmese politics.

Apparently, what broke the ice between Thein Sein and Suu Kyi was the warm reception she received from his family. Thein Sein invited Suu Kyi to his house, where his wife and children greeted Suu Kyi cordially. As the story goes, Suu Kyi was so delighted she remarked "a husband of such a wonderful woman could not be bad".[34] If true, this confirms another truth about Burmese politics: it is all personal.

It also meant one thing. Thein Sein, backed by Shwe Mann, had prevailed over 'hardliners' within the regime for whom Suu Kyi was already "a dead tiger".[35] The 'moderates' understood that bringing Suu Kyi on board was essential, albeit very risky, to make the reforms possible by restoring domestic and international legitimacy. For hardliners, the reformers "were veering away from the original script", which was to "take things in a reformist direction without going too far" (read: without Suu Kyi who "wasn't meant to be part of the picture at all").[36] Their dissent "was based not on a strategic analysis or a clear alternative agenda, but on gut instinct".[37] In a hidden, though 'epic' battle of wills between reformers and hardliners within the regime, by mid-2011 the former gained an upper hand (and cemented their dominance by 2012).[38] This meant a fundamental adjustment of the regime's policy towards Suu Kyi: from marginalization to co-optation.

After the Suu Kyi–Thein Sein summit, change was in the air. Myanmar hit the headlines on 30 September 2011, when Thein Sein – to Beijing's shock and disbelief – suspended the controversial Chinese-backed Myitsone Dam, citing a previously unheard of reason: the will the people.[39] Meanwhile, the thaw between the regime and Suu Kyi intensified. Behind-the-scenes talks between Aung Kyi and Suu Kyi continued; press censorship of articles on her (and on her father) was lifted, which was the first sign of censorship relaxation until its suspension in August 2012. In September Khin Aung Myint said Suu Kyi would be "welcomed" if she joined the parliament.[40] She made steps to do so. In October Suu Kyi agreed to the NLD standing in parliamentary by-elections scheduled for April 2012, thus returning to the official fold. Her party was subsequently re-legalized: it was re-registered in December by electoral commission, with Suu Kyi's personal presence during the procedure. Myanmar hit the international headlines when Hilary Clinton came to visit (29 November – 2 December 2011), being the first US State Secretary since John F. Dulles to do so. She had a productive meeting with Thein Sein and a cordial one with Suu Kyi.[41] Apparently Suu Kyi told Clinton "I don't want to be an icon, I want to be a politician", to which Clinton pithily replied, "Get ready to get attacked".[42]

By late 2011/early 2012 events accelerated even more. Starting from late 2011, the presidential envoy and one of Thein Sein's closest 'lieutenants' – Aung Min – secured a series of new ceasefire agreements with ethnic guerrilla groups, temporarily breaking the deadlock in ethnic relations. For a while it indeed looked like guerrillas would switch guns for laptops.[43] On 13 January 2012, Thein Sein's administration released more than 600 of Myanmar's political prisoners, including the most famous ones, such as Min Ko Naing, Htay Kywe, Zaw That Htwe, Khun Tun Oo, U Gambira ... and Khin Nyunt. By early 2012 Thein Sein had become the unexpected face of Myanmar's reforms. In the meantime, the society's mood changed considerably. People not only ceased to fear speaking Suu Kyi's name in public, but her face suddenly appeared on street vendor stands in Yangon's – on posters, pictures, photographs, calendars, even trinkets and keyrings.[44] For anyone who remembered the pre-2011 atmosphere, it was an amazing development. When the by-elections in April 2012 were decisively won by the NLD and turned out to be free and fair, it was clear to all, Burmese and foreigners alike, that the reforms were real.

Understanding the Burmese Spring

Why did the generals, after decades of stagnation and irreconcilable isolation, decide to initiate reforms? There is no single answer to that question, yet one may dare to suggest that it was the (unexpected) outcome of four simultaneous processes coupled with one dominant tendency in Burmese politics.

The first was the Tatmadaw's planned withdrawal from direct policymaking into a comfortable position 'above politics'. If the Tatmadaw's declarations are to be taken seriously, this was what they had wanted all along since the coup of 1988: military leaders constantly emphasized that their rule was temporary (however, what this precisely meant was never disclosed as no exact timetable was ever set). Yet before 2010, the conditions were not ready for them to withdraw and they could have done it only from a position of strength, never weakness. By early 2011, having marginalized Suu Kyi and contained, though not eliminated, other domestic and international threats, the generals felt comfortable enough to pursue their long-planned exit strategy. Thus, in the elite-driven, top-down transition process "from within" Myanmar, carried out by the Tatmadaw as its key institution, the generals transformed themselves from praetorians' into 'arbitrators': guardians of the political system they established.[45]

Another process went hand in hand with this: liberalization within the regime. There had always been 'moderates' in the junta. Or to be exact people (Khin Nyunt, Hla Min, Win Aung, Nyan Win, Aung Lin Htut or Kyaw Thu) who did not want to relinquish power but understood the importance of appearances in both domestic (and especially) international policymaking. The regime would have been less delegitimized domestically, and Myanmar would have been less isolated internationally, had the SLORC/SPDC paid a little more than scant attention to political decorum.

The number of more open-minded individuals within the Tatmadaw ranks had been increasing; a process that had begun in the 2000s, though it was invisible to foreign observers. A gradual replacement of narrow-minded commanders with better educated military technocrats proceeded within the middle and high ranks of the military administration. It culminated in changes between 2011–2015. With Thein Sein, Shwe Mann and Min Aung Hlaing coming to power, accompanied by an entourage of reform-minded ministers, legislators and other subordinates (Soe Thane, Aung Min, Tin Naing Thein, Hla Tun, Nay Zin Latt, U Myint, Aung Tut

Thet, Aung Kyi, Nyan Tun, Ye Htut, Set Aung and others), these elite-driven, top-to-bottom reforms became possible. Broad minded individuals within the Tatmadaw initiated the process, overcame the 'hardliners' (Tin Aung Myint Oo, Htay Oo, Zaw Min, Kyaw Hsan, Ko Ko, Aung Thaung, Maung Thaung, Lun Thi and others) and became modernizing actors.[46]

These internal dynamics within the army and army-based institutions (the USDP, the Hluttaw), were accompanied by two processes external to the Tatmadaw. The first one was small, almost invisible to the outside world. It was the process of socio-political change in Myanmar. An inner-system approach of tentative steps towards reforming the country was initiated by conscious individuals in the mid-2000s. There, civilian reformists – Nay Win Maung, Hla Maung Shwe, Tin Maung Thann, Kyaw Yin Hlaing, Sonny Nyunt Thein, Kyaw Ni Khin, Ye Mya Thu (founders of the Myanmar Egress organization) – were joined by other, sometimes very diverse, individuals (Khin Zaw Win, Kyaw Thu, Aye Mya Hlaing, Ma Ja Nan Lahtaw, Maung Zarni, etc.) and organizations (e.g. the Shalom and Metta Foundations). This phenomenon, which gained momentum after Cyclone Nargis, during the 2008 referendum and after the 2010 elections was labelled 'the third force'. In the polarizing political scene of Myanmar, the third force was controversial: they were nearly (or bluntly) traitors to the NLD and to the exile Burmese community as well as suspicious to the Tatmadaw. Accused of complicity with the regime – the very nature of their activity forced them to lean towards the junta, not to the politically weak NLD – they nevertheless instilled new ideas into the minds of the ruling military class. They prompted change, though we will never estimate how much exactly as their influence has been overestimated by supporters and underestimated by their opponents. Many of the third force members jumped on the bandwagon once reforms kicked in, joining Thein Sein's reformers formally and informally. Together with a group of exiles and/or overseas returnees, both Burmese and ethnic minority influencers either incorporated themselves into the ranks of Thein Sein's network as policy advisors or assisted informally. Among the Burmese returnees were people such as Thant Myint-U, Min Zaw Oo, Aung Naing Oo, Nyo Ohn Myint, Zaw Oo and many others; among the ethnic group, Harn Yawnghwe, Lian Sakhong, Naw Zipporah Sein, and Ja Nan Lahtaw stood out the most. Together they made a team of reformers, who helped Myanmar make a comeback after six decades of military misrule.[47]

Finally, the last process, and the only external one, was subsidiary. In the late 2000s, growing understanding that sanctions did not work began to spread amongst Western policymaking circles. However, since sanctions are always easy to introduce and difficult to lift, and because pro-democracy groups continued to exert pressure with their pointless, moral support for them, few Western policymakers risked changing their policies (after all, it was not their people who suffered). Obama's administration in 2008 admitted to the failure of sanctions and tried to reach out to the Burmese junta. Initially this did not work out, but 'pragmatic engagement' finally paid off once Thein Sein's reforms started in 2011. Such international support strengthened the reformers vis-à-vis hardliners. Although international standing had never been the most important benchmark in the Tat-madaw's policymaking, it mattered symbolically. Their pariah status irritated the Burmese, military and civilians alike. The possibility of restoring international legitimacy was an important, even if secondary, incentive for reforms.[48]

All that said, one should be cautious to retrospectively paint a picture of a grand scheme of reforms. Politics in general, and Burmese politics in particular, is full of ad hockery. It was true with these reforms as well, especially after 2011.[49] Visions and plans look nice in history textbooks, but the reality is usually much more murky. Decisions are driven by particular interests, emotions and hopes, a lack of (or insufficiency of) knowledge, short-sightedness, incompetence, and at times stupidity, personal sympathies, animosities as well as blind chances. Reforming a country, especially one undertaking systemic transition, is like a walk in the dark without a clear direction or plan. The bumpy road to post-authoritarianism, full of ambiguities, shades of grey and disorientation about its direction, may perhaps be fully understood only by those who went through it, in this country or another.

Furthermore, the Burmese Spring would not have been possible had not Suu Kyi decided to give it a chance in mid-2011. The new political circumstances, however, put Suu Kyi in a challenging position. She had to take her biggest political risk since 1988.[50]

Notes

1 Taylor, *The State in Myanmar*, pp. 481–484.
2 "Prime Minister General Khin Nyunt clarifies future policies and programmes of state", *The New Light of Myanmar*, 31 August 2003.
3 Popham, *The Lady and the Peacock*, pp. 345–365. A slightly different account can be found in Ye Htut, *Myanmar's Political Transition*, pp. 20–21.
4 Quoted in: Pederson, *The Burma Spring*, p. 425.
5 Personal legacy; the 1990 elections' shock and the reformists defeat, Kyaw Yin Hlaing, "Political impasse in Myanmar", pp. 21–27; other explanations point out personal issues (Than Shwe's dislike of Suu Kyi), cultural reasons (the generals' xenophobia) and the inward-looking identity of the Tatmadaw.
6 Clements, *The Voice of Hope*, pp. 29, 35 and 183, 256–258, 300; *Daw Suu's 25 Dialogues*, p. 187.
7 Kyaw Yin Hlaing, "Political impasse in Myanmar", pp. 27–29.
8 'Burma was a "boutique" issue in US politics', Steinberg, "Aung San Suu Kyi and U.S. policy", pp. 35–59.
9 Details about this purge: Andrew Selth, *Secrets and Power in Myanmar: Intelligence and the Fall of General Khin Nyunt* (Singapore: ISEAS, 2019), pp. 56–81. Khin Nyunt's fall had unintended positive consequences: with the removal of his intelligence network, space emerged for civil society, Marie Lall, *Understanding Reform in Myanmar. People and Society in the Wake of Military Rule* (London: Hurst, 2016), pp. 10–29.
10 One can argue that just like "Aung San amnesia" set in in the 1990s (see: Houtman, *Mental Culture*, pp. 26–32), so "Suu Kyi amnesia" set in in the 2000s.
11 While dislike towards Suu Kyi was evident in the SPDC, the reasons for it are disputable. It was popular to accredit Than Shwe with dislike, or even detest, towards Suu Kyi. For a feminist interpretation, see: Harriden, *Authority of Influence*, p. 216. For an argument about xenophobia, see Pederson, *The Burma Spring*, p. 432.

12 Yet, "the darkest hour is just before the dawn": it was then in mid-2000s when the first bottom-to-top, initiatives from within Myanmar emerged to reform the country, see: Lall, *Understanding Reform in Myanmar,* pp. 13–67.
13 Thant Myint-U, *The Hidden History of Burma,* pp. 107 and 110.
14 Renaud Egreteau, *Caretaking Democratization. The Military and Political Change in Myanmar* (London: Hurst, 2016), pp. 3–13.
15 Robert H. Taylor, "Myanmar's 'pivot' toward the shibboleth of 'Democracy'", *Asian Affairs,* vol. 44, np. 3 (2013), pp. 392–400.
16 Ye Htut, *Myanmar's Political Transition,* pp. 3 and 217.
17 Lall, *Understanding Reform in Myanmar,* pp. 58, 65; Egreteau, *Caretaking Democratization,* p. 36.
18 In 2015 I asked Suu Kyi whether she agrees with Than Shwe being the founder of the political system in Myanmar. Displeased, she answered: "Than Shwe is almost forgotten", quoted in: Michał Lubina, *Pani Birmy. Biografia Polityczna Aung San Suu Kyi* (Warszawa, PWN, 2015), p. 432.
19 "Constitutional reform in Myanmar: Priorities and prospects for amendment", *Bingham Centre Working Paper* No 1 (2014), p. 8.
20 Suu Kyi was originally sentenced to 3 years in jail, but the verdict was immediately shortened to 18 months of house arrest.
21 "Suu Kyi criticizes NDF faction", *The Irrawaddy,* 15 April 2010.
22 *Progress Report of the Special Rapporteur on the Situation of Human Rights in Myanmar,* 7 March 2011, GA A/HRC/16/59.
23 "A shot in the dark", *Prospect,* 20 October 2010; "Suu Kyi's influence wanes as party splits", *Sunday Times,* 17 October 2010; Popham, *The Lady and the Peacock,* p. 369; Zöllner, *The Beast and the Beauty,* p. 480.
24 Thant Myint-U, *The Hidden History of Burma,* pp. 133–135.
25 Ye Htut, *Myanmar's Political Transition,* p. 1.
26 Lall, *Understanding Reform in Myanmar,* pp. 56–57. The second Panglong (Pinlon) conference took place in February 1947 between Aung San and the leaders of many (though not all) ethnic minorities. The agreement reached there paved way to formation of the Union of Burma. It is now a national holiday in Myanmar (Union Day, 12 February) and Panglong has been mythologised as the apparent concord between the Bamars and the ethnic minorities. Although chronologically speaking the 1947 Panglong was the second Panglong conference, the first conference (that took place in March 1946) was less important and is often forgotten. It is popular to understand the second Panglong conference (1947) as the Panglong conference and call Suu Kyi's Panglong as the Second one (although it is chronologically the Third).
27 "Sanctions, Daw Suu Kyi and NLD", *The New Light of Myanmar,* 13 February 2011; "To quarrel or to be reconciled," *The New Light of Myanmar,* 30 June 2011.
28 Kyaw Yin Hlaing, "The unexpected arrival of a new political era in Myanmar", in: *Prisms on the Golden Pagoda. Perspectives on National Reconciliation in Myanmar,* ed. Kyaw Yin Hlaing (Singapore: NUS Press, 2014), pp. 218–220.
29 "President U Thein Sein, Daw Aung San Suu Kyi vow to cooperate for national interest", *The New Light of Myanmar,* 20 August 2011.
30 "Suu Kyi Says Burma President wants 'real change'", *BNN,* 24 August 2011; "Suu Kyi 'satisfied' with Thein Sein talks", *The Irrawaddy,* 20 August 2011.
31 Ye Htut, *Myanmar's Political Transition,* pp. 50–53. Thein Sein's administration "went so far as to publicise the NLD's success, but did not go so far as to acknowledge that the SLORC had failed to transfer power". Derek Tonkin, email correspondence, 16 February 2020.
32 Lall, *Understanding Reform in Myanmar,* p. 72.
33 Popham, *The Lady and the Generals,* p. 98.
34 Kyaw Yin Hlaing, "The unexpected arrival", p. 220.
35 Ye Htut, *Myanmar's Political Transition,* p. 53.
36 Thant Myint-U, *The Hidden History of Burma,* pp. 145–153.

37 Ibid.
38 Lall, *Understanding Reform in Myanmar*, p. 65.
39 Ye Htut, *Myanmar's Political Transition*, pp. 159–160. Suu Kyi, on the other hand, joined the protests by writing her "Irrawaddy Appeal" (11 August 2011), which strengthened dissent, but she was not the driving force behind the movement itself.
40 "Burma: No objection to parliament bid", *RFA*, 20 September 2011.
41 Hillary R. Clinton, *Hard Choices* (New York, NY: Simon & Shuster, 2014).
42 "The Burmese Spring", *The New Yorker*, 6 August 2012.
43 "All must try to see national race youths who brandished guns using laptops", *The New Light of Myanmar*, 2 March 2012.
44 Visit to Myanmar, January–February 2012.
45 Egreteau, *Caretaking Democratization*, pp. 3–26; Robert H. Taylor, "The armed forces in Myanmar's politics: A terminating role?", *ISEAS Trends*, no. 2 (2015), pp. 5–33; Mary Callahan, "The generals loosen their grip", *Journal of Democracy*, vol. 23, no. 4 (2012), p. 120; Maitrii Aung-Thwin, "Reassessing Myanmar's "Glasnost"", *Kyoto Review of Southeast Asia*, no. 14 (2013).
46 Egreteau, *Caretaking Democratization*, pp. 3–13; Narayanan Ganesan, "Interpreting recent developments in Myanmar as an attempt to establish political legitimacy", *Asian Journal of Peacebuilding*, vol. 1, no. 2 (2013), p. 254; Marco Bünthe, "Burma's transition to quasi-military rule: From rulers to guardians?" *Armed Forces & Society*, vol. 40, no. 4 (2014), pp. 757–8.
47 Lall, *Understanding Reforms in Myanmar*, pp. 13–65; Kyaw Yin Hlaing, "The political impasse in Myanmar", pp. 32–40; Egreteau, *Caretaking Democratization*, pp. 5 and 33–35; Narayanan Ganesan, "The Myanmar Peace Center: Its origins, activities, and aspirations", *Asian Journal of Peacebuilding*, vol. 2, no. 1 (2014), pp. 130–1.
48 Taylor, "Myanmar's 'pivot' toward the shibboleth of 'democracy'", pp. 392–400; Bünthe, "Burma's transition to quasi-military rule", pp. 757–8; Egreteau, *Caretaking Democratization*, pp. 12–14; Thant Myint-U, *The Hidden History of Burma*, p. 162.
49 Egreteau, *Caretaking Democratization*, p. 14. See also: Khin Zaw Win, "Myanmar in political transition," in: Kerstin Duell (ed.) *Myanmar in Transition: Polity, People, and Processes* (Singapore, KAS 2013), p. 10.
50 When she said: "what we are doing now involves a lot of risk but it is time to take the risk because in politics there is no 100 percent assurance of success" – she meant it, "Suu Kyi's party to register for Myanmar elections", *AP*, 17 November 2011.

6

THE POKER GAME

By deciding to take part in the 2012 by-elections, Suu Kyi switched her tactics from a struggle against the military-dominated system into an attempt to change it from within. By doing so, she risked everything.

Hard choices

By March 2012 Suu Kyi stepped forth into Myanmar again, starting her new triumphal tour. She designated Kawhmu, a Yangon suburb, as her constituency to candidate from. In the West, a candidate who chooses a constituency previously seldom frequented would have to strive hard to convince local voters that he/she is not a parachute candidate. But in Burmese dynastic, personalized politics, Suu Kyi's choice of Kawhmu was understood by almost all (if not all) villagers as an incredible privilege. She could have singled out any place in Myanmar, but she granted them this honour. Consequently, it mattered little that it was the military who had undertaken some developmental projects in the village, and that they proved to be major ones (the NLD did much less for Kawhmu) in years to come, or that it was a USDP candidate who the local community deemed a respectable figure.[1] Suu Kyi is the mother of Myanmar and the village voted for her in subsequent elections ceaselessly. This micro case study shows the electoral logic in Myanmar quite well.

Back then, in early 2012, the mass enthusiasm that surrounded Suu Kyi's campaign – as everywhere she went, she attracted huge crowns (average of 10,000 per rally)[2] – showed that despite 15 years of house arrest, including most of the previous decade, Suu Kyi was still unquestionably the most popular person in the country. Her fame shone brightly once again. The by-elections were just another one of her shows.

Politically, however, Suu Kyi's breakthrough decision to contest the by-elections was a concession. A major, fundamental one. After 23 years of struggle with the generals, she made the best out of a lousy bargain and accepted the Tatmadaw-enforced rules of the game. What else, if not a concession, was her choice to reject the dreams of restoring the results of the 1990 elections? For 20 years, with endeavour, persistence bordering on stubbornness, high personal cost, and after almost losing her life at least twice (at Danubyu and Depayin), Suu Kyi tried to force the generals to transfer power to her party. It never happened. Step by step, the Tatmadaw enforced its vision – its roadmap. For so many years, the generals could not break her. And now, after all this, she yielded and decided to concede to 10 per cent of a parliament controlled by the Tatmadaw. In a way she did exactly what the NDF (NLD splinters) did, to her outrage, in 2010: she agreed to an allotment of political space by the regime instead of demanding a transfer of power.[3] To use a Hegelian thought, Suu Kyi finally understood that "rational is real". Or, in simpler words, she belatedly accepted the Tatmadaw's non-level playing field. Why? And why so late? Given the fact that the conditions generals offered were more or less similar, why did she not accept them in 1989, 1995 or 2002? For what sake did she waste two decades for both herself and the country?

We will probably never know why. As one veteran Burma-watcher commented, "no one else can explain except Aung San Suu Kyi herself, why she decided to lead her party into the political process under a constitution she had denounced as totally unacceptable just two years before".[4] I was unable to get the answer from Suu Kyi,[5] and on other occasions she offered only vague, quasi-aphorist comments like: "if you want to bring an end to long-standing conflict, you have to be prepared to compromise",[6] or that she operated on the premise of "compromise based on principles",[7] or populist remarks ("If I'm going to be used for the sake of the nation, that's fine by me)".[8] Her party was no better at explaining. I have been asking this question ('why?') to many interlocutors in Myanmar and, after 8 years of doing so, I am no nearer to the answer. Some of my interviewees pointed out that there was substantial, domestic and international, pressure on her to become more flexible. Others said she understood that time was running out for her; speculating that she needed to go out on a limb.[9] Others still pointed to her character, personal instincts and political ambitions:

> Equally important may have been her internal processes, by which I mean her character and her political instincts. By character I focus on her hubristic conviction that she was born to rule, on her stubbornness, belief in her own infallibility and high-handedness. When you combine this with her political ambitions, she has shown herself quite capable … of making a complete U-turn when faced with realities. What was sacred dogma only yesterday can be tossed overboard in a trice when other interests come into play. She is not, in short, a person for whom principles are enduring, except her own personal self-interest.[10]

I find all these explanations valuable yet insufficient. This forces us to speculate.

Presumably, the combination of the four processes (the Tatmadaw's planned exit strategy; liberalization within the regime; social change; and rapprochement with the West) left Suu Kyi with a hard choice. Had she kept her high moral ground position (one rising above politics), rejecting the unfair roadmap, she would have been marginalized. Politically sidelined – as liberalization would have gone on without her (perhaps not as far, but far enough to re-engage with the Western world) – Suu Kyi would have been respected only. She would be admired, certainly (she would have kept her iconic position within and outside Myanmar), yet politically of little relevance. A 'Burmese Dalai Lama' – a universally esteemed figure yet too powerless to reach set political goals, so to say.

Being a real politician, Suu Kyi wanted power; so she had to catch the momentum before it was lost. She had to board the 'reform' train before it was too late: it would depart with or without her. Therefore, after 23 years of futile struggle to force out the generals, she made a strategic U-turn. Suu Kyi changed her tactics from confrontation to cooperation and agreed to function within the rules determined by the regime. One should not underestimate this fact: it finally allowed Myanmar to break the two-decades-long deadlock. Unsurprisingly, previous UN Secretary Ban Ki-Moon, who remembered the pre-2010 situation in Myanmar and Than Shwe's snubs well, hailed Suu Kyi for her "flexibility and wisdom and compromise".[11]

By no means was it surrender, though. Suu Kyi now wanted to change the system from within. Her goal was to get to the parliament, later win majority, amend the constitution, and gain access to real power.[12] That is why she agreed to "become part of the new system"; however, "this was meant as an expedient, not an endgame", as she "decided to join the system in the belief that the government would not only continue reforms but also reform the constitution itself".[13] In short, it was just a modification of means, not objectives. This was pragmatism pure and simple and the best reflection of her father.

A hazardous one. To evoke the football metaphor once again: Suu Kyi restarted the match against (ex) generals with no assurance at all that the referee would not show her a red card once more or nullify a correctly scored goal yet again. This was the single bravest decision in her political life after entering politics in 1988. She bet all her cards – her credibility, her influence, her prestige – on it, knowing too well she could be outplayed by the (ex) generals. Like a poker player, Suu Kyi risked everything.

Initially, events seemed to confirm her decision. On 1 April 2012, the NLD secured a landslide in the by-elections, winning 43 out of 44 contested seats and producing nationwide euphoria. Suu Kyi was triumphant: "we even won in the military constituencies" – she later boasted during a closed meeting with Poland's Speaker of the Senate – "our candidate won with the military one in Thein Sein's constituency; it means even president's staff voted for us".[14] She had once again proved she held the Burmese people's hearts and minds. The joy was not even spoilt by being reminded of the rules of the game: once elected, Suu Kyi again tried to test the limits of the (post) generals' power by demanding a change to the oath (from 'protect' the Constitution to 'abide by'), but facing their uncompromising stance, she backed down after several days of deadlock. Despite this incident, it was a historical moment for her and for the country.

Even more symbolism awaited her during her debut foreign trip to Thailand (29 May–3 June 2012) and especially her second one to Europe (13–29 June 2012). For the first time since the beginning of her political career, she could leave Myanmar without anxiety that she would not be allowed to come back. This fact in itself showed how much had changed within barely a year. Her visits to Thailand, Switzerland, Norway and the UK, as well as her American follow-up in September, were in fact her one grand tour de force.

In Thailand, Suu Kyi quickly noticed the developmental difference between Bangkok and Yangon, visited refugee camps and participated in the World Economic Forum; stealing the show by upstaging Thein Sein's planned visit (the president cancelled it fearing less publicity). In Europe, among everlasting fanfares, she collected the Nobel Peace Prize and Oxford's honorary degree, spoke (as the first woman from abroad and as the first non-leader of state ever) in the British parliament, visited the BBC and celebrated her 68th birthday with her family in Oxford. Accompanied by a chorus of very American turgid speeches, she picked up the Congressional Gold Medal at the Capitol and met President Barrack Obama. This was not only her "carpe diem" moment – she described it as "one of (the) most moving days of her life".[15] These events also marked the zenith of her global influence. Never before (and never after) was she feted so overwhelmingly by various members of the international community. For this single moment, her hybridity seemed the perfect match between local and international, Burmese and Western, Asian and global. Suu Kyi offered the world what it needed: a political moralist preaching vaguely enough to touch the hearts and sufficiently shallow enough to remain universalist and intelligible. It suited the audience perfectly well. As one long-time Myanmar observer commented on the British part of her tour, it did not matter much that Suu Kyi did not say anything particularly insightful. This was because: "so infatuated were the ruling classes in Britain that what she said was less important than the fact that she was able to speak in such excellent English, of the old school variety".[16] Not only in Britain but also elsewhere in the West impression trumped substance. Suu Kyi was the fairy tale the world wanted to believe so much, especially in times of uncertainty.

The consequences for Myanmar could not be underestimated. After the by-elections, the West returned to Myanmar, welcomed by it with open arms. Beginning in spring 2012, US, Canadian, Australian and EU sanctions were suspended (later lifted) and a 'gold rush' commenced. The country was flooded with foreign businesspeople, investors, consultants, activists, experts, politicians and many, many other believers of the idea of 'last frontiers' and 'El Dorado'. This influx of foreign sources and expertise, along with loans, grants, and debt cancellations from top international institutions and member donors, provided the cash flow and know-how so deeply needed by Myanmar. "Capital is coming" remarked a beaming, philosophically-inclined businessman from the tourism sector, interviewed by me in mid-2012.[17] He had reasons for his optimism: tourism sky-rocketed after lifting the boycott (Suu Kyi had changed her mind on it too).

In just one year, Myanmar turned from pariah to darling of the international community, becoming one of (if not the) most politically-interesting countries in the world. Myanmar's diplomacy reinvigorated to a scale unseen since the 1950s. Myanmar's government initiated a series of economic reforms: floating the kyat rate, establishing special economic zones (Dawei, Thilawa, Kyaukphyu), expanding and modernizing the banking sector, introducing new laws on microfinance, trade unions, foreign investments, farm land, export and import, anti-corruption, central banking, telecommunications, minimum wage, anti-money laundering, new tax legislation, SMEs. These and many more were just a few of the most important reforms enacted in 2011–2015.[18]

Yangon quickly transformed (for good and for bad) from a postcolonial (charming) backwater into a Bangkok-style pretender, with shopping malls glitter-ing downtown, advertisements (like Pepsi's "good to be back") giving colour to the previously greyed streets, and traffic jams becoming the showcase of the town. Throughout the country, roads were improved, infrastructure developed, con-nectivity enhanced and the environment polluted even more. Internet services exploded from one of the slowest in the world to being fast and widely available.[19] Sim cards ceased to cost a thousand dollars, WiFi no longer was an unknown word and smartphones became accessible to almost everyone (soon Facebook would revolutionize Myanmar, again for good and for bad). Socio-political space expan-ded significantly in the country. Most of the political prisoners were released (including ex-members of the regime); exile dissidents were welcomed home; civil society, grassroots civil organizations, including humanitarian, educational and religious institutions (the latter controversially, as religious extremism soon clouded the blue sky of a reforming Myanmar) sprouted in big cities; and political parties re-legalised. The 2012 by-elections were free and fair, with the NLD allowed (albeit belatedly) to hold mass rallies throughout the country during the campaign period (compare with 1989 and especially 2003!). Censorship was eased and then formally lifted. But self-censorship remained; in a media dominated by the cronies, criticism of the Tatmadaw still reminded any Burmese journalist of entering a mine field. Even so, Myanamar media recalled their best 1950s heritage and overtook many Southeast Asian neighbours in freedom and quality of media coverage. Dis-sent and public discussion became tolerated again, exiled media was allowed to function (it was a shocking experience to read *The Irrawaddy* inside Myanmar without anxiety) and reports by human rights agencies (AI, HRW and others) were no longer blocked. Trade unions and the right to strike and protest publicly, including during rallies were reintroduced. This was another shocking develop-ment. Demonstrations, including those against confiscated land, soared country-wide (Suu Kyi learned the cons of it for herself it 2013), and although some were cracked down upon (student protests in 2015), the balance sheet is incomparable to the pre-2011 era. Most importantly, after decades of brutal dictatorship, the people of Myanmar were revived and unleashed unprecedented energy. Political discussions in the public sphere (especially in tea houses) became a norm once again, with citizens discussing without fear of being overheard or prosecuted. Yet the latter aspects did not matter that much. The public majority got a well-deserved break from politics (which had complicated their lives enough in the last six decades). After years of poverty and stagnation, Myanmar could finally reintegrate with a rapidly developing Asia and make up for the lost time. That is why, obvious cons notwithstanding (unresolved ethnic issues, emerging communal tensions, Buddhist–Muslim violence, the rise of Buddhist extremism and the Tatmadaw's entrenchment in various key segments of socio-political life to name just a few), the reforms and opening up were positive for Myanmar.[20]

For Suu Kyi, however, the balance sheet has been more mixed.

In search of one brave soldier

The reconciliation process between the regime and Suu Kyi began with Thein Sein and Suu Kyi's meeting on 19 August 2011. They "decided to cooperate with each other in the areas they could and leave the matters they could not then agree on with each other for future discussions".[21] The ad hoc decision was constructive in this particular moment, yet it concealed two irreconcilable political objectives. The regime wanted Suu Kyi to accept the rules of their game and support their reforms; she wanted to change the system from within. What they understood as her coming to sense with reality, she treated as a concession that needed to be reciprocated.

Initially all went (almost) well. Suu Kyi – to use a Chinese expression– granted Thein Sein 'face' (*gei mian*) by saying she believed he wanted reforms, agreeing to registering her party, and taking part in the by-elections. They let her campaign freely and allowed her to win (by not falsifying and not cancelling the results); they also issued her with a passport, allowing her to travel abroad without repercussions. It seemed that the process of mending fences was well on its way.

Yet already back then, the first cracks began to appear. The regime was irritated by Suu Kyi's constant usage of the name Burma instead of Myanmar,[22] which symbolically signalled her lingering opposition to the political system. Suu Kyi was not delighted about lifting sanctions, as she wanted to remove them step by step in a quid pro quo with Thein Sein's administration. Thus, she called for easing, not removal, of sanctions and warned against "reckless optimism"[23] and about a "mirage of success"[24]; she was half-hearted about foreign investments in Myanmar and kept resisting informal pressure exerted upon her by Western governments. This was all to no avail. The free and fair by-elections were the drop that broke the dam: Western governments lifted sanctions on a much bigger scale than Suu Kyi anticipated or apprehended, depriving her of a strong political weapon. She noticed the consequences almost overnight: with most of the sanctions lifted, she lost the battle over the constitutional oath. Once she realized the game with sanctions was over, she behaved in the way of a true politician: she made a virtue out of necessity, presenting sanctions as the reason behind making Burmese reforms possible.[25] In a similar manner, she initially tried to oppose Obama's visit to Myanmar in 2012, claiming that it was politically too early for it. However, once it became clear that she could not resist the US and other Western countries' pressure to re-engage with Myanmar, she jumped on the bandwagon, securing headway. Meetings between Suu Kyi and visiting Western leaders (including Bill Clinton, Barack Obama, and David Cameron) overshadowed their formal encounters with Thein Sein and his reformers.

Nevertheless, despite these cracks, the Suu Kyi–Tatmadaw rapprochement continued. Suu Kyi's 'charm offensive' towards the army was enacted with a clear objective in mind. Given the 25 per cent of Tatmadaw delegates in parliament and the overall political system of Myanmar making the Tatmadaw a 'gatekeeper' for its Constitution, Suu Kyi needed to befriend the army if she wanted to amend Article 57f that barred her from presidency. What Suu Kyi searched for was – to quote her own (not very diplomatic) words – "one brave soldier" to support her cause.[26]

She did much to win the generals and ex-generals over. "I'm not that bad, they should try me first" she told me, adding that they were "nervous about losing the grip of power", but their anxieties were ungrounded, since the NLD "from the very beginning wanted reconciliation, not revenge".[27] In her remarks one sees a typically authoritarian equation between the leader and the party. Suu Kyi herself, indeed, never wanted revenge and did not try to enact it after 2016. But the same cannot be honestly said about the NLD. From the very beginning, there had been strong revanchist sentiments in the party (talk of "Nurnberg" in 1990!). The NLD's radical wing, although weakened, never ceased to exist. Under Win Tin it favoured a much more confrontational stance: non-acceptance of the roadmap, continuous call for sanctions and retaliation when chance arose. "Some of us would like to push the military into the Bay of Bengal" announced Win Tin, aptly summarizing the difference between him and Suu Kyi – "She only wants to push them into Kandawgyi Lake".[28] Suu Kyi, to her credit, did much to halt these revanchist, politically suicidal, tempers. She pushed her re-engagement with the regime vision through (e.g. she enforced her decision to re-register in November 2011 and to participate in by-elections despite strong opposition from the radicals) and kept the party in line. Yet these sentiments never ceased to exist.

Disciplining the party along the moderate line was just the first step in Suu Kyi's long march to convince the junta into accepting her as Myanmar's next political leader. Soon more steps followed. At the turn of 2012 and 2013, Suu Kyi sat silent during the Tatmadaw's offensive against the KIA. She offered – to the Kachins' disappointment – only moral platitudes ("I don't like any kind of war or violence").[29] She then accepted hefty donations (totalling the equivalent of US$235,000) from former cronies of SPDC (Tay Za, Kyaw Win and Zaw Zaw), generously declaring that they should be given a chance; Zaw Zaw reciprocated instantly by arguing: "I don't want to be a bad crony. I want to be a good one".[30] This miraculous redemption helped him to get removed from the US sanction's list in 2016.

In early 2013 Suu Kyi hit international headlines by declaring a couple of times that she remained "fond" of the army; she linked this statements to her declaration of wanting to be a president, leaving no room for misunderstanding.[31] She defended herself against accusations of siding with the army by repeating that she had loved the army ever since she stepped into politics. Indeed, the first time she declared her fondness towards the Tatmadaw was during her Shwedagon speech and those who talked in length with her about it confirm her respect for the Tatmadaw as an institution ("the army is like sons and daughters of the nation, so the army should be treated like the nation").[32] "I still love the army, I hold deep respect for it", she told me in 2015, nonetheless adding: "it is not the problem of the army, but the way it has been used. There must be good commands and the army should remain professional".[33] What she meant was that the army should stay away from politics. One may conclude that Suu Kyi is not against the Tatmadaw "per se".[34] Rather, she is against military "usurpers", who have wrested away the power destined for her. "She may dislike certain individuals, but she respects the army as an institution and does not want to weaken it".[35] That is why, as she told Clinton in 2011, she "can do business with them".[36]

Whatever the reason, by publicly repeating that she "likes the army", Suu Kyi sent a clear political signal in early 2013. And, since actions speak louder than words, for the first time ever, Suu Kyi attended the military parade on 27 March 2013 – the showcase of the Tatmadaw's might – stirring attention both at home and abroad.

Suu Kyi most probably wanted to reassure the military establishment that she would not challenge the status quo, both in domestic and foreign policies. The 2013 Letpadaung copper mine issue turned out to be the first test of Suu Kyi's rapprochement with the regime (and her leadership skills). Letpadaung mine was perhaps a typical case of pre-2010 business and social conditions in Myanmar. Due to the joint venture company (the regime's MEHL and Chinese Wanbao), villagers were removed from their lands with little compensation, while investors polluted the environment. Since previously this kind of behaviour was the unholy norm, few cared (in the establishment) and none dared to protest (in the society). After the suspension of the Myitsone Dam project, however, people became bolder, and boosted by the newly granted right to strike, protested against the mine. Unfortunately, the villagers learned the limits of their newly acquired rights the hard way: after staging protests, they were brutally beaten. As word spread, Letpadaung became a national issue. The USDP formed a commission to investigate and invited Suu Kyi to head the inquiry. With the commission's final verdict, which recommended keeping Chinese investment (under the conditions of compensating the villagers and becoming environmentally friendly), Suu Kyi passed the political realism and geopolitics test – she met the Chinese ambassador to Myanmar a day earlier and declared that Myanmar had to "get along with the neighbouring country whether we like it or not".[37] However, she did not pass the test on public relations. Foreign policy imperatives did not speak to the people who pleaded: "Mother, give us back our mountain!"[38] Suu Kyi, experiencing a novelty – a hostile crowd – reverted to anger. She corrected them, quarrelled with the crowd and scolded them, which looked quite bad in the eyes of the media.[39]

Other, similar actions reflected Suu Kyi's strategy of reassuring the generals about herself: she distanced herself from the nationwide (failed) student protests in 2014 and even expelled a NLD veteran who had criticised Buddhist nationalists for being in an informal alliance with the regime. By doing all this, Suu Kyi risked her credibility in order to convince the generals to amend the Constitution.

Her search for 'one brave soldier' started with Thein Sein. The president initiated changes and he – against the advice of "hardliners"[40] within the army – brought Suu Kyi on board, understanding that without her the reforms would be a challenging, if not impossible, thing to do.[41] In turn, she initially praised his will to reform the country and apparently hoped he would be her "Burmese Frederick de Klerk".[42] Thein Sein returned the favour by going as far as saying he would "accept her as president", suggesting amending the Constitution.[43] Initially (in 2011 and early 2012) their relations were good and there was even a plan to nominate her as minister in Thein Sein's cabinet.[44] Another sign of good terms was an idea to set up a direct telephone line between them, given the frequency of their meetings in 2012.[45] Unfortunately, with time, their relationship deteriorated, which was clearly visible in the decreasing number of their bilateral meetings (officially they held one meeting in 2011, three in 2012, one in 2013, and one in 2014, not counting multilateral talks).[46] Different reasons for the rift are cited. Some say Thein Sein "indulged her without conceding anything",[47] was "indecisive or unwilling to cooperate with her",[48] or set a trap for her.[49] Others claim it was her fault (a 'change of heart') based on misunderstandings, different personalities and her leaning towards Shwe Mann.[50] In Thein Sein's eyes, Suu Kyi betrayed him: she "did not play a constructive and responsible role" of the "loyal opposition", which should support the government in the reforms instead of criticising and, especially, siding with his colleague-turned-archenemy, Shwe Mann.[51] Suu Kyi felt just as betrayed.[52] From her perspective Thein Sein got much, thanks to her support – domestic and international credibility – yet he gave little in return.

Disillusioned with Thein Sein, whom she no longer trusted, Suu Kyi around mid-2012 took the side of his competitor and rival, *thura* Shwe Mann, Pyithu Hluttaw Speaker. Initially the personal rivalry between Thein Sein and Shwe Mann was beneficial for the changes within Myanmar. They competed over which of them was the greater reformer. With time (around 2013), however, their enmity – "more a personal falling-out than a difference in worldview"[53] – obstructed the modernization drive.[54] Suu Kyi entered this dynamic and sided with Shwe Mann. He gave her chairmanship of Hluttaw's committee of the rule of law, which she clearly enjoyed.[55] He also "tried hard to make her feel at home in her new Naypyitaw surroundings, treating her as a partner, gaining her confidence. There was good personal chemistry, something Aung San Suu Kyi never had with Thein Sein".[56] By 2013 they openly allied with each other: they met frequently, formally and informally, held joint press conferences, declared their political partnership as the way to national reconciliation, their representatives voted together on several bills in the Hluttaw (e.g. one that increased salaries of MPs) and foreclosed changing the first-past-the-post voting system (favouring the NLD); Shwe

Mann even backed her dream of amending the Constitution, while she called him "an ally" in return.[57]

For Thein Sein's camp within the UDSP, all this was prime evidence of Shwe Mann's duplicity. Apparently, in 2011 when Thein Sein faced objection from regime hardliners over bringing Suu Kyi in ("giving a dead tiger new life"), Shwe Mann backed his decision ("tigers are controlled with the whip in a circus. I can control her"). Now he was using her (Suu Kyi "had fallen into a Shwe Mann trap") to upset Thein Sein's supporters, distance Suu Kyi from Thein Sein, build his own profile based on Suu Kyi's popularity in the media, among the elites and society, and possibly secure presidency or other high posts for himself after 2015.[58] On the other hand, the Suu Kyi–Shwe Mann rapprochement seemed to move beyond a political marriage of convenience (their continued cooperation after 2016 might indicate so, too). This must have crossed the red line not only for Thein Sein, but apparently for Than Shwe (the old dictator supposedly called Shwe Mann "a traitor") and others in the regime.[59] With tacit support from Min Aung Hlaing, the Tatmadaw's commander-in-chief, Thein Sein spectacularly purged Shwe Mann and his men from the USDP on 12 August 2015. He did so by seizing the party headquarters in Naypyidaw and exiling e.g. Maung Maung Thein, in order to prevent "a Shwe Mann–Aung San Suu Kyi coalition from assuming power".[60] This was a clear signal to other top ranking officers. If they did not understand that Suu Kyi could not give them anything they didn't already have (money, privileges, impunity, all guaranteed by status quo), then Shwe Mann's enforced political retirement reminded them of the value of corporal solidarity and the perils of breaking away from it. Indeed, Shwe Mann was the closest thing to an ally Suu Kyi ever had in the Tatmadaw. But even Shwe Mann, in the peak of his power (2013–2015) was unable (or unwilling) to amend the Constitution for her.

Simultaneously, Suu Kyi had tried to approach the commander-in-chief of the Tatmadaw, Min Aung Hlaing, the third (or perhaps the first) political figure in post-2011 Myanmar. Suu Kyi, during one of the closed-door meetings in the Polish parliament in 2013 said: "the commander-in-chief is the most important figure, he decides about everything, he is much more important than the president".[61] Min Aung Hlaing initially was reluctant even to meet with Suu Kyi.[62] Eventually he did, meeting with her during few 'window-dressing', multilateral summits in 2014 and 2015, which ended with inconclusive results for Suu Kyi. Hence, despite all her concessions and notwithstanding her alliance with Shwe Mann, Suu Kyi proved unable to find her "one brave soldier".[63]

Notes

1 Zöllner and Ebbighausen, *The Daughter*, pp. 216–217.
2 "Burma's April parliamentary by-elections", *CRS Report for Congress*, 28 March 2012, pp. 4–6.
3 Interview with Khin Zaw Win, Yangon 14 November 2019.
4 Robert Taylor, *Foreword*, in: Ye Htut, *Myanmar's Political Transition*, p. xii.

5 The closest reply to an answer I received was that thanks to engaging with the regime, "we are present in the legislative. The legislative is the root of democracy. This will lead to changes, this is how changes start", quoted in Lubina, *Pani Birmy*, p. 485.

6 She said this about the ethnic conflict, but it may be understood in the context of her struggle with the regime, too, "VOA interview with Aung San Suu Kyi", *VOA News*, 17 September 2012.

7 "Suu Kyi: I am neither saint nor icon", *The Sydney Morning Herald*, 28 November 2013.

8 Quoted in: Popham, *The Lady and the Generals*, p. 115.

9 Personal interviews in Myanmar, 2012–2019.

10 "She is not, in short, a person for whom principles are enduring, except her own personal self-interest", Derek Tonkin, email correspondence 18 February 2020.

11 *Joint Press Encounter by Secretary-General Ban Ki-moon and Daw Aung San Suu Kyi*, UN Secretary General, 1 May 2012.

12 "Aung San Suu Kyi eyes leading in Myanmar despite constitutional ban", *RFA*, 5 November 2015.

13 Thant Myint-U, *The Hidden History of Burma*, p. 148.

14 Quoted in: Lubina, *Pani Birmy*, p. 481.

15 "Aung San Suu Kyi awarded congressional gold medal", *The Guardian*, 20 September 2012.

16 Derek Tonkin, email communication, 9 September 2019.

17 Interview, Yangon, September 2012.

18 Andrzej Bolesta, "Post-socialist Myanmar and the East Asian Development Model", *Central European Economic Journal*, vol. 5, no. 52 (2019), pp. 172–185; Andrew Engvall and Soe Nandar Linn, "Myanmar economic update: Macro-economy, fiscal reform, and development options", in: *Debating Democratization*, pp. 159–181; Sean Turnell, "The glass has water: A stock-take of Myanmar's economic reforms: Exchange rate, financial system, investment, and sectoral policies", in: Ibid., pp. 181–205.

19 When I was in Myanmar for the first time (September 2010), it took me 1 hour to send two emails.

20 Visits to Myanmar: 2011–2014; Egreteau, *Caretaking Democratization*, pp. 39–65, 81–115; *Metamorphosis. Studies in Social and Political Change in Myanmar*, eds R. Egreteau and F. Robinne (Singapore: NUS Press, 2016), pp. 69–103, 209–260; *Debating Democratisation in Myanmar*, eds N. Cheesman, N. Farrelly, and T. Wilson (Singapore: ISEAS, 2014), pp. 3–11, 19–43, 75–93, 109–159, 205–229; *Myanmar in Transition*, pp. 9–19, 57–67, 97–111, 121–131.

21 Kyaw Yin Hlaing, "The unexpected arrival", p. 220. Similar view: Ye Htut, *Myanmar's Political Transition*, p. 53.

22 "Announcement of informing NLD to use name of State", *The New Light of Myanmar*, 29 June 2012.

23 "The Lady Abroad".

24 "Barack Obama warned", *Daily Telegraph*, 19 November 2012.

25 "A conversation with Daw Aung San Suu Kyi", *The New York Times*, 30 September 2012.

26 "Myanmar: Suu Kyi's search for 'one brave soldier'", *Financial Times*, 8 February 2015; "The lady's predicament", *The Irrawaddy*, 31 March 2015.

27 Quoted in Lubina, *Pani Birmy*, p. 485.

28 "In Burma, democratic 'conscience' still wears blue", *The Washington Post*, 12 March 2013.

29 "Suu Kyi says Kachin War should 'stop Immediately'", *The Irrawaddy*, 16 January 2013.

30 "Give cronies a chance to reform, says Suu Kyi", *The Irrawaddy*, 11 January 2013; "Suu Kyi: Burma's constitution must change", *DVB*, 10 January 2013.

31 "Why Suu Kyi still loves Burma's army", *The Independent*, 27 January 2013.

32 She said this in late 2010 to former Polish Ambassador to Myanmar, Jerzy Bayer (himself an ex-military man). Bayer told me that Suu Kyi not only respected the army, but wanted it to remain (to paraphrase communist phraseology) "the leading force" in

Burmese politics, providing, naturally, that Suu Kyi's leadership was respected. A conversation with Bayer in Berlin, 25 November 2019. I have heard similar opinions from several people from her circle of acquaintances, who requested anonymity.

33 Quoted in: Lubina, *Pani Birmy*, p. 486. She said something similar to BBC just after her release, "Aung San Suu Kyi aims for peaceful revolution", *BBC News*, 15 October 2010.
34 Steinberg, "Aung San Suu Kyi and U.S. policy toward Burma/Myanmar", pp. 35–59.
35 Conversation with one of Thein Sein's advisors, Yangon 16 November 2019.
36 Clinton, *Hard Choices*, p. 107.
37 "The Letpadaung saga and the end of an era", *The Irrawaddy*, 14 March 2013.
38 Sengupta, *The Female Voice of Myanmar*, p. 241.
39 "Suu Kyi confronted by hundreds of anti-mine protesters", *The Irrawaddy*, 4 August 2015.
40 Again, I reinstate that this term should be used with caution, see: Thant Myint-U, *The Hidden History of Burma*, p. 214.
41 Ye Htut, *Myanmar's Political Transition*, pp. 22, 50–53.
42 Popham, *The Lady and the Generals*, p. 252.
43 "Burma's Thein Sein 'would accept Suu Kyi as president'", *BBC*, 29 September 2012.
44 Ye Htut, *Myanmar's Political Transition*, p. 54.
45 It never materialized, Soe Thane, *Myanmar's Transformation*, pp. 322–323.
46 They met nine times during his tenure, ibid., p. 322.
47 "The lady's predicament".
48 Ye Htut, *Myanmar's Political Transition*, p. 54.
49 "Icons bid for power", *The Independent*, 17 April 2017.
50 Ye Htut, *Myanmar's Political Transition*, p. 54.
51 Ibid., p. 55.
52 Thant Myint-U, *The Hidden History of Burma*, p. 216.
53 Ibid., p. 161.
54 Ye Htut, *Myanmar's Political Transition*, pp. 68, 103–119, 123–147.
55 Ibid., p. 54. For a more neutral view, see: "Myanmar: Storm clouds on the horizon", *Report no. 238*, Crisis Group Asia (2012), p. 13.
56 Thant Myint-U, *The Hidden History of Burma*, p. 215.
57 "The lady's predicament"; "From General to Politician", *The Irrawaddy*, 25 October 2013; Ye Htut, *Myanmar's Political Transition*, p. 54. "Shwe Mann: Article 57 not our priority", *The Irrawaddy*, 23 January 2014. Suu Kyi called him an ally once he was ousted from USDP's chairmanship on 13 August 2015, "Aung San Suu Kyi hails Shwe Mann as an 'ally'", *BBC*, 18 August 2015.
58 Ye Htut, *Myanmar's Political Transition*, pp. 53–55, 109–114, 147, 212. Soe Thane also used the "dead tiger" comparison, though with less details and less candidly, *Myanmar's Transformation*, p. 31.
59 Apparently, Suu Kyi held 36 closed-door meetings with Shwe Mann; Ye Htut, *Myanmar's Political Transition*, pp. 55, 118 and 217.
60 Thant Myint-U, *The Hidden History of Burma*, p. 216.
61 Quoted in: Lubina, *Pani Birmy*, p. 488.
62 "Army Chief defends constitution, says meeting Suu Kyi problematic", *The Irrawaddy*, 24 November 2014.
63 She admitted it in 2015, 'with regard to hopes for genuine negotiations with the government, there has been disappointment', "Aung San Suu Kyi: a painful metamorphosis", *Channel 4*, 18 June 2015.

7

A POLITICAL TO-BE-OR-NOT-TO-BE

Seeing her failure to align with the regime, Suu Kyi did not give up. She tried to use her two ace cards once again – popular support and foreign backing – to force the ex-generals to change the Constitution. At the same time, while testing the limits of the political space allotted to her in the early 2010s in Myanmar, Suu Kyi never lost sight of the ultimate goal – the prospect of the 2015 general elections.

Dreaming of amendments

The NLD wanted to amend Article 57f, Article 109 and Article 436. During their course of action, the NLD concentrated its efforts on changing Article 436, instead of 57f, although amendment of 436 would effectively pave way to other changes, including 57f.[1] Suu Kyi presented amending the Constitution as a citizens' democratic right.[2] Yet in Burmese conditions, where personal is political[3] and vice versa, it was all about Suu Kyi wanting to obtain the presidency for herself. She declared her desire to become president unequivocally and repeated it a number of times,[4] which was just dotting the 'i'. From the very beginning, it was evident to all – herself, the (ex) generals and the people included – that the campaign for the amendment of the Constitution was all about lifting the clause blocking Suu Kyi's presidency, nothing else. In Myanmar, it is all about the leader and her/his mission to upgrade the country understood as his/her dominion. The distinction between personal and public is blurred, at best. Only the leader, not Myanmar state's institutions or their mechanisms, can secure goals important for societal growth: progress, development, prosperity, standing, etc. This is how it is likely understood by Suu Kyi: with all her self-imposed burden of a 'mission', 'duty', 'responsibility' and so on, she – and only she – must carry Myanmar's fate on her shoulders. Only she can guarantee success, for this is her country, inherited after her father, and this is a personal, a family, issue: she feels an imperative to clean up what the usurpers messed up. And for that, she needs the full power available, which for a civilian in post-2010 conditions, happens to be presidency; otherwise her mission of completing her father's task and making Myanmar great again cannot be completed. This could be the Burmese structural core behind Suu Kyi's reasoning. Crucially, this has been a reciprocal relationship, understood similarly by the other side, the people, as well.[5]

To amend the Constitution, the NLD joined hands with 88 Student Generation leaders and established a joint committee, which – via NLD offices – started collecting signatures of citizens who supported the amendments. From 27 May 2014 to 19 July 2014, the party staged a campaign of rallies in support of changing the Constitution in several Burmese cities (Naypyidaw, Yangon, Mandalay). In the speech inaugurating her campaign, Suu Kyi urged the people "to test parliament",[6] returning to her favourite tactics of testing the limits of space allotted by the regime. Throughout the campaign, Suu Kyi came out with outspoken criticism, unseen since 2003.[7] Six months later, when I interviewed her, she remained quite critical: "I supported these so called reforms only at the beginning, and that with reservations, but already in 2012 I warned about it. Now the so called reforms stalled, if not regressed".[8]

The rallies drew an average of a few thousand supporters; the biggest one in Mandalay was estimated at 25,000 people. The NLD, too, collected more than 5 million signatures. That was a considerable achievement, but too little to frighten the regime. The (ex) generals responded by warning Suu Kyi via electoral commission and through lawyers, and by conceding to bogus concessions. In August 2014, they set up a parliamentarian commission on reviewing the Constitution, which did its best not to amend it. On 31 October 2014, just before Obama's second visit, they organized roundtable talks with Suu Kyi and ethnic minorities. By doing so, in theory, they answered Suu Kyi's repeated calls for four-party talks. In reality, the regime played a simple trick: by enlarging the number of participants in the talks to 14, the (ex) generals stalled deliberations as there were now too many actors and too many topics to reach a conclusive statement. Suu Kyi called it "just for show"[9] and she was right: it resembled pre-2010 actions undertaken in order to appease the West. Suu Kyi kept pressuring, at one point even threatening to boycott the forthcoming 2015 elections,[10] so the regime repeated its tactics of apparent concessions, this time organizing six-party talks in April 2015. Again, these led to nothing. Despite Suu Kyi being apparently backed by Shwe Mann, this was too little to counter the emerging alliance between Thein Sein and Min Aung Hlaing. On 25 June 2015, the Hluttaw voted the constitutional amendments down, burying Suu Kyi's hopes. Although the results clearly indicated that many USDP members, possibly Shwe Mann supporters, backed the amendments, it was not enough to overrule the Tatmadaw's veto. The ousting of Shwe Mann in August 2015 was the last nail to the coffin of the NLD's hopes to convince the regime to let Suu Kyi become President.

Foreign backing was not enough either. While all those talks and negotiations were taking place, Suu Kyi simultaneously used her second trump card:

international support. In 2013 and 2014, she undertook several trips abroad (Singapore, Eastern Europe, Western Europe, Australia) ostensibly to collect the fruits of her decades of non-violent struggle (to collect the Sakharov Prize and an honorary degree in Sydney, lecture at Sandhurst and at other places). In reality though, behind closed doors, she asked international leaders to support her cause of constitutional amendments. But the prevailing intellectual mood in the West was now different. Back then, Burma was a success story. Barack Obama, for whom Myanmar was the achievement of his "pivot to Asia", proclaimed gaining a "a new partner without having fired a shot".[11] Western governments were not only jostling for lead positions in Myanmar's market for their companies, but politically Myanmar represented much needed good news. Suu Kyi still had red carpet receptions worldwide and politicians from left to right jumped to take photos with her and compliment her non-violent struggle. Yet, all they offered was moral support. Why die for Suu Kyi?

The Rohingya trap

There was one more reason for the West's half-hearted support for Suu Kyi. Around 2013/2014 (the exact date is difficult to pinpoint as it was a gradual process). Suu Kyi's image slowly but steadily began sliding from that of an exceptional moral icon into that of an ambiguous politician.

There was one, single reason: her stance on the Rohingya crisis. Communal violence erupted in Rakhine (Arakan) state in late May of 2012, though the history of the conflict spans decades. May 2012 made the world aware of the long-lasting problem of the unrecognized Muslim group, which calls itself the Rohingya and that has hostile relations with the Buddhist Rakhine majority in Rakhine state. This had started to become a serious problem as early as 1978 during the first exodus of the Rohingyas, though effectively it originated in 1942 with communal violence between Muslims and Buddhists in World War II and perhaps even prior to that with the Muslim colonial migration to Arakan. Widely disliked, if not detested by Burmese society, the Rohingya people, after decades of neglect, found much sympathy and publicity in the West. From 2012 onwards, the plight of the Rohingya dominated international media coverage of Myanmar, overshadowing the (better, but still sorry) state of the Buddhist Rakhines' existence. To this the Burmese reacted with disbelief and anger. They perceived such global news coverage of Myanmar as biased and one-sided. International, Western and Middle Eastern criticism of Myanmar's stance on the Rohingya united the society in an anti-Muslim stance. This was coupled with re-emerging communal tensions, especially between Buddhists and Muslims. These hostilities reignited all the more after the easing of decades of an iron-clad authoritarian grip – in some cases with dire consequences. The Burmese proved to be ill-equipped to resist the twin plagues of fake news and hate speech. Both of these phenomena went viral on Burmese Facebook, contributing to a continuation of violence in Rakhine (October 2012, September 2013) and, in 2013, to Buddhist–Muslim communal clashes and anti-Muslim pogroms in 'Myanmar proper' (Meikhtila, Okkan, Mandalay, Moenyo, Letpadan, Gyobingauk, Kantbalu) and Shan State (Lashio).

The creeping Islamophobia sweeping through Myanmar, the xenophobic turn in some Burmese Buddhist groups and the 'siege mentality' atmosphere had taken their toll on Suu Kyi's stance. With the crucial 2015 elections approaching, speaking out in support of the Rohingya people equalled committing political suicide in Myanmar. On the other hand, Suu Kyi, as a hybrid politician, was surely aware of the human rights-based intellectual climate in the West and its consequences: Westerners had certain presumptions based on her iconic image, and expected her to behave in a certain way. And even if at the beginning she was somehow unconscious of the scale of problem, she was quickly reminded of her ordained role as 'the conscience of a country'. The first demands for her to use her moral leadership to solve the Rohingya problem started to pop up in mid-2012. Initially, they were quite innocent but with time, as the Rohingya issue became the most highlighted problem of Myanmar, they gained momentum. This was very bad news for Suu Kyi. Speaking out in favour of the Rohingya meant jeopardizing her popular support; not doing so equalled the risk of losing external backing. It was a real 'Rohingya trap'.

Suu Kyi did her best to avoid the trap. She did not say a word in support of the Rohingya nor did she ever use this politically incorrect name inside Myanmar. At the same time, she never called them by the term 'Bengali' – a derogative in Myanmar – either. In accordance with the finest eristic methods, she generalized, digressing from the Rohingya's plight into broader issues: peace, reconciliation, rule of law as well as calls against violence and prejudice. This she coupled with her favourite psychological explanations (violence motivated by fear).[12] The Nobel Laureate self-pitied herself by posing as an impartial figure who, by representing the middle way, became a victim of this situation.[13]

Suu Kyi's balancing act was what one may expect from a realist politician. Whatever she would have said, would have been bad. A realist politician in such a situation tries to say nothing much about anything and/or presents the issue in a vague, murky way, so that no one can accuse him/her of anything. Thus, Suu Kyi passed her test on Realpolitik-type prudence, yet did not escape criticism from both sides.

She was accused of sympathizing with Muslims by some in Myanmar and 'Photoshopped' pictures depicting her dressed in a hijab went viral on Burmese Facebook.[14] Many passed on this fake news without even checking it, including – ironically – the wife of Thein Sein's minister of information, Ye Htut (known as the "Facebook minister" due to his fondness of using social media).[15] Bazaar rumours (and now Facebook posts) spread about her alleged personal liaisons with Muslims. An old accusation – of Suu Kyi being not Buddhist and Burmese enough – also resurfaced. This time, it re-emerged in the mouths of Buddhist nationalists, grouped in the Ma Ba Tha (Protection of Race and Religion) association: an offspring of the 969 movement which was responsible for Buddhist–Muslim violence in 2012 and for the xenophobic turn of some segments of

Burmese society. According to the mouthpiece of the movement, Ashin Wirathu, who is an (infamous) twenty-first century equivalent of a 'political monk', if Suu Kyi "became the president, the governance would be in chaos. Racial and religious conflict would deteriorate".[16] On another occasion, he suggested that Suu Kyi was 'surrounded' by Muslims (read: not Buddhist enough).[17] Wirathu's criticism – a moderate one in his case, as he was capable of far worse remarks – must be understood in the context of his lobbying for a set of nationalist, discriminatory laws. These were later known as the four "Protection of race and religion" bills, for which he wanted to secure Suu Kyi's consent. Ma Ba Tha was surprised and displeased that Suu Kyi's NLD did not support the four laws. Suu Kyi did not approve them and faced accusations from Ma Ba Tha of being "too focused on human rights" and too soft on protecting "race and religion" (read: on Buddhism).[18]

The relations between the NLD and Wirathu deteriorated so much before the elections that Win Htein (a close aid of Suu Kyi) said Wirathu "should go to hell".[19] Disappointed with the NLD, the Buddhist radicals sided with Thein Sein's wing of the USDP (Htay Oo, Tin Naing Thein, Khin Yi, Myat Hein, Ye Htut and others), reinforcing popular rumours that the regime was behind the Buddhist nationalist movement from the very beginning. Although in Myanmar it was popular, if not universal, to ascribe the military's hand (or hardliners' hand within the military) to founding and leading the Ma Ba Tha movement, there is no undeniable proof of that, only indications (albeit strong)[20] and conventional wisdom. An unholy alliance, however, between the USDP and Ma Ba Tha did indeed take place from at least 2015 onwards. It was consecrated by the Thein Sein administration's support for the four laws, adopted in September 2015 (two months before the elections) and Wirathu's call to vote for the USDP in the November 2015 elections.

Suu Kyi was well aware of what was going on. She told me in February 2015: "the president is tactically supporting the extremists, that is why he is so popular", adding, in her classic moralistic way, that "we cannot support their actions, we would not win by compromising our values. We could, but we don't want to".[21] If we look past the high moral ground of her remarks, what Suu Kyi said and did was simple: she refused to play the regime's game. The regime wanted "to force her into a position where she has to make a pro-Rohingya public statement, that could damage her popularity".[22] Given the overall atmosphere in Myanmar, "standing up for human rights" meant "siding with the Muslims and not supporting the place of Buddhism in the nation",[23] which was a suicidal move from a political perspective. Suu Kyi realized what would happen if she supported the Rohingyas. Ultimately, she chose silence, then ambiguity … and was proven right in Myanmar. She won the elections by a landslide, despite criticism from Buddhist radicals.

Thus, Suu Kyi's stance was just secure enough to keep her first trump card – public support. Nevertheless, maintaining foreign support – her other ace – proved to be much more problematic. Yesterday's foreign advocates did not buy her

Realpolitik logic. As political realism has never been a guide for human rights groups and likeminded mainstream media in the West (previously they would not have supported Suu Kyi otherwise), Western human rights groups and journalists witnessed "the moral giant" becoming "a calculating politician".[24] And this was just a token of things to come.

Suu Kyi, who evidently wanted to keep foreign support, as she must have gotten used to – if not taken for granted – the universal admiration flowing from abroad, reacted to this new tendency with irritation and incomprehension. "Some NGOs think they can decide everything. They are so strong to have their own policies" she told me, adding that, in her opinion, "there should be a joint effort to build a whole new society" (under her escort, naturally). When I inquired about her stance on the accusations of her recently becoming a politician, she did not mince words: "I've always been a politician. I was born a politician. What do these journalists think I was doing all along in these 27 years? If Mandela and Havel could have been politicians while being in prison, … why not me?"[25] At other occasions she expressed similar sentiments.[26]

Naturally, she was correct. It is fair to admit that she described herself as a politician as early as 20 years ago.[27] This is all true. Yet such strong statements did not help her. Deconstructing her status as an icon was not the game she should have played. Her Western backers supported her, not because she was a politician (even if an honest one) but because she was considered 'the beacon of hope' of a better world. If it turned out she was not a beacon, then why support her? The world was not Myanmar, where (the majority of the) people worshiped her for just being Aung San's daughter and being worthy of his legacy. In the West, she was admired for what people believed she represented. This is a fundamental difference. She should have been aware of it.

Or perhaps on the contrary? Suu Kyi might have come to realize that her iconic status brought her more bad than good. Perchance she was frustrated that global admiration did not translate into political influence within Myanmar. Imaginably, she grasped that she could not gain power in Myanmar with the help of the Western media. Or maybe she was just tired of having to meet all those foreigners (and answering their identical questions). Or perhaps, it was all of these factors combined.

Whatever the reason, starting from around 2012/2013 (as it was a process, it is hard to pinpoint a date) Suu Kyi ceased to be an accessible politician, stonewalling herself from wanted and unwanted visitors alike. Most of these protective measures were taken by her secretary, dr. Tin Mar Aung, a member of her inner circle. It did not win her or Suu Kyi many friends. If Western journalists fell in love with Suu Kyi at the cusp of the 1980s and in the 1990s, now their love affair slowly but irreversibly came to an end. Again, this was not in Suu Kyi's interest – she lost her ability (and/or the will) to handle journalists, and this had consequences. Leniency ended, as many people turned their backs on Suu Kyi and started taking notice of things previously overlooked. Fortunately for the Nobel Laureate, inside Myanmar she still has the indulgence of the media. Globally however, even if much of the foreign criticism originated from bruised egos, there was something to it.

The incompetence of Suu Kyi's staff has become proverbial.[28] It has led to serious consequences at times. During her 2012 trip to Thailand, Suu Kyi's staff forgot to inform of their plans not only to the Thai hosts but also … to president Thein Sein. Once he learned (from the media) that Suu Kyi would be visiting there, he cancelled his trip.[29] Who knows, maybe this was yet another nail in the coffin for Suu Kyi and Thein Sein's relationship? Or perhaps it was the very first?

Thein Sein was hardly the last leader affected by her staff's poor management. The list of inadvertently (or otherwise) discouraged figures is long. If not answering the Dalai Lama's letter, demanding the president of Mongolia's, Tsakhiagiin Elbegdorj, CV or offhandedly handling the president of Maldives, Mohamed Nasheed, was rude, senseless (but perhaps politically inconsequential), then not honouring George Soros, who supported Suu Kyi's movement financially for many years, was reckless.[30]

As a consequence of this kind of behaviour, complaints about the NLD's incompetencies became common by mid-2010. Suu Kyi's personal staff was small, inefficient, disorganized and overworked. Foreign friends tried to suggest to Suu Kyi that a certain level of division of labour was not only beneficial but was required in the modern world. To no avail. Suu Kyi hired a personal assistant, Tin Mar Aung, only in late 2012. The Rakhine assistant brought a certain level of organization into Suu Kyi's schedule, but this came at the price of becoming her only gatekeeper, which made Tin Mar Aung (and, by extension, Suu Kyi) many enemies.[31] It did not change Suu Kyi's habit of micromanaging everything by herself however, which resulted in her being "overworked, struggling to delegate power and not always getting accurate information about the day-to-day decisions within the party".[32] Furthermore, the NLD itself was hardly a model organization either.

Cadres (not) deciding everything

Burmese political parties are organizationally and structurally weak. They usually function as appendixes to their leaders. This is true for all Burmese parties, regardless of their ideological goals: democracy, unity, solidarity, development or otherwise. The NLD is not an exception here.

When Suu Kyi was finally released in 2010, the NLD seemed more of a relic than a battle-hardened political party ready for another clash. The party's 2012 by-elections programme was built on three important – but vague – issues: rule of law, internal peace and constitutional amendments. Yet the party did not develop a detailed approach to more concrete issues, such as the ethnic conundrum, their relationship with the Tatmadaw, the role of the private sector, foreign investors and the government in the development process.[33] Ideologically, the NLD was just the extension of Suu Kyi, who after getting to parliament and indulging in Naypyidaw politicking paid less and less attention to her own party.[34]

No serious refreshment of member cadres commenced. Although Suu Kyi accepted some young members into the party after 2011, they were not admitted into decision-making positions and were kept away from her inner circle (the latter even narrowed). Party leadership remained in the hands of Suu Kyi's loyal veterans of the anti-regime struggle. This caused some unrest,[35] yet did not influence Suu Kyi's policymaking. During the NLD's first congress in March 2013 – which confirmed Suu Kyi's official leadership in the party – Aung San Suu Kyi hand-picked members of the Central Committee (120) and the Central Executive Committee, which now expanded from 7 to 15.[36] She chose individuals on the basis of "their past performance, current contributions to the party and their potential leadership skills".[37] Only four new members (Aung Soe, Myo Aung, Phyu Phyu Thinn and Zaw Bwe) were included into the CEC (and some of them were only auxiliary members); the ratio of new members vs old ones remained 1 to 3. By doing so, Suu Kyi "dashed" hopes, that "some 'younger blood' would be included in the NLD leadership", but she explained, it was "impossible to leave the old, experienced members behind".[38] In intra-party policymaking everything continued in the old way: in Suu Kyi's authoritarian "my-way-or-the-highway approach to managing her party".[39] All decisions were made unilaterally by her, based on her own assessments, their loyalty (her most valued quality in politics),[40] their previous contributions and, sometimes, competencies. She rarely valued other people's advice.[41] The structure of the NLD recalls the Leninist model of democratic centralism. It is top-down, hierarchical, centralized, non-transparent, inaccessible, inflexible, personalized, intolerant of internal dissidents and prone to factionalism (not unlike her father's AFPFL).[42] Because of this, the NLD was called "little more than a club of Suu Kyi loyalists" unable and unwilling "to reach out to other influential groups in Burmese society"; a club which "failed to rise above the level of amateurish management, with poor public relations and even worse mechanisms for attracting and cultivating real political talent".[43] Before the 2012 by-elections, Suu Kyi personally chose candidates seemingly based on "how much time they had spent in jail".[44]

This situation repeated itself on a much grander scale before the general elections in 2015. Suu Kyi rejected nominations of many local leaders and veteran democracy activists (e.g. Myo Khin), which were proposed by provincial NLD branches, putting her trusted candidates in their place. This decision produced rare public criticism (Suu Kyi predictably expelled defiant members from her party) and some defections (e.g. Khin Phone Wai, Kyi Min, Ko Mya Aye). She, too, crossed out some distinctive figures, such as Nyo Nyo Thin or Ko Ko Gyi (and other 88 Student Generation candidates), deeming them potentially disloyal and troublemaking, and – just in case – scrapped all Muslim candidates. Additionally, as a sign of things to come, she forbade the NLD candidates from speaking to the media.[45]

Replying to a long unseen criticism of her decision, Suu Kyi reminded the people of Myanmar about the rules of her game; she came out with her very own pure and simple understanding of democracy: "the responsibility of the people is simply to vote for the party, not the name of the candidate".[46]

For some, Suu Kyi's autocratic style was proof of her disconnection with the West. As one Australian Burma watcher summarized already in 2014,

> Suu Kyi is not a democratic person. The West really wanted her to be but she is known to be rather despotic, bad at taking advice and intolerant of dissent. She no doubt has a vision for her country, but I don't think that vision corresponds to the West's vision or rather visions for Burma. She speaks impeccable English and may have lived in a democratic country but I think her politics is a continuation of her father's independence struggle and that struggle is inherently anti-Western and promotes a localized version of democracy, which diverges greatly from both the definition and practice of democracy around the free world.[47]

Another observer added a similar interpretation:

> Suu Kyi is not a Westernized Burmese, a global citizen, but a continuator of Anglicised postcolonial elites, who thinks about Myanmar the colonial way. We seem to think that she is just like we – she speaks impeccable English and she has royal manners – but it is a mask only. Inside there, she thinks the colonial way. What proves it, is her condescending attitude towards subordinates and servants; she unconsciously replicates colonial patterns, this is how she was brought up.[48]

While not agreeing with some of these judgments, these observations are in line with what is, in this book, conceptualised as postcolonial hybridity. That is why in her party policy style, Suu Kyi is closer to figures such as Jawaharlal Nehru, Zulifikar and Benazir Bhutto or Sirimavo Bandaranaike, than to Western equivalents.

The inability to build a team of competent staff and the lack of qualified assistants remains the NLD's ultimate weakness – and this exposes Suu Kyi's biggest post-2010 political conundrum. The elimination of competent, yet potentially undevoted collaborators continues to secure Suu Kyi's paramount position. Nevertheless, if "cadres decide everything" (as Stalin put it), her ability to produce long-term reforms is structurally hampered by the incompetent, understaffed NLD. Suu Kyi cannot micromanage and do everything personally.

On the other hand, fortunately for her, cadres do not decide electoral victory in Myanmar.

The plebiscite

The November 2015 general elections were Suu Kyi's to-be-or-not-to-be in politics. If she did not win these elections, she would be marginalized and all her concessions would be in vain. She needed to win, and win decisively. It was the necessary yet insufficient precondition of her coming to power. In Suu Kyi's long march to political power, winning the November 2015 general elections was key.

She needed to secure at least 67 per cent of the seats in both houses of the Hluttaw (or 329 seats). Only this guaranteed a majority, which would enable outvoting military MPs and other deputies (the USDP; other parties) in all but constitutional matters. Yet even such potentially spectacular results were just a prelude to negotiations with the (ex) military establishment. The ex-junta establishment may or may not have allowed her to come in to power. However, to sit at the negotiating table at all, Suu Kyi needed to score a landslide victory.

In the months leading up to elections, the outcome did not seem obvious at all. Most importantly, there was no guarantee that the elections would take place. Furthermore, opposing parties were not sure whether or not the regime would rig the vote or, more probably, just cancel the results yet again. Finally, the NLD's success was not guaranteed automatically. Criticism and dissatisfaction grew as the elections approached. Suu Kyi lost many supporters due to her heavy-handedness in ruling the party, her controversial alliance with Shwe Mann, her unwillingness to form a coalition of democratic forces and negligence of ethnic parties. Voices of many Burmese people breaking the informal self-censorship on criticising Suu Kyi started to emerge. Critics stated that Suu Kyi was turning friends into enemies, lacked strategic thinking or forward planning, was detached and did not understand the ordinary people of Myanmar. This conjoined with dissatisfaction among Yangon elites, as many members of the Burmese 'middle class' were quite disappointed with her and became disillusioned much quicker than the rest of society.[49] It was obvious that Suu Kyi enjoyed unrivalled popularity – people once again flocked to her rallies in mass numbers during the 2015 campaign – but it was far from certain whether this would prove enough to secure the needed 67 per cent. Given the logic of Myanmar's non-level playing field, the USDP started from a better position: the military appointed 166 MPs were their natural allies. The USDP did not have to win the elections, they just needed to score enough to block the NLD's majority. Thein Sein's party had at least three strong trump cards.

The president's reforms, though incomplete and not fully successful, had made a breakthrough. Moreover, the regime had finally made some progress in settling ethnic issues. Finally, and perhaps most importantly, Thein Sein formed a contemporary nationalist equivalent to 'two wheels of dhamma' with Ma Ba Tha. This had enormous potential to influence the electoral results, or at least spoil the NLD's victory. The generals and ex-generals had most probably wanted and hoped to see a divided Hluttaw, where the NLD would be at worst a *primus inter pares* and at best would sink among the many other parties. However, if they indeed thought so, they repeated the same mistake as in 1990.

When I asked her whether she was afraid of becoming part of a perpetual opposition to the system, Suu Kyi replied:

> They will not marginalize us, they will not make it. We will not be forever in opposition, we will finally win, the people support us. Go to the marketplaces, see how many my father and mine pictures are there. And how many pictures of Than Shwe or Thein Sein are there?[50]

She was correct.

When she started her long struggle to come to power within-the-system, she made many concessions needed to make her electoral victory possible. In her view these were "relatively trivial matters that can be addressed once she and her party are in power".[51] She was again right. She won and nothing else mattered. All her political concessions paid off.

Although the NLD became intellectually shallow, with many party members becoming politically impotent, Suu Kyi turned her party into an effective political machine concentrated on winning polls. The NLD's 2015 campaign was professional.[52] It was a Burmese-styled version of electoral campaigns in Western countries.

The NLD's 2015 manifesto was neither sophisticated nor realistic. It promised a fool's paradise: the amendment of the Constitution, national reconciliation, rule of law and the end of corruption. Additionally, they promised things that mattered to all people: improvement of the economy, health care, education etc. The party fell short on details of how to achieve these goals. It was, as always, vague. All in all, it did not matter. The NLD's slogan spoke volumes: "time to change". With such a catchphrase, the NLD could do without any programme, as this motto effectively made the elections a plebiscite on the previous military rule.

Suu Kyi cut off all independent candidates and surrounded herself with yes-men. Again, it mattered next to nothing. It was she who bore the biggest responsibility. Tirelessly travelling from one part of the country to another during their campaign, she stretched herself to the limits in order to ensure that the elections followed precolonial patterns of electing Maha-Sammata.[53] In Myanmar, where the political is personal, elections were a referendum on Suu Kyi herself – she saw to that herself. Aung San's daughter triumphed, proving once again that she is the mother of the nation. This unique, unclear to foreigners, Burmese relationship between the ruler and the ruled, based on karmic logic, expectations of proper, moral behaviour and an ineffable 'something else', guaranteed a thunderous victory for her and her party.

In the fully free elections, the NLD won by a landslide, securing 79.4 per cent of contested seats in the two-chamber national legislature (255 seats in Pyithu Hluttaw, 135 in Amyotha Hluttaw and 496 in regional Hluttaws), or 57 per cent of the popular vote. The NLD knocked out its competitors: the USDP and smaller parties. Suu Kyi won almost everywhere. In cities more than in the countryside. She succeeded in Myanmar proper more than in ethnic minority regions. She made headway there too, however, except for in Rakhine. Minority groups also saw a chance of removing the (post) military establishment from power through the elections. This trumped all reservations they might have had about the NLD. At the end of the day, the elections proved to be a dual, interconnected plebiscite: a plebiscite on Suu Kyi as a leader and on the military rule.

The jubilant Suu Kyi knew, however, that this spectacular triumph was just a prelude to negotiations that could pave her way to power.

Notes

1 Lall, *Understanding Reform in Myanmar*, pp. 87–88.
2 "Suu Kyi says Myanmar should amend charter for equal rights", *RFA*, 10 January 2014; Aung San Suu Kyi, *Politics and Education*, Kapuscinski Lectures, 12 September 2013.
3 "When the personal is political", *New Age*, 10 December 2019.
4 "Suu Kyi: 'I want to be president'", *BC*, 7 June 2013.
5 "Suu Kyi says Myanmar should amend charter for equal rights", *RFA*, 10 January 2014.
6 "Myanmar: Suu Kyi urges public to 'test parliament' with charter change campaign", *RFA*, 27 May 2014.
7 "Suu Kyi calls on public to join demonstrations for constitutional reform", *The Irrawaddy*, 24 March 2014; "The lady rallies the masses once again", *Foreign Policy*, 5 June 2014.
8 Quoted in: Lubina, *Pani Birmy*, p. 489.
9 "Suu Kyi denounces 'just for show' 12-party charter talks", *The Irrawaddy*, 15 December 2014.
10 "Opposition party leader is considering an election boycott", *The New York Times*, 4 April 2015; Suu Kyi threatened to boycott the elections already in late December 2013. These were all empty threats.
11 *Remarks by the President at the United States Military Academy Commencement Ceremony*, The White House, 28 May 2014.
12 "Burma's sectarian violence motivated by fear", *The Guardian*, 24 October 2013.
13 Suu Kyi, *Politics and Education*, 12 September 2013; "Aung San Suu Kyi explains silence on Rohingya", *VoA*, 15 November 2012.
14 "Aung San Suu Kyi: a painful metamorphosis", *Channel 4*, 18 June 2015.
15 "Minister's wife shares fake Facebook photo of Suu Kyi in Islamic headscarf", *The Irrawaddy*, 6 June 2014.
16 "A Suu Kyi presidency would bring 'chaos,' says firebrand monk", *The Irrawaddy*, 28 November 2013.
17 Jordt, "Breaking bad in Burma".
18 "Religion looms large over poll as NLD, Ma Ba Tha trade words", *Myanmar Times*, 31 July 2015. In Burmese human rights is *lu a kwint a ye*, where the word *a kwint a ye* means opportunity, blurring the sense of human rights/opportunities, Elliott Prasse-Freeman, "Conceptions of justice and the rule of law in Burma," in: ed. D.I. Steinberg, *Myanmar: The Dynamics of an Evolving Polity* (Boulder, CO: LRP, 2015), p. 98.
19 "Myanmar radical monk endorses ruling party in election, raps opposition", *Reuters*, 4 October 2015.
20 "Exclusive: 'Strong evidence' of genocide in Myanmar'", *Al Jazeera*, 28 October 2015.
21 Quoted in: Lubina, *Pani Birmy*, p. 494.
22 "Is Burma's regime inciting Rakhine conflict to discredit ASSK", *The Week*, 12 June 2012.
23 Jordt, "Breaking bad in Burma".
24 "There's a kind of hush in Myanmar", *The New York Times*, 5 June 2014.
25 Quoted in: Lubina, *Pani Birmy*, p. 494.
26 "Suu Kyi: I started as a politician not a human rights defender", *Equality Myanmar*, 29 October 2013.
27 When she talked with Bill Richardson, she said "'I look upon myself as a politician.' She smiled. 'And that isn't a dirty word, is it, Congressman?'", quoted in: Victor, *The Lady*, p. 134.
28 "Amid disorganization, Aung San Suu Kyi visits Thailand", *The New York Times*, 29 May 2012.
29 Ibid.
30 Popham, *The Lady and the Generals*, pp. 238–240.
31 Ibid., pp. 244–247; Pederson, *Burma Spring*, p. 505.

32 "Myanmar democracy icon finds herself assailed as authoritarian'", *The New York Times*, 28 September 2015.

33 "Aung San Suu Kyi must transition too", *WSJ*, 20 June 2012.

34 Popham, *The Lady and the Generals*, pp. 245–246.

35 "500 NLD members to quit in Pathein", *The Irrawaddy*, 23 October 2012; "Suu Kyi's party told it's too authoritarian as Burma's activists quit", *The Independent*, 12 November 2012.

36 Suu Kyi, Nyan Win (secretary), Hantha Myint (secretary), Ohn Kyine, Win Myint, Tun Tun Hein, May Win Myint, Win Htein, Zaw Myint Maung, Aung Moe Nyo, Daw Khin Htay Kywe, Nan Khin Htwe Myint, Kyaw Khin, Nyi Pu, Myo Aung; plus auxiliary members Mann Johnny, Thein Lwin, Aung Soe, Zaw Bwe and Phyu Phyu Thin.

37 "Suu Kyi re-elected as NLD leader", *The Nation*, 13 March 2013; "Suu Kyi elected NLD Chairperson at historic congress", *The Irrawaddy*, 10 March 2013.

38 Lall, *Understanding Reform in Myanmar*, p. 86.

39 "Myanmar democracy icon finds herself assailed as authoritarian".

40 Beech, "What happened to Myanmar's human-rights icon?"

41 Lall, *Understanding of Reform in Myanmar*, p. 86.

42 Ibid., p. 68; "Milestone for Myanmar opposition", *Bangkok Post*, 3 March 2013; "Governing Myanmar", *The Diplomat*, 24 February 2017; "NLD 'iron rules' stifle new parliamentarians", *Myanmar Times*, 25 April 2016.

43 "Can Suu Kyi lead?", *The Irrawaddy*, 10 October 2012.

44 Lall, *Understanding Reforms in Myanmar*, p. 77.

45 "Myanmar democracy icon finds herself assailed as authoritarian"; "Aung San Suu Kyi urges support for NLD amid Myanmar candidate row", *RFA*, 10 August 2015.

46 "Myanmar: NLD members must follow party rules: Aung San Suu Kyi", *RFA*, 11 August 2015.

47 Conversation with Anna Zongollowicz, Yangon, 17 February 2014.

48 Interview with an American Burma Watcher, Yangon, 3 February 2015.

49 Interviews, Yangon, February 2015.

50 Quoted in: Lubina, *Pani Birmy*, p. 432.

51 "The lady's predicament".

52 Popham, *The Lady and the Generals*, pp. 337–342 and 363.

53 Zöllner and Ebbighausen, *The Daughter*, pp. 243–246.

8

THE STATE COUNSELLOR

Politically speaking, the NLD's electoral triumph was not the turning point in Suu Kyi's road to power. The breakthrough was achieved afterwards, in a series of behind-closed-doors meetings between Aung San Suu Kyi and high-ranking (ex) generals.

Above the president

The extent of the NLD's victory was a surprise to all, including the NLD, who expected to win, but by a lesser margin. Knocked out, the USDP was totally shocked: this was not what they forecasted in their darkest dreams. Top leaders – Htay Oo, Aung Min, and many others – lost their seats (Shwe Mann, contending as an independent, lost too). Nobody anticipated such an outcome. None was prepared. What happened afterwards was classic Burmese political ad hockery.

After coming round, the regime succumbed to internal finger-pointing while representing itself as well-mannered to the public. Thein Sein and Min Aung Hlaing congratulated the NLD on its victory and announced that they would respect the results. Despite internal disunity, the regime was politically beaten but not broken. The fact that now the Tatmadaw itself (not any proxy party) would be the opposition to the NLD, was not ideal, but it was tolerable. Because of the biased Constitution, the Tatmadaw could check and balance every government and, in the worst case, it could topple it, too, if the government misbehaved (Myanmar is always one coup away from a military government). Though empowered, the NLD still had to cooperate and cohabitate with them anyway.

The spectre of 1990 haunted Myanmar. The lack of trust – Suu Kyi and the (ex) generals did not speak to one another frequently in the period leading up to elections – might have led to a grave repetition of history (many the NLD members indeed feared it). Fortunately, lessons had been learnt on both sides. The NLD understood it needed to convince the regime to relinquish power by means of confidence building measures and thus assuring the former generals that retribution was not an option. The military realized that the NLD in power was not the end of the world; it did not threaten the Tatmadaw, just enforced the need for military forces to be watchful.

Suu Kyi called for reconciliation and univocally rejected 'Nurembergs', and the (ex) generals agreed to meet her.[1] In a series of behind-the-scenes talks in early December 2015, Suu Kyi met with both Thein Sein and Min Aung Hlaing (2 December 2015) and – crucially – with Than Shwe (4 December 2015). Apparently, she used Than Shwe's beloved grandson Nay Shwe Thway Aung[2] as well as Shwe Mann as go-betweens to secure a meeting with the former dictator. This confirmed rumours that Than Shwe, although he had withdrawn from everyday politics, was still the person consulted when landmark decisions were at stake – loyalty within the Tatmadaw did not expire with retirement. The negotiations between Suu Kyi and the (ex) generals remained – and still remain – secret: no media were present and no communiqués were published, and the exact details (what was discussed and what was agreed on) are still unknown. Aside from smiles for the press and short remarks, most was revealed by Nay Shwe Thway Aung. He posted on Facebook about the Than Shwe – Suu Kyi meeting. It was supposed to last 2 hours and the ex-dictator was said to have declared "It is the truth that she will become the future leader of the country. I will support her with all of my efforts". Accompanying this post was a picture of a 5,000 kyat banknote, signed by Than Shwe, Thein Sein and Suu Kyi, with a vague explanation: "The significance of this note is ... they signed only before they became the head of the country or while they were head of the country".[3] And, that was it. Apart from this mysterious banknote story – worth a James Clavell novel – nothing more was elaborated on.

Thus, it is unknown what decisions were made. Suu Kyi and the (ex) generals must have agreed on basic principles of cooperation; the regime endorsed a transfer of power to the NLD. Whether it was a transitional pact[4] however, is more doubtful. It was rather an ad hoc, unwritten short-term deal, with a general understanding that the NLD would take over power and respect the Tatmadaw's red lines, without concrete details, which would have to be worked out later in practice. Despite the fact that there was no tradition of systemic transformation in Myanmar, the process went by relatively smoothly and enabled a peaceful transfer of power. It was an achievement Myanmar should be proud of, especially when compared with 1990.

However, it does not mean there were no strains. The whole process was shrouded in mystery and the unknown, which enhanced uncertainty and allowed conspiracy theories to flourish. Whatever Suu Kyi and the (ex) generals decided on – and it seemed that they agreed on a transfer of power, but not on constitutional amendments – Suu Kyi tried to push the limits of this unwritten deal. Suu Kyi was empowered by her newly gained conviction that the NLD would be allowed to take governance. The long period of transition of power between elections in November and formally taking office in February/March 2016 – a Burmese equivalent of political horse trading[5] – gave the NLD extra time to negotiate a settlement. The Nobel Laureate knew the stakes were much higher for the Tatmadaw to stage a coup after a period of reforms. She tried to manoeuvre herself as much as possible in these favourable circumstances. By late January/early February 2016 Suu Kyi seemed to go all in: she tried to secure presidency for herself, despite the Tatmadaw's veto.

The first eligible date for a presidential election (the President is elected by the Hluttaw) was 8 February 2016. Just a few days earlier, Myanmar was electrified by news that Suu Kyi wanted to circumvent the constitutional limitations. The Tatmadaw, however, was opposed. After that, the presidential nomination was postponed. Suu Kyi negotiated hard – where, how and with whom is again unknown – while society, diplomats, commentators and investors held their breaths. Anything was possible, including a coup. From the Tatmadaw's point of view, amending the Constitution was a bridge too far. Facing the Tatmadaw's opposition, Suu Kyi backed down and returned to her previous idea – first revealed just before the 2015 elections ("I already made plans") – of her being "above the President",[6] nominating a proxy.

Who would that be? The rumoured list included, among others, Suu Kyi's physician Tin Myo Win, Tin Oo, U Lwin's daughter Su Su Lwin and her husband Htin Kyaw, as well as Tin Mar Aung. It was a hard choice for Suu Kyi. In politics – especially in Burmese politics – one could never be sure of anything (read: anyone); she needed to pick an unambitious candidate. She did, placing her trust in Htin Kyaw, a respectable intellectual from a good family (his father was a popular writer), who was a retired economist and civil servant and Suu Kyi's long acquaintance – though not her driver as some media announced.[7] Htin Kyaw was an NLD veteran, with good connections (his father-in-law, U Lwin, was the NLD's founding member and one of the party's 'uncles'). Only briefly arrested in 2000, Htin Kyaw harboured less ill-feelings towards the Tatmadaw than other NLD members (read: he was acceptable to the army). Along with the NLD-nominated vice-president Henry Van Thio – a Chin – the choice of Htin Kyaw who is half-Mon from his paternal side was a symbolic (even if empty) gesture towards ethnic minorities. All in all, Suu Kyi chose wisely. From his first inaugural speech (during his swearing-in on 30 March 2016 he mentioned Suu Kyi)[8] until his resignation in March 2018, Htin Kyaw was a loyal, unambitious protégée, who executed his ceremonial duties with grace. A perfect puppet.

Suu Kyi, however, was unsatisfied. The Tatmadaw's veto over her presidency spoiled the fun. She still hoped to bring the military round – apparently she convinced Htin Kyaw that his term would be a short one, as she would be able to persuade the Tatmadaw to allow her to assume the office herself[9] – but in the meantime she kept concentrating the power in her hands. As rumoured, she became foreign minister. This was not at all because of her interest in foreign affairs. As it later turned out, her ministerial tenure was very modest, with only sporadic trips abroad, to such extent that a new Ministry of International

Cooperation was founded in 2018; its minister took over the duties of a foreign minister in all but name. Suu Kyi needed to be foreign minister to be a member of the National Defence and Security Council (NDSC), potentially a powerful council. According to the Constitution, the President in extraordinary circumstances, after consulting with the NDSC, could declare an emergency and hand over power to the army (read: reintroduce military rule). Therefore, Suu Kyi needed to be on the NDSC to keep an eye on the army; a consideration that trumped any potential negative consequences such as the resulting inefficiency of the foreign ministry. The Ministry of Foreign Affairs (MFA) was, however, not her only portfolio entry. She took seats in three other ministries as well: the Presidential Office (to have an eye on the president), the Ministry of Education (a logical choice given her 'educating the nation' agenda) and the Ministry of Electricity and Energy. The last one was intriguing – Suu Kyi is not a trained technician but she probably realized the importance of the energy problem in Myanmar (read: she wanted to deal with it herself). Later she relinquished the last two posts because in the meantime she had carried out a brilliant move that checkmated the military and stunned the public. During the new parliament's first session on 30 March 2016, in its first legislative initiative, the NLD proposed a bill that circumvented constitutional limitations placed on Suu Kyi. It did so by introducing a new post of State Counsellor with power effectively exceeding that of the President (the right to oversee the President's office, determine foreign policy and coordinate decision-making between the executive and the legislative). The bill was formulated precisely with Suu Kyi in mind (it even mentioned her by name) and proposed a period equalling that of the President's term. The bill indirectly circumvented the Constitution as it did not contradict any causes; it simply filled a loophole. Suu Kyi outplayed the military establishment in style. This chancellor-style post was a bold political move, an outstanding piece of ad hoc tactical manoeuvring (allegedly, the NLD lawyers invented it in the last moment when it became clear that Suu Kyi would not be allowed to become President).[10] The army was taken aback; military MPs stood up and protested – military leaders apparently were impressed by Suu Kyi's shrewdness in private though[11] – but were outvoted; the bill was passed and quickly signed by the President (6 April 2016). Suu Kyi had secured a position not only above the President but above the emerging political system as well. She was not, however, above the army. In a country where power was personalized, it made sense. It showed that in a world of backstage Burmese politics, Suu Kyi was a skilful player, at least when it came to tactical games. If she was equally capable in long-term strategies, in competent governance or in improving people's lives, she would be a stateswoman.

All's well that begins well

To paraphrase Suu Kyi's remarks from 1996,[12] her government started off with a lot of *metta* from both inside and outside the country. The Burmese believed that electing Suu Kyi – the proper heir – would make things right in their country.

Foreigners believed pretty much the same (although from a different standpoint) and for a while, forgot about some of the reservations they held about her.

Goodwill helped to overlook the disconsolate reality on the ground as well as the first warning signs. The NLD government faced the monumental challenge of reforming a deeply dysfunctional state and uniting a torn country. Despite Thein Sein's legacy, Myanmar was still (and still is) an underdeveloped country with deep structural obstacles, such as ethnic tensions; an unstable economy; and a lack of adequate structures and institutions (e.g. ineffective bureaucracy).[13] Reforming Myanmar after six decades of the Tatmadaw's misrule was a Herculean task for anybody.

Yet the NLD made their life even harder by "creating many of their own problems".[14] The NLD promised many things they could not deliver. Pledging to achieve national reconciliation with ethnic minorities was "evidence of monumental hubris" given the scale of problems and the necessity of bringing the Tatmadaw and their enemies on board.[15] Even in the most optimistic scenario, it was going to be a long process, certainly not one completed in one term. Promising to be able to fix it quickly was imprudent, at best. Secondly, amending the Constitution had been Suu Kyi's number one dream, yet "to put in Machiavellian terms: why indeed would armed men obey unarmed ones?"[16] Again, it required much time, patience, concessions and its final outcome was uncertain. Thirdly, ending corruption. Although, to her credit, Suu Kyi was (and still is) a clean politician herself and did her best to keep her government clean, too,[17] corruption did occur. To purge the party, barely after a year in power she forced the resignation of her Mon chief minister, Min Min Oo, and in 2019 she spectacularly sacked and arrested her Tanintharyi chief minister, Lei Lei Maw (a member of the NLD's CEC). But rooting out cultural patterns is a task for generation(s). In Southeast Asia, so far only Singapore has managed to root out corruption. And Myanmar – despite all of Suu Kyi's declarations to catch up and overtake it[18] – is not Singapore.

After taking over power, two of Suu Kyi's ministers – finance minister Kyaw Win and commerce minister Thant Myint – were caught holding fake diplomas from non-existing universities.[19] Her cabinet members – mostly the NLD veterans, ex-generals (from Shwe Mann's faction) and retired bureaucrats – were quite old; averaging above 70 in years (Suu Kyi was 71 then), making it the oldest government in modern Burmese history.[20] It was not a bad thing per se – though an ironic twist of history given Suu Kyi's opposition to Nu's octogenarian 'government' in 1988. However, their lack of competence in law-making or executive experience raised questions: "they had little understanding of how a democracy worked in practice".[21] Nobody doubted their benign intentions, but do good people automatically make a good government? Myanmar was to learn the answer soon enough. Curiously, too, they were all men. Again, certain cultural norms favoured that – Myanmar is not Canada, men held more offices – but the governmental structure did little to help the cause of Burmese female political representatives.[22]

Most importantly, when the NLD took over, the party seemed ... unprepared to govern.[23] They had no strategy, no reform plan, and few, if any, detailed or articulated policies to be implemented, even on the most fundamental issues: "it was almost as if the party's overriding goal was to win government, and little thought had been given to what might follow after that".[24] There were two reasons for this. Firstly, the NLD members were unsure to the last moment that power would be theirs; some even feared arrest when entering parliament.[25] In a way, it recalled precolonial times, when a *wungyi* (minister) summoned to the palace could have expected a promotion or execution; and everything in between. The USDP government did not make the NLD's life easier, either. By obstructionist policies (not handing over documents or forbidding civil servants from talking to the incoming team) and overspending the budget in its last months in power, the USDP made transition more difficult.[26] Secondly, ill-preparation was a logical result of the dominance of ad hockery in Burmese politics. Although ad hoc actions, even such spectacular ones as the State Counsellor bill, could secure tactical goals and impress spectators, they did not work well in articulating and implementing medium and long-term policies.

Suu Kyi made a bad situation even worse by rejecting many of the non-NLD staff. Out of distrust she dismantled the microcosmos of think thanks and analytical centres, the 'brain' of Thein Sein's reforms. Staffed by reform-minded military and former third force members, Suu Kyi viewed them as enemies or traitors at worst, or suspicious and insufficiently loyal at best. The same applied to civil society organizations not associated with the NLD, exiles and other individuals. With these NLD-exclusive HR policies, Suu Kyi went overboard when she dismissed many competent, qualified and eager to work for her people – and wasted their energy.[27] Had Suu Kyi already possessed an abundance of qualified personnel, this might have made sense. But she did not. Her shortage of qualified candidates was previously evident and was probably the real reason behind reducing the number of ministries from 36 to 23 (efficiency of government was quoted).[28] Thus, the spectre of Stalin's cadres formula would haunt Suu Kyi for a long time.

In mid-2016, however, all these things were unnoticed or overshadowed. Enthusiasm and optimism trumped everything. Initially enthusiasm and optimism seemed validated. Suu Kyi spoke much about national reconciliation (read: NLD–Tatmadaw reconciliation) and she meant it. She went above and beyond to reassure the Tatmadaw to rest easy. Her government increased Myanmar's defence budget to 14 per cent of the annual budget.[29] She started mending fences with Min Aung Hlaing. Thanks to these actions, the perception of Suu Kyi within the Tatmadaw started changing from "a formidable threat" into "a pragmatic leader".[30] Critics claimed that gestures such as Suu Kyi visiting the Defence Services Museum in Naypyidaw (a personal guided tour with Min Aung Hlaing) or inviting Min Aung Hlaing to both public and private commemorations of Martyr Day were done in order to convince the Tatmadaw of lifting the veto of her presidency.[31] Even so, it was a good thing: anything that soothed the military's fears and anxieties brought Myanmar a step further to separation of the military from politics. If the result was the NLD's over-cautiousness – tolerance to criticism of the Tatma-daw decreased significantly, with media freedom becoming the first casualty of that – it was a necessary price to pay. The army's cooperation, or at least a lack of disturbance by them, was the first precondition to rule Myanmar effectively and resolve pressing issues.

Already by 2016 Suu Kyi had begun to tackle the single most difficult problem faced by Myanmar: the ethnic conundrum. Decades of brutal civil war had built a wall of distrust and a conflict economy benefitting local Tatmadaw commanders, Ethnic Armed Organizations (EAOs) and Myanmar's neighbours. Since 1948 no government had been able to successfully resolve this Gordian knot, or indeed even where to begin. Politically and historically speaking, the Bamar majority is too strong (and too unwilling) to share power and privileges, and yet it is too weak to enforce its vision of society completely. An exclusive nation-building project beyond Burmese dominance had never come into existence; there was no Myan-mar-styled 'unity in diversity'. No Burmese leader ever resolved this problem, Aung San included. His Panglong conference was a step in the right direction, yet it was incomplete, hardly sufficient and never materialized – instead of solving the ethnic issue, Panglong became a myth.[32] Suu Kyi wanted to build upon this myth, or rather establish ethnic peace in the country for the first time. Policymaking based on mythmaking is not a bad thing per se providing that politicians do not believe in the myths (Suu Kyi probably does believe in the Panglong myth because she over-idolizes her father). Judging by her public statements,[33] she seemed to have hoped that simply repeating a Panglong conference in a new form would pave way to ethnic reconciliation. Consequently, she called a second – though chronologically third – Panglong conference, named the 21st Century Panglong. To her credit, she was able to bring representatives from almost all EAOs to the conference. To secure such a feat, she travelled to Beijing, and Zhongnanhai ordered its informal, covert clients, such as the China-bordering Wa minority, to appear in Naypyidaw.[34] When the 21st Century Panglong kicked off in style on 31 August 2016, there was much optimism.

Unfortunately, after a few days of discussions, it turned out that bringing all the actors to one conference, though needed, did not provide the necessary conditions to end seven decades of ethnic strife. Expecting the opposite was naïve, given the conflicting agendas of so many stake-holders, some of whom were quite unwilling to compromise (the Wa left on the second day of the conference citing protocolary issues and reinforcing doubts about the militant Wa's intentions).[35] However, Suu Kyi believed in two things from the beginning. First, she could do it alone. Second, she could do better than Thein Sein's new ceasefire agenda. Thus upon taking office, she dissolved the Myanmar Peace Centre (MPC) and dismissed Aung Min's negotiation team (including their contacts and influence), instead nominating her trusted physician Tin Myo Win to negotiate with ethnic minority peoples.[36] While this idea should not immediately be rejected, as personal communication channels are an essential condition of peace-making on Myanmar soil, Tin Myo Win's lack of know-how in dealing with ethnic issues proved a hindrance.

Coupled with the NLD leader's unnecessary rejection of the institutional experience gathered by the MPC, this complicated Suu Kyi's task instead of easing it. Most importantly, however, Suu Kyi did not seem to be able to propose a way out of the fundamental, structural contradiction between the Tatmadaw's priority (demanding ethnic armies to disarm and demobilize) and the EAOs' federal agenda. Although in her defence one may say that it requires a political genius to resolve this ethnic issue, the result of her actions – failure – still stands. Her Panglong conference did not produce results. To save face, it was rebranded as a cyclical event (it convened twice more, in 2017 and in 2018, still inconclusively). Soon new clashes dashed hopes for a quick reconciliation and the idea of a miraculous ethnic issue-solving conference was conveniently forgotten.

Back then, however, in mid-2016, power transition and governance were still so far, so good (or at least not so bad). The lack of substance coming from the Panglong Conference was overshadowed by Suu Kyi's stylish foreign policy. Soon after, she travelled to Washington. During her symbolical farewell visit – the last one with Obama and the final one as a democracy icon – she managed to have economic sanctions on Myanmar lifted. History came full circle: these sanctions were introduced mostly due to Suu Kyi and now it was she who secured their cancellation. It was an unequivocally positive outcome for Myanmar. Suu Kyi made it happen just in time. Soon Hillary Clinton lost the elections, which brought forth a Myanmar-disinterested Trump presidency. But even in post-2016 USA, Suu Kyi did not achieve bad results: she was criticised much less in the USA about her stance on the Rohingya issue than elsewhere in the West.[37] US media, especially liberal ones, were no less disapproving of her actions in 2017 than other Western outlets, but, crucially, American politicians remained much more constrained in their responses. Keeping many of her American friends despite deteriorating circumstances remains her achievement.

More importantly, in the longer perspective, Suu Kyi mended fences with Beijing, re-approaching Myanmar's top neighbour after post-Myitsone uneasiness. The process had already begun when Suu Kyi was in opposition: she flew to Beijing for the first time in June 2015 and, since assuming power, regularly continues to call on the Zhongnanhai 'court' accompanied by an entourage of ministers and deputies. If for the West, Suu Kyi's apparent transformation from a democracy icon into a Realpolitik player was a painful, shocking metamorphosis, then for China, it was the opposite: back to normal. For China, it was a sign of Suu Kyi's political maturity: she came back to her senses, left behind her democratic illusions of youth and returned to their Asian traditional model of policy-making. She became a responsible partner with whom one could do business. One only needs to wait for the Chinese to award Suu Kyi with the Confucius Prize for this transition process to be complete. Additionally, there was a dynastic link: for Xi Jinping, the leader of princeling faction, Suu Kyi is the closest a foreigner can get to be on par with a Chinese leader. The son of Mao's moderate 'lieutenant' and the daughter of Burma's independence father understand one another without words.

China reached out to the NLD too and provided kudos-hungry NLD members with what the Middle Country did best: red carpet receptions during sponsored trips, seminars, conferences and other events, with compliments announced in public, sweet offers whispered into their ears and red envelopes given as reimbursement. This Chinese-styled 'soft power' significantly improved China's bad image in Myanmar, or at least diminished its PR losses abroad. Moreover, dropping the Myitsone case and concentrating on the Kyaukpyu pipeline and economic zone as well as on other investment issues, all helped Beijing restore grounds for Chinese influence in Myanmar after Thein Sein's 'turmoil'. The process empowered Suu Kyi as well: from then on, she could count on China – in the UN Security Council for example – which would prove to be personally priceless for her while also being beneficial for Myanmar. "A tender gourd among cactuses" – as Nu called Burma in 1954 – cannot change its geography and has to live well with China while struggling not to fall into neo-colonial dependency. Whoever manages this delicate balancing act – Suu Kyi has done so far – fulfils Burmese national interests.

The other cactus proved welcoming, too. Although falling behind China in importance and influence in Myanmar, India had ambitions to catch up. Its Act East policy – a new incarnation of Look East – is yet to materialize, but there is mutual understanding, though no excitement, between Modi and Suu Kyi. Modi would be the last person to criticise Suu Kyi on the grounds of human rights abuses. India's invisible influence was apparently instrumental in convincing Bangladesh to accept Rohingyas fleeing persecution in 2017; a hypothetically firmer stance from Dhaka might have complicated the situation even further. Regardless of the reason, at the end of the day, Suu Kyi enjoyed friendly relations with both of Myanmar's big neighbours. Good for her, and good for Myanmar.

Wooing Japan was successful, too. Suu Kyi seemed to have found common issues with Abe. Japan is eager to restore its dominant position in Myanmar, or at lessen the political distance between itself and China. Japanese investments (Thilawa and beyond), coupled with assistance and diplomatic support, were important to Suu Kyi. She was not alone vis-à-vis the West – the recent remarks of the Japanese Ambassador supporting Myanmar's stance on ICJ was good evidence of that[38] – and she was not at the mercy of China. She could balance Beijing against Tokyo, looking out for her and Myanmar's best interests.

Additionally, good relations with Seoul, Bangkok and Singapore (and not bad with Jakarta) compensated the complicated relations with the West and even more complicated relationship with Kuala Lumpur. All in all, the balance of Suu Kyi's foreign policy is positive.

The ARSA and other political earthquakes

On 24 August 2016 an earthquake struck Myanmar damaging many (ill-restored) temples in Bagan. In a country where such signs were traditionally interpreted as forewarnings of problems to come, it was considered a bad omen.

And indeed, between Autumn 2016 and Autumn 2017, Suu Kyi experienced her worst period, with mounting domestic-cum-international problems. In November 2016, Burmese military and police posts in Northern Shan State were attacked by forces from a new EAO alliance – called the Northern Alliance (NA) – consisting of Kachin's KIA, the Arakan Army (AA), Kokang's MNDAA and Palaung's TNLA (informally backed by UWSA). The Alliance launched a coordinated offensive, inflicting heavy losses upon the Tatmadaw and provoking its subsequent counteroffensive. Effectively they sent Suu Kyi's Panglong idea packing. Since then, the situation in Shan, Kachin and Rakhine states has deteriorated , with alternating periods of fighting and negotiations. Moreover, the EAOs generally preferred to deal directly with the Tatmadaw and bypass a helpless Suu Kyi altogether. She herself noticeably sided with the Tatmadaw's position on ethnic issues, reaching a "cynical simpatico" with the army.[39] Regardless of who was more to blame, the result is evident: the demise of 21st Century Panglong. At the end of the day Suu Kyi not only did not achieve more than Thein Sein's NCA, she actually achieved even less.

A little earlier, in October 2016, for Suu Kyi an even worse political catastrophe commenced on the western edge of Myanmar. On 9 October 2016 a new Rohingya guerrilla group, ARSA – onerous to fight with due to their use of civilian outfits – attacked Burmese military posts in Rakhine by surprise, prompting severe retaliation. Enraged, the Tatmadaw reverted to a version of its traditional 'four cuts' tactics to strike back at ARSA and punish the Rohingya community collectively. Although successful in military terms, the tactics came with a price. It was no longer the 1960s and the (Western) world reacted with strong diplomatic condemnation centred, predictably but unfairly, on Suu Kyi. Criticism, much harsher than there had been pre-2015 – including from fellow Nobel Peace Prize laureates – was apparently a shock for her. "She's angry (…) she doesn't 'get it' why the world doesn't understand" one source revealed; Suu Kyi instantly sensed danger for her cabinet: she warned Western diplomats that establishing a UN Fact Finding Mission on Rohingya would "bring down her government".[40] In her mind, she did her best: she appointed the Kofi Annan Commission and tried to manoeuvre the Rakhine minefield. It was not quite so easy – she made several diplomatic mistakes while implementing her (inconsequential and incompetent) Rakhine policies – but her actions were indeed rational from a Burmese perspective. She could not allow herself to alienate the Tatmadaw as it potentially would be politically fatal to her. Additionally, the first cracks between her and Min Aung Hlaing appeared (despite the Tatmadaw's wish, the NLD was unwilling to convene a NDSC, fearing it might lead to coup).[41] Furthermore, Suu Kyi could not stand up against her (anti-Rohingya) nation and lose her major trump card: popular support. She had to walk an ever more swinging tightrope in the rapidly deteriorating atmosphere.

On 29 January 2017, a prominent NLD Muslim lawyer (a constitutionalist and one of the authors of the State Counsellor bill), Ko Ni, was killed in broad daylight; shot while waiting (with his grandson in his hands) in front of a taxi stand before Yangon's Mingaladon airport. This brutal, macabre and blatant murder triggered an avalanche of speculations and theories – some elements within the Tatmadaw were considered probable though unproven accomplices. Regardless of whether Ko Ni was killed for being a Muslim or for being a constitutionalist (or for both), the assassination "sent NLD reeling", as it seemed to confirm their worst fears: fears of the old regime's schemes and plots to overthrow them.[42] Certainly, it deprived the NLD of one of its brightest (and most independent) minds. Succumbing to the anti-Muslim atmosphere, Suu Kyi did not attend Ko Ni's funeral, making yet another personal sacrifice, aka choice, in service of her political cause.

By 2017, the first signs of disappointment with what the NLD had done, or rather had not done, emerged in society and (especially) abroad. The NLD came to power with the overarching slogan "time for change", yet little had changed after the first one and half years (and thereafter) of its governance. Sweeping reforms modernizing the country never materialized. Their top goals of national reconciliation, peace, achieving constitutional amendments and economic development were not realized. The unimpressive progress on these issues undercut the NLD's credibility. Expectations were always too high, if not impossible to meet – "we are not magicians" Suu Kyi's spokesman Zaw Htay pleaded[43] – but the party had done little to tone down the optimistic promises it had made during its electoral campaign. The April 2017 by-elections marked the first political warning to Suu Kyi. The NLD won, but only modestly (securing 9 out of 19 contested seats), suffering a telling defeat in ethnic minority areas. History repeated itself in the 2018 by-elections when the NLD won 7 out of 13 seats (54 per cent).

Many groups were disenchanted for different reasons. The business community complained about the NLD's inability to formulate concrete plans or strategies. A long awaited NLD-backed economic programme was finally published in June 2016, yet it satisfied few. The NLD undermined investors' confidence with bureaucratic delays or arbitrary and contradictory administrative and legislative measures, which led to the slowdown of economic growth and decrease in FDI inflow. This was coupled with the kyat's loss in value, soaring prices, and energy blackouts which all affected ordinary people's lives. "Economy is clearly not this government's top priority", one manager summarized.[44]

Ethnic minorities expressed their grievances for what they saw as Suu Kyi patronizing them. Previous charges of condescending remarks, endorsing Burman-centric historiography and using Burmese Buddhist cultural symbols,[45] were now joined by accusations of not listening to ethnic voices, neglecting their feelings and dominating administration cadres (the NLD nominated all chief ministers even in regions where they did not win).[46] In early 2017, in an event that symbolically spoke volumes, Mons staged a protest against naming a new bridge in Mawlamyaing after Aung San. Suu Kyi's Panglong on her turn, suffered from heavy moral rhetoric and few specifics: Suu Kyi neglected personal diplomacy, while she kept preaching and sloganeering to EAOs about values, which did little to win their trust.[47] Gen. Gun Maw, KIA's vice leader, told me a few words, which summarize ethnic peoples' feelings quite well: "we can't say she helps the ethnic minority peoples just because she dresses in their clothes. That's much too little".[48]

Ethnic minorities were hardly the last dissatisfied group. Many Burmese disliked Suu Kyi's 'Tatmadaw first' policy. Alignment with military interests and making concessions towards the army in key areas resulted in her following the footsteps of the old regime in many ways.[49] If this argument seems a bit detached from reality – Suu Kyi had to appease the Tatmadaw in order to remain in power at all – then let's just say that, at the end of the day, there was little difference between the old regime and the new NLD one.

Democrats, both Burmese (and especially Western) expressed concerns about the insufficiency of democracy in the NLD's governance. Suu Kyi banned the NLD MPs from talking to the media ("iron rules"),[50] forbade public criticism of her or her party, and limited debates, MPs' initiative and democratic practices within Hluttaw. The NLD did not undo the old system of repression. It kept previous laws (e.g. Telecommunication Law, section 66 d) and imposed some new restrictions on journalists and citizens. Occasionally, it reverted to censorship and arrests of critics for their remarks in media and on Facebook.[51]

The NLD's rule meant a "reduction in the country's degree of authoritarianism, not a qualitative change to its political system".[52] This probably had to do with the simple fact that, unlike the USDP, the NLD did not have to prove its 'democratic credentials', they just took their legitimacy for granted.[53]

The harshest criticism came from abroad as a result of the treatment of the Rohingya people and because of the NLD government's defensive narrative towards foreign criticism, mirroring SLORC/SPDC's approach. In an ironic twist of fate, the 26 years (1989–2015) of Suu Kyi's calls for exerting pressure on the government came to haunt her now, as the world continued to pressure Myanmar's government – this time hers. Again, it was just a prelude of what was to come.

To make matters worse, to paraphrase an Eastern European catchphrase, the NLD had been "heroically overcoming self-created difficulties". If the concentration of power in the hands of Suu Kyi made political sense, then her over-centralisation and governance practices led to serious administrative deficiencies. Aside from being the State Counsellor and two ministers at once, at the beginning of her rule Suu Kyi chaired two important sub-cabinet committees (security, tranquillity and rule of law; economic affairs). Later the number increased to around 30 committees, important ones and less so (like the BRI committee). Her autocracy; tendency to micromanage everything (in a 'schoolmarm' style – she introduced a performance evaluation report system for subordinates); the need for her consent to every decision, big or small; her want to vet every bill before its submission to parliament; and her unwillingness to delegate authority to others, all led to her inability to cope with many tasks, which led to bureaucratic and legislative inertia and administrative inefficiency.[54] Her lack of inclusiveness towards outside groups (ethnic organizations, civil society groups, grassroots activists and others) resulted in their perception of negligence. They felt unwelcome; she rarely met with local media and even less frequently with civil society, instead coordinating policies from only within her own inner circle of the NLD veterans, key bureaucrats, diplomats and ex-officers.[55] Her tokenism and tendency towards moral preaching; propensity to defy public grievances (protests were either ignored or suppressed); poor PR communication; a puritan streak (that led to the unpopular and ultimately revoked decision of restricting the purchase of betel) and her concentration on symbolic yet cosmetic issues (anti-litter campaign), all took the shine off of her.[56] Suu Kyi recognized this, offering what was interpreted as a sort of self-criticism. In reality, it was an intelligent neutralisation of accusations. During her anniversary speech, where she defended herself ("One year is not a very long period"), she offered to "step aside" if the people found her work unsatisfactory.[57]

Suu Kyi knew her nation well and so she was well aware that goodwill towards her had not eroded so much by then as to seriously trouble her. If each new government in the world had a proverbial 100 days of immunity, then in Myanmar, Suu Kyi had 1000 days. People complained, but did not rebel against the mother of their nation. In 2016 and 2017, I frequently heard: "give her time", together with "the military disturbs her and conspires against her" (blaming the old regime became the favourite excuse of the NLD supporters). The latter claim, although unsubstantiated,[58] showed one tendency: "while the hoped-for change has not taken place yet, no one wants a return to authoritarian rule – not even the army itself".[59]

Besides, the NLD government was not a total disaster. Firstly, it survived, which was not an obvious thing at all at the beginning of 2016. Secondly, it normalized relations with the Tatmadaw and consolidated administrative power, by founding a modus operandi with bureaucratic nomenclature.[60] It lifted US sanctions and improved, albeit modestly, Myanmar's infrastructure, education and health services; it reduced rural poverty (a bit); it started the restructuration of state banks and enterprises, undertook financial and legal reforms and exercised fiscal restraint.[61] All in all, the balance sheet of the NLD government was negative in August 2017, but it was not a total failure. It still did not risk repeating the fate of Nu's Pyidawtha plan, which promised miracles and ended up becoming an object of jokes in society. There was widespread hope that Suu Kyi would still be able to make things right.

And then ARSA attacked again.

Notes

1 "Military concedes election to Aung San Suu Kyi in Myanmar", *The New York Times*, 11 November 2015.
2 The one who allegedly wanted to buy Manchester United.
3 "Myanmar's ex-dictator sees Suu Kyi as country's 'future leader' – relative", *Reuters*, 6 December 2015.
4 Egreteau, *Caretaking Democratization*, pp. 15–28.
5 Interview with Khin Zaw Win, Yangon, 13 November 2019.

6 "Aung San Suu Kyi, long a symbol of dignified defiance, sounds a provocative note", *The New York Times*, 17 November 2015.

7 "Driving Miss Suu, try again CNN", *The Irrawaddy*, 10 March 2016.

8 "Prescript: President U Htin Kyaw's inaugural address", *The Myanmar Times*, 30 March 2016.

9 Thant Myint-U, *The Hidden History of Burma*, p. 221.

10 Private conversations, Yangon 2017 and 2019.

11 Ibid.

12 Clements, *The Voice of Hope*, p. 47.

13 Selth, "Be careful what you wish for", pp. 6–7.

14 Ibid.

15 Ibid.

16 Egreteau, *Caretaking Democratisation*, p. 82.

17 "Patience tested", *The Nation*, 1 May 2017.

18 "Aung San Suu Kyi calls for close economic ties with Singapore in official visit", *The Strait Times*, 30 November 2016.

19 'Myanmar approves cabinet nominees, but some face questions over credentials', *The New York Times*, 24 March 2016.

20 Thant Myint-U, *The Hidden History of Burma*, pp. 224–225.

21 Selth, "Be careful what you wish for", p. 8.

22 For more about the consequences of Suu Kyi's iconic position for Burmese female political representatives, see: Sengupta, *The Female Voice of Myanmar*, p. 322.

23 "As hope for a bright future dims, what are the prospects for Myanmar", *Nikkei Asian Review*, 28 April 2017.

24 Selth, "Be careful what you wish for", p. 8.

25 Thant Myint-U, *The Hidden History of Burma*, p. 223.

26 "Patience tested".

27 "Sideshow in Myanmar", *The New York Times*, 10 April 2017; Thant Myint-U, *The Hidden History of Burma*, p. 225.

28 Selth, "Be careful what you wish for", p. 9. In 2018, the number was increased to 25.

29 "It is good to be Tatmadaw", *The Diplomat*, 11 May 2017.

30 "Army to rebrand itself as new political reality sets in", *The Irrawaddy*, 16 May 2016.

31 Thant Myint-U, *The Hidden History of Burma*, p. 225.

32 Matthew J. Walton, "Ethnicity, conflict, and history in Burma: The myths of Panglong", *Asian Survey*, vol. 48, no. 6 (2008), pp. 889–910.

33 I write more about it (and quote speeches) in my previous book, *The Moral Democracy*, pp. 337–351.

34 "How 'One Belt, One Road' could smooth out rocky China–Myanmar ties", *WPR*, 20 April 2017.

35 "As hope for a bright future dims, what are the prospects for Myanmar".

36 Thant Myint-U, *The Hidden History of Burma*, pp. 226–227.

37 Conversation with Bridget Welsh, Kuala Lumpur, 26 February 2020.

38 "Japan backs Myanmar's claim that no genocide occurred in Rakhine State", *The Irrawaddy*, 27 December 2019.

39 "Suu Kyi stirs ethnic pot ahead of Myanmar elections", *Asia Times*, 12 February 2020.

40 "Defiant and defensive"; "Myanmar's 'Great Game' enters volatile new phase", *Asia Times*, 7 April 2017.

41 Thant Myint-U, *The Hidden History of Burma*, p. 236.

42 Ibid., pp. 234–235.

43 "After Aung San Suu Kyi's first year in power", *The New York Times*, 8 April 2017.

44 "Myanmar business sector disappointed with pace of reforms", *Nikkei Asia Review*, 7 April 2017. See also: "Suu Kyi's NLD has a growth problem", *Nikkei Asian Review*, 6 April 2017; "Myanmar's government — time for course correction?", *Nikkei Asian Review*, 21 March 2017.

45 Sengupta, *The Female Voice of Myanmar*, pp. 320–325.

46 "Not even Aung San Suu Kyi can fix the world's longest-running civil war', *The Washington Post* 13 April 2017.

47 "Aung San Suu Kyi's quiet, puritanical vision for Myanmar", *Nikkei Asia Review*, 29 March 2017.

48 "Burma always follows the strongest country", *Polska-Azja*, 13 May 2014.

49 Selth, "Be careful what you wish for", pp. 11–15.

50 "NLD's iron rules stifle new parliamentarians".

51 Selth, "Be careful what you wish for", pp. 12–13.

52 "The new Burma is starting to look too much like the old Burma", *Foreign Policy*, 28 June 2017.

53 Thant Myint-U, *The Hidden History of Burma*, p. 249.

54 Ibid., p. 9; "Aung San Suu Kyi's year in power"; "Defiant and defensive".

55 "The new Burma is starting to look"; Thant Myint-U, *The Hidden History of Burma*, p. 249.

56 Selth, "Be careful what you wish for", p. 4.

57 "Aung San Suu Kyi's speech on the occasion of the one year anniversary of the government", *State Counsellor Office*, 1 April 2017.

58 "Why Myanmar's military is not planning a coup", *Nikkei Asian Review*, 8 May 2017.

59 "Patience tested", *The Nation*, 1 May 2017.

60 Kyaw Sein and Nicholas Farrelly, "Myanmar's evolving relations. The NLD in government", *Asia Paper*, Stockholm, October 2016, pp. 62–63.

61 Selth, "Be careful what you wish for", p. 17.

9

FALL FROM GRACE

With the Rohingya crisis, Suu Kyi hit a brick wall. Until now, she had been trying to keep her twin trump cards of domestic support and foreign backing. The latter was eroding, but until September 2017 there were still illusions, hopes (that she would combat the Rohingya issue) and goodwill in the West, which prevented people from crossing her out. After September 2017, due to the scale of the crisis, these considerations ended. To the global public, Suu Kyi became the villain – the fallen icon.

The Rohingya crisis

On 24 August 2017 the Annan Commission officially submitted its report: a compromise, which offered the Rohingya a path to citizenship (by revisiting the 1982 law), while not using the name 'Rohingya' in the document.[1] The NLD accepted the report. However, the next day, ARSA attacked 30 military and police facilities in Rakhine state, effectively sabotaging the Annan Commission's efforts and triggering the worst ever retaliation from the Tatmadaw. Tired of waiting for NDSC to be conveyed, Min Aung Hlaing allowed his field commanders (Aung Kyaw Zaw, Maung Maung Soe, Khin Maung Soe and others) to act as they pleased. They did so; pushing ARSA back to Bangladesh along with approximately 700,000 civilians, committing ethnic cleansing and crimes against humanity with "genocidal intent"[2] along the way. In the West, a passive Suu Kyi was blamed for the tragedy: the crisis was a game changer in her relations with the West.

Apparently, the situation blew in up Suu Kyi's face: she was hardly prepared for it. Since the very beginning of global media attention on Rakhine, Suu Kyi considered it a secondary issue compared to more important priorities. From the moment she had assumed leadership, not much had changed. She simply swept the Rakhine problem under the rug so that the issue did not disturb her policymaking in Naypyidaw. True, she appointed the Annan Commission, but thought that that alone would take care of the problem. As Ye Min Zaw told me, "she had a good plan with the Commission, but she played it out badly".[3] Suu Kyi did not invest much of her domestic capital into convincing the Rakhines and the Rohingyas about the Annan Commission's intentions. She visited the region only once and met only with selected representatives, local 'yes men'. In August 2017, her long-time negligence and disinterest in the Rakhine issue backfired.[4] The crisis over-whelmed her, proving that in a watershed moment she failed to act as a successful stateswoman.

Incompetent and taken by surprise, Suu Kyi "mishandled the crisis".[5] She was overshadowed by the Tatmadaw. The army did what it pleased without asking (or perhaps even informing) Suu Kyi. Once the unprecedented scale of the tragedy became globally evident, media attention concentrated on Suu Kyi, not on the army. The "Man bites dog" motif worked again. A brutal army massacring mino-rities in a Global Southern country was not news: the world knows too many of such stories. Besides, who could pronounce and remember Min Aung Hlaing's or Maung Maung Soe's names? However, a genocide in a country governed by a famous Nobel Peace Laureate was definitely news. Western and Middle Eastern media were quick to condemn Suu Kyi (although it was not she who was killing Rohingya people), repeating their well-known accusations with a double-barrelled fury.

The deluge of criticism forced Suu Kyi to react. In her speech on 19 September 2017 Suu Kyi played dumb. She claimed that her government did not know the reasons behind the Rohingyas' flight ("we want to find out why this exodus is happening") and that the human rights violations would be "addressed in accor-dance with strict norms of justice".[6] Her tactics were intelligent, if desperate: after all, it would be much better to be portrayed as a detached from reality ruler, than as a powerless leader. She, too, downplayed the direct causes of the Rohingyas' exodus by placing the crisis in a wider context of more important domestic prio-rities, including the economic development of Rakhine. This was not incorrect in a wider sense, yet it was badly timed. While media showed satellite images of scorched villages and footage of hundreds of thousands of refugees crossing the Naf river, the foreign public demanded actions to help them, not Suu Kyi outlying developmental strategies for the region. The NLD's leader either underestimated the problems of Rakhine once again or spoke the way she did to enhance the false image of an ill-informed politician.

These image-protecting measures were to no avail. After that fatal speech she was condemned even more for her words and (in)action. It completed the process of her 'fall from grace'. This did not mean she lost all friends in the West – some influential characters, such as Mitch McConnell and Boris Johnson remained. Furthermore, till this day, she has better contact (and understanding) with Christine Burgener, the Special Envoy to the UNSG, than with Yanghee Lee, the former UN's Special Rapporteur on Myanmar. And she received much more under-standing from Western politicians, than from Western media; reactions from politicians and diplomats concerning her actions to the Rohingya crisis have been much more constrained than those of the media. In a way, by using her contacts in the West, she was able to reduce and neutralise negative political responses towards the Rohingya crisis.[7] If not for her, the world's political reaction might have been even harsher given what happened in Rakhine. But thanks to her backstage diplomacy, the criticism on Myanmar, albeit rhetorically harsh, remained symbolic and confined to the media sphere.

Nevertheless, that said, from now on associating with Suu Kyi became a burden, not a boost, for any Western politician. If previously Suu Kyi was the person to have a photo with, it now became fashionable to condemn her and distance one-self from her, especially among certain activist groups and their supporters. Their pressure prompted such actions as the futile attempts to take away her Nobel Peace Prize, revoking prestigious international awards and Canadian honourable citizen-ship and – in a very academic styled gesture – removing Suu Kyi's portrait from her Oxford College's hall of fame. Although these were only symbolic gestures – it would have been far worse for Suu Kyi if Mitch McConnell had removed her picture from his office – when it came to Suu Kyi's until-now second trump card, unequivocal foreign support, it was game over.

There was no global understanding for the following issues she had to consider.

First, even now, there is widespread abhorrence towards the Rohingya people in Burmese society. These feelings stem from several issues: the colonial legacy of anti-Indian sentiment; as a consequence of the postcolonial bloodbath in Rakhine; and the anxiety towards 'encroaching' Islam and the fear of Islamic terrorism. These and other factors make the Rohingya – their very name a centre for dis-pute – the scapegoat for all the social and political ills of Myanmar. I suspect every Burma scholar has a personal collection of anti-Rohingya remarks heard from people in Myanmar. I certainly do. Comments ranging from "dump them all into sea", via historical findings ("they are not from this land, they came here") to philosophical questions ("is it possible to Burmanize Rohingya?").[8]

This atmosphere alone would force any politician to take these public sentiments into consideration: why (politically) die for the Rohingya? Unfortunately, in August/September 2017, hysteria about the "Islamist terrorist threat" reached its climax. It was no longer just a "multidimensional disconnect"[9] between responses inside and outside Myanmar. Burmese reactions were "not only different but dia-metrically opposed" to Western ones.[10] If it was all about "the most persecuted minority in the world", expelled *en masse* amid crimes against humanity in the West, then in Myanmar it was reported as a Burmese version of 9/11.[11] The cir-cumstances were such that society was (and still is) not only understanding, but openly supportive, of the Tatmadaw's stern measures – on this issue "the military and the wider public find themselves blissfully aligned".[12] On top of that, Suu Kyi still needed to have public backing to balance the army's position. If she went against the feelings of her people, she would commit a spectacular political *seppuku*.

Second, and combined with the first issue, was Suu Kyi's imperative not to rattle the Tatmadaw if she wanted her government to continue to exist. In private she was supposedly angry at the Tatmadaw – about the army deciding to resolve the Rohingya problem by force and not peacefully as she herself preferred.[13] Even so, her relationship with the Tatmadaw was too precarious to risk it for the Rohingya minority. Given the Tatmadaw and the people's shared resentment of the Rohingya, Suu Kyi's hypothetical support for these Muslims would be like scoring a spectacular own goal. At best it would lead to a significant decrease in her support causing a deterioration in her position vis-à-vis the Tatmadaw; at worst it could even justify an anti-Suu Kyi coup.

Third, she did not necessarily disagree with the public sentiments. While accusing Suu Kyi of Islamophobia is unfair, she nevertheless seemed to share many anxieties of her compatriots (albeit in a softer form). Already in 1979 she had spoken publicly about the "dislike of Muslims" within society and the "irrational fear" of the Muslims "swamping the Burmese". She referred to societal distaste of ritual killings, commenting that "in Burma it was alright to cut a man's throat, but to do the same to an animal was a heinous crime".[14] Even if she did it with irony, she did not distance herself from it. In 2013 she said there was a "climate of fear" originating from "worldwide perception that global Muslim power is very great".[15] Apparently she held a "not-unfounded sense" that "aggressive and chauvinistic voices within the international Muslim community … have deliberately fuelled a hate campaign against her".[16] In the early 2010s she told the Polish Ambassador "look what Islam has done to India", meaning: Myanmar did not want to experience the same problems of communal discord and conflict.[17] If true, this means she was not against Islam per se, but in Myanmar would rather keep at arm's length. Over one million Rohingya with their Bengali origin (regardless of whether their ancestors were Mrauk-U's captives or colonial or postcolonial immigrants) did not fit this worldview well. It did not mean she deliberately wanted to harm them or harboured ill-feelings towards them. No, nothing personal here. But it is easier to toss away foreigners (perceived or real) than compatriots. Suu Kyi most probably does not consider the Rohingya as fellow Burmese (but as Bangladeshis).[18] From her perspective, reforming and upgrading her country mattered much more than their plight (however sorry). She was "not a Mother Teresa"[19]; Myanmar, and her conviction that she was indispensable to it, was much more important than improving the world. If the Rohingya had to be sacrificed for Burma's greater good, so be it. Suu Kyi was able to give up her husband, children and so many friends and loyal supporters for her cause, now she did the same to a million of unwanted foreigners.

It seemed fair enough to the Burmese (it still does even now) but not to the (Western) world. No one expected her to behave like that. Of all people, Suu Kyi was supposed to support repressed minorities. She was supposed to take moral leadership and prevent massacres like, say, Gandhi, who saved Muslims in 1947 Calcutta. Suu Kyi failed dramatically. This was the first, fundamental reason for condemning her. Her stance remains indefensible from a liberal-internationalist point of view.

The second fundamental reason behind denouncing her is much more personal. Since she left house arrest in 2010, Westerners "would simply love to see her revert to her role as icon of democracy, rising above party politics, and even offering the unfortunate Rohingya a modicum of support", as Derek Tonkin correctly summarized.[20] Suu Kyi was expected to give hope, call for peace in the world and give advice on how to live life fully – something akin to the Dalai Lama. She did the opposite: she chose the fully ambiguous road of 'politicalness'. And she spectacularly spoiled the fun. This explains what Andrew Selth called "the extreme nature" of some criticism, "often highly personal (in) tone" of analysis and with a "strong sense of loss, even betrayal" – especially among human rights activists – who "feel badly let down" by someone who was supposed to be "different from other politicians". Consequently, critics in Selth's view behaved as "spurned lovers": "lashing out with extra force against someone once held dear, giving particularly sharp edge to their comments".[21] Today's condemnations of Suu Kyi – just like her previous idealisation – tell more about the commentators and their hopes projected onto her than about Suu Kyi herself.

It shows, too, the negative consequences of the celebrification of politics. It is the flip side of earlier depoliticization, which later rebounds. Criticism of Suu Kyi operated (and still operates) on the same logical basis as media attention that follows movie stars, singers and other celebrities: from praise to condemnation. This was simply the media's melodramatic soap opera called 'the icon's fall', a second season to the previous series, 'the beacon of hope'.

Finally, and most importantly for this book, it shows the delusions and delusiveness of postcolonial hybridity. Suu Kyi was considered 'ours', 'Western', etc., and expected to follow Western values and patterns accordingly. International audiences understood that her goal was to ensure civic rights so that everyone in Myanmar could live a dignified life, unrepressed by authorities. This was the reason international supporters backed Suu Kyi, not because she fought for power (why should they care about her otherwise?). If she bailed out on her most repressed people, relinquishing the goals she (allegedly) had been fighting for, then she was betraying previously set values. Suu Kyi responded to these accusations by emphasising that she has been a politician all along (meaning: back off, don't expect an activist's behaviour). This is true; she had acted like a politician from the start, a certain level of opportunism[22] in courting the Western world (e.g. in her initial charming stance towards journalists) notwithstanding. Yet, from a Western perspective, this is a weak justification. Being a politician does not absolve one from respecting human rights. A politician should use their power to fight for them.

But from the start, these were not necessary her values or ideas.

Suu Kyi understands the way the Western world operates and wants to implement some – not all – of its civilizational achievements into Myanmar. But she is not Western, she is a hybrid politician, someone inbetween worlds. The fundamental misunderstanding between the Western perception of her and reality had much to do with the fact that Suu Kyi had been socialised in the UK, speaks impeccable English and knows European cultural patterns, leading to many to take for granted that she shared the values of the Western world. Yet, the similarity was only surface level – in phraseology, declarations, slogans. Deeper inside, there lies the uncomfortable truth, that human rights, democracy, rule of law etc., matter differently to the Burmese than to Westerners. Suu Kyi, to her credit, never succumbed to talk of 'Asian values', yet in one thing she was quite similar to many Asian elites (who reject human rights while valuing Western education). She understood Western-cum-universal values as ways to improve her country, not as autotelic values. Since the beginning of her career, she looked for external ideas to reform Myanmar: to use what is needed and discard what is not. So, when a decisive moment came and universalist values clashed with domestic (personal) interests, she chose the latter. The Rohingya crisis spectacularly showed that, for Suu Kyi, human rights had their limits when Myanmar's and Burmans' (and her personal) interests were at stake. Human rights mattered very much when she was in opposition; when she came to power, however, emphasizing them would do more harm than good to her interests.[23] In short, her country (and her role in it) came first; universal values – second.

From a liberal internationalist perspective, national reconciliation should apply to all people living in Myanmar, regardless of whether they are part of the Burmese nation or not. In postcolonial Myanmar, however, where colonial categories were and still are based on a hierarchical concept of *taingyintha* [24] and where ethnic designations were tied to issues of national unity,[25] the Rohingyas not belonging to the nation was (and still is) an essential issue. These colonial categories decided about the life and death of a community over one million strong. The fact that she still does not consider the Rohingya a 'Burmese people' –like the vast majority of her nation – is just as important to her political choices as her Realpolitik imperatives. Suu Kyi was no more immune to this post-mortem symbolic colonial violence than her nation.

Finally, the Rohingya issue is precisely the point where her postcolonial hybrid path and the liberal universalist West spectacularly diverge. The issue itself shows the limits of hybrid policymaking. For two decades Suu Kyi skilfully navigated the stormy waters of both Burmese and international politics, capably connecting two aspects of her heritage for her own political good ... until the crisis broke out. It became a turning point: she had to choose between Myanmar and the world. Picking one meant losing the other. Her unenviable choice had consequences. Suu Kyi's fall from grace had finally deprived the leader of one of her twin aces – unequivocal foreign support. Although she played it cool in public, referring to the Buddhist law of *annica*, or impermanence (she stated, that: "actually, nothing is surprising, because opinions change and world opinions change like any other opinion"),[26] she must have been aware that this was a serious setback for her. Truly her foundation was shaken. She had to bid farewell not only to the international admiration she got used to and to valuable political support but also, most importantly, she lost the leverage she had over the (ex) generals. Now some (though not all) foreign friends, like Bill Richardson, were turning into enemies.

However, not all was lost. She received a political blessing in disguise.

Ms Suu Kyi goes to The Hague

Western and Middle Eastern criticism of Suu Kyi finds little understanding in Myanmar. For the majority of the Burmese, Suu Kyi is the mother of nation, who sacrificed herself for the Motherland. Down with those, who would raise their hands against the mother! "We stand with Aung San Suu Kyi!", they rallied. The Burmese reacted with anger and rejection of foreign criticism to a scale much larger than in 2012 or 2016. For Suu Kyi, who was weakened by her so-so governance, this was a new revving of the engine, so desperately needed to stay in power. She successfully positioned herself as the protector of her country against foreign aggressors. Convenient battle lines were set: she as the leader of Myanmar vs. the hostile world.

Intriguingly, by not allowing the UN's fact finding mission and rejecting its report as well as bluntly dismissing international accusations (she rejected some accusations as "fake news" and a "huge iceberg of misinformation")[27] and calls for accountability, Suu Kyi mirrored SLORC/SPDC's pre-2011 actions and phraseology. Before, it was she who called for pressure and sanctions to influence the regime; now the international community used the same tactics against her. In this example of political bad karma – the Rohingya issue as "Suu Kyi's nemesis"[28] – there is an important difference however. The military regime's message did not receive traction neither at home nor abroad. It did not resonate in society due to the Tatmadaw's insufficient legitimacy. This time, Suu Kyi's narrative was shrugged off in the West, too – it even enhanced condemnation of the Peace Nobel Laureate – yet it found perfect understanding and support at home. No more was needed. A Burmese version of 'rallying around the flag' provided Suu Kyi with both long-lasting domestic support and became a convenient excuse for her partial competence at governance. The more foreign media slanders her over the years, the more Suu Kyi's popularity blossoms at home. With Myanmar constantly attacked, condemned and vilified from abroad, nobody (or few at best) inside the country ask questions about tangible results of Suu Kyi's governance. All unite behind the symbolic mother of their nation. Those who did not do so, like two Reuters' journalists Wa Lone and Kyaw Soe Oo (2019 Pulitzer Prize winners, who uncovered the mass murder of Rohingya in Inn Din and spent more than 500 days in jail), faced ostracism and misunderstanding. Even if in private conversations the Burmese agreed that the Reuters' journalists were set up by the Tatmadaw-controlled police,[29] the majority (Yangon elites and individual cases excluding) considered them (at best) little more than traitors. The nation and the leader were almost single-minded about that too. For Suu Kyi, who could have granted them amnesty much earlier and did so only after lengthy outside pressure, they "must suffer for the glory of Burma".[30] In yet another example of hybridity, her stance mirrored governance in colonial times, where, although some freedoms were ultimately granted to colonies, those who crossed the red lines of colonial security landed in jail. Suu Kyi's restrictions on freedom of speech could be interpreted the same way. Just as in colonial times, when "doctrines of liberty" could not be "transferred nor applied to the East" until "a higher order of general civilization"[31] permitted it, full implementation of these freedoms had also not as yet happened in Myanmar. Up until now, political expediency had not allowed for it.

Paradoxically, then, the nature of Western and Middle Eastern criticism over the Rohingya issue favoured Suu Kyi in the local context. Condemnation, directed at the country and at Suu Kyi, and not at the real culprits – the Tatmadaw – united the Burmese in a 'siege mentality'. Media logic (accusing a Nobel Laureate) kept the Suu Kyi-centric narrative about Myanmar. For two decades Suu Kyi's dominance in coverage of Myanmar tremendously helped her political cause … and, it is still favourable for her even now. As long as she remains the main target of criticism, she can play the convenient role of a nation's shield.

This was best seen when Myanmar was accused of committing genocide against the Rohingya people by Gambia at the International Court of Justice in The Hague in November 2019. In a rare spectacle of unapparent political outcomes (not often does a Peace Nobel Prize Laureate defend their policies against accusations of genocide and even less often do such accusations serve their own interests) Suu Kyi once again showed her political talents. The Laureate, known for her quick-thinking skills and brilliant out-of-the-box ad hoc actions, announced she would personally defend her country at The Hague, although she did not have to do it. By doing so, however, she turned this process into a 'we' versus 'them' issue and stationed herself as the symbolic protector of her country against evil foreigners. Additionally, she made her trip to The Hague a political show: media covered her every move and her defence speech was broadcast on live TV. A huge screen constructed near the town hall in Yangon also showed the live transmission. Pro-Suu Kyi rallies spontaneously sprouted in Yangon and other cities: the Burmese united once again behind the mother defending their country. Consequently, her popularity reached new highs. Unveiling a year before (another bevy of) crucial elections, the ICJ case was heaven-sent for Suu Kyi.

Against these benefits, the cons – another deluge of international criticism (the new season of 'the icon's fall' media series) – mattered little. After initial (well-hidden) personal gloom over the loss of Western support (she acted withdrawn and retreated),[32] Suu Kyi reconciled herself with Western criticism. As for the West, critics noted "she has given up trying", while in the past they stated "she cared for her adulation", now she no longer needed this as she knew that "their infatuation has given way to disillusion"; she just did not see "how she can possibly get back into general Western favour, and neither does she wish to".[33] Instead she found new admirers: Asians. At present, she feels "a lot more secure in an Asian environment. She is as at home in Singapore and Beijing today as she used to be in Oxford and London, but isn't any more. She has simply swapped her intellectual base"; she "can say what she likes around Asia, and no one will contradict her".[34] This new arrangement is more than enough compensation.

Gains in popularity were not the only benefits from the ICJ for Suu Kyi. As in the Chinese game *weiqi* (or Go), she played various moves at the same time. She protected the army internationally, gaining the Tatmadaw's reluctant appreciation, while domestically checkmating it at the same time. By taking control of the defence process, she could now use it as leverage against the Tatmadaw in crucial negotiations for constitutional amendments (her dream of presidency!) or, at worst, to limit the Tatmadaw's influence. She pushed the USDP onto the defensive and dominated the political scene, significantly empowering her civilian government vis-à-vis the Tatmadaw.[35] In short, it was a win–win for her.

Finally, by going to The Hague Court Suu Kyi proved once again her hybridity. There was much talk of how she had Burmanized (or re-Burmanized) herself since she came back to Myanmar in 1988: she allegedly changed and tossed away her universalist heritage. But when a political chance arose, she presented a vivid understanding of how the world functions. She gathered a good team of lawyers, headed by William Schabas, she knew what to say and what to write,[36] and she had (and still has) good tactics. They were based on inaccuracies in the UN fact finding mission report, difficulties of proving genocide, the long-running pace of the process (which favoured Myanmar) and, if all fails, the necessity of the UN Security Council enforcing the ICJ's verdict on a member state. In short, Suu Kyi, a hybrid politician, had not forgotten her international skills at all. Yet another example of her cautiously navigating international waters can be found in her June 2019 trip to Hungary to meet Victor Orbán: she was deliberately 'cocking a snook' at her erstwhile liberal supporters by meeting with the 'bad guy' of the liberal West.

In the meantime, she did not forget her domestic skills either, particularly her ability to keep her subordinates on a short leash.

The cadres' reshuffle

On 21 March 2018 president Htin Kyaw unexpectedly resigned a few days before his second anniversary. The news caught analysts off guard, once again proving how little insight there was (and still is) into Suu Kyi's decision-making process. Initially Htin Kyaw's deteriorating health was interpreted as the main reason for his resignation. He visited clinics during his foreign trips. During Pope Francis's 2017 pilgrimage to Myanmar – a barely concealed diplomacy effort to resolve the Rohingya issue – Htin Kyaw was fragile, even though few noted it (they rather focused on whether Pope Francis would use the name Rohingya). Journalists only later took notice of his condition, prompting Suu Kyi – in her unique style ("we have the first lady who will take care of him") – to deny speculations.[37] By doing so, Suu Kyi proved once again the adequacy of Prince Alexander Gorchakov's maxim ("I don't believe in news that has not been denied"), as indeed Htin Kyaw resigned soon after.

However, if health was the reason for his resignation, it was only partially true. His exasperation with being a ceremonial president treated offhandedly by Suu Kyi was probably more significant.[38] International criticism of Myanmar might have taken its toll too. It is not comfortable to be the president of a country accused of genocide (especially if one is a gentleman with traditional values). For all this speculation, the main reason was possibly different. When Suu Kyi nominated Htin Kyaw she did so hoping that it would be a temporary solution until she attained the Tatmadaw's consent to amend to Cconstitution.[39] Given the army's unwillingness to change the charter, the 'above the President' mechanism, instead of being an interim measure, proved to be much more durable. Now Suu Kyi decided to place another subordinate on the presidential seat.

There was a bit of uneasiness with the replacement process. According to the Constitution, when a President resigns his duties are taken over by the first Vice President, who in this case happened to be gen. Myint Swe, a hardliner nominated by the Tatmadaw. The NLD's nightmare scenario was that Myint Swe, while acting president, could convene meetings of the NDSC and declare an emergency (read: stage a legal coup). Nothing of the sort happened. The transition went smoothly and Htin Kyaw was replaced by another of Suu Kyi's loyalists, Win Myint. A lawyer and an NLD veteran (MP from 1990, 2012 and 2015 and Pyithu Hluttaw Speaker since 2016), Win Myint knew the price of the struggle against the regime. In a personal story mirroring Suu Kyi's own drama, Win Myint also faced the dilemma of family vs. politics. When he was in jail for dissident activity, his only son became terminally ill and the military intelligence offered him a pact with the devil: release in return for relinquishing politics. He refused and was doomed to never see his son again. In Suu Kyi's eyes, Win Myint passed 'the ability to sacrifice for the cause' test,[40] along with the loyalty and trust tests,[41] which are the essential requirement for her subordinates. Win Myint, 5 years younger than Htin Kyaw, is more energetic – he's a real politician, not an intellectual – but, crucially, he is no less loyal to the NLD leader.[42] Just like his predecessor, Win Myint is her yes man. This verifies, for the second time, that Suu Kyi chose the correct candidate for a ceremonial presidency, showing once again that she continues to prudently pick the members of her inner circle.

Along with this presidential reshuffle, the NLD underwent reorganization. Immediately prior to assuming presidency (30 March 2018), Win Myint was nominated as vice chairman no. 1, while Mandalay chief minister, Zaw Myint Maung (known as the NLD's most dynamic minister along with Yangon chief minister Phyo Min Thein) was given the position of vice chairman no. 2. At the time, both new deputies were 66 years old. Another veteran, Win Htein (76 years old), who rigorously made sure members towed the party line, was moved to honourable retirement, becoming a member of the NLD's board of patrons.[43] Myo Nyunt and Zaw Myint Maung were nominated to be NLD spokespersons. This restructuring marked an important intra-party reshuffle. When Suu Kyi became State Counsellor, she left party issues to five members of the secretariat (Win Htein, Win Myint, Zaw Myint Maung, Nyan Win, and Hantha Myint), which resulted in many tensions. From now on Zaw Myint Maung was responsible for managing everyday party affairs while Win Myint was responsible for state administration.[44] This reconfiguration of the NLD was completed during the NLD's second congress (23–24 June 2018) when the party expanded CEC members from 15 to 21[45] and CC members from 106 to 148 (plus 30 alternate members, totalling 178 members). Yet, not much changed in intra-party politicking. Initial steps to "cultivate and infuse fresh ideas into the party faltered leaving younger members frustrated".[46] Dissident voices were repressed as usual: three MPS were suspended and two (Thet Thet Khine and Kyaw Zeya) spectacularly sacked (from the NLD's Yangon township committee) for open criticism of party policies.[47] During the 2018 Congress, CEC members were this time chosen by secret ballot, but apparently delegates "received a closed letter listing the people they should vote for". Furthermore, there were no illusions that one of the objectives of the Congress was to "follow the leadership of Daw Aung San Suu Kyi".[48]

The cadres' reshuffle, especially the nomination of the NLD vice chairmen, was widely interpreted as Suu Kyi's succession strategy. This may well be so, but one must be cautious to remember that any one of Suu Kyi's subordinates may fall out of favour at any time and lose their strong position overnight. As was reported, Suu Kyi "disposes of them without a twinge of conscience, if it suited her whims; loyalty meant nothing".[49] Or rather, it is a reminder that loyalty in the NLD works only one way: the subordinate must be staunchly loyal to Suu Kyi, but she does not have to be grateful at all.[50] This happened to Tin Mar Aung, the all powerful personal assistant of Suu Kyi, who had already fallen from grace in the first year of Suu Kyi's rule.[51] Currently, Suu Kyi's inner circle consists of CEC members – some more powerful, like Win Myint, Zaw Myint Maung, Tin Myo Win, others less so. Additional members like Htin Kyaw and his wife Su Su Lwin, Pyone Mo Ei (wife of Tin Myo Win), Ohmar Moe Myint (Michael Moe Myint's wife), security advisor Thaung Tun, construction minister Win Khaing, minister Kyaw Tin Swe (serving in her office), and probably some others also make up the number of individuals 'in the know'.[52] In addition, there are some foreign consultants both formal (Sean Turnell) and informal (Robert Cooper, Lord Ara Darzi etc.).[53] Yet, all of these individuals have but an auxiliary voice. Suu Kyi consults her inner circle, but decides on her own and she always has the last word in every committee (especially in important ones such as the NLD's economic committee) and every decision she deems important. When she chairs TV-broadcasted public meetings with her ministers and other subordinates, she emulates (albeit in softer form) Vladimir Putin's style of roasting subordinates for their incompetency, which enhances the image of her intellectual and political paramountcy. There is only one leader. Even if labelling Suu Kyi as a Burmese '*Duce*'[54] is morally unfair, in terms of describing her governing style, it is quite an adequate designation.

The Burmese twins

Since coming to power, Suu Kyi has had to walk on thin ice: to rule without alienating the Tatmadaw. Otherwise her government would be doomed. She has managed this; mending fences with the Tatmadaw (read: political survival) remains her most important political achievement. At the same time, she has tried to limit the influence of the Tatmadaw without provoking it. This rational consideration trumped every other aspect of her governance. Consequently, the NLD's actions implemented a Burmese version of 'crab tactics', with steps forward, backward and to the side, depending on the situation. After five years of governance, the NLD and the Tatmadaw seemed to reach a certain level of understanding, if not developed a shared worldview. At the end of the day, the family quarrel in Burmese politics – the more than two decades-long political struggle between a father's daughter and (successors of) a father's comrades – finally dimmed.

At the beginning of its rule, the NLD was all about caution: it did all it could to block any criticism directed at the Tatmadaw from both within party ranks and from society; it did not dare touch the Tatmadaw's privileges; and it kept the military-era bureaucracy intact, despite modest attempts to infuse new blood into the state apparatus. The NLD's policy became a necessity, too, given Suu Kyi's distrust of Thein Sein's reformers and wariness of almost anyone outside the NLD. Consequently, she had to rely on the existing state bureaucracy in everyday governance. In many units there was only one NLD member: the minister or director, with no administrative experience. The result was predictable for anyone at least partially acquainted with the work of any bureaucratic structure anywhere: *nomenklatura* swallowed the NLD, not the other way round. After a few years in power, the "NLD was caught up the vortex of Naypyidaw".[55]

This is not to say the NLD did nothing over the years to replace the military-era cadres. It cautiously pushed its men (rarely women) up the ladder and secured some noticeable achievements. In early 2019 the General Administration Department, the administrative 'brain' of the Burmese state (which manages the whole administration of the state – more than 30,000 civil servants – down to township levels), was transferred from military oversight (Home Ministry) to a civilian one (Cabinet Office), marking "the big victory of Aung San Suu Kyi".[56] The NLD also managed to introduce legislation enforcing soldiers to vote in town and not in barracks. The NLD, too, limited the Tatmadaw's influence in many aspects of everyday life that are invisible to foreigners. To give just two examples: in the 1990s the Burmese had to rely on low-quality palm oil imported by UMEC while Yangoners had to travel by the Ma Hta Tha poor public transportation supervised by UMEC's daughter company, Bandula. Currently the public no longer has to rely on UMEC or other military-affiliated business for the palm oil and Yangoners travel by the – still criticised but considerably better – YBS Bus service.[57] There are many more examples of such tiny issues that make life more bearable for the Burmese. Overall, in many aspects of socio-political life, the Tatmadaw was 'tamed' to civilian governance.[58]

These little steps that keep limiting the Tatmadaw's omnipresence have been possible thanks to the fact that "the generals do not want to run Myanmar – at least not directly".[59] The generals initiated reforms and allowed for the opening up of Myanmar. They did not anticipate the scale of Thein Sein's reforms and they were outplayed by Suu Kyi's State Counsellor bill, but these are ultimately minor, sec- ondary issues. The generals want to protect the Tatmadaw (and its interests, including economic ones) and its political centrality, and they could respond should their Three National Causes be endangered. But otherwise they are fine with leaving governance to civilians, providing they respect the Tatmadaw's red lines. Naturally, it would be better if a military proxy, like the USDP, was in power, but a NLD that behaves in a non-confrontational manner towards the Tatmadaw is tolerated: "within those bounds they want the NLD government to succeed as they share many of its goals".[60] They all want their country to be successful, prosperous and globally respected.

None of these goals has so far materialized. The Rohingya crisis tarnished Myanmar's image, hampered reforms and complicated the geopolitical situation. But again, for some actors it had a positive side. The generals saw that Suu Kyi – whom they had always suspected of siding with foreign interests at the cost of Burmese ones – chose to defend Myanmar (and them by extension). This was her acid test in their eyes. In this regard, the Rohingya crisis was a positive breakthrough for the Suu Kyi – Tatmadaw relationship.

It does not mean there are no tensions left. The Suu Kyi – Min Aung Hlaing relationship is workable, but nothing more: it is formal and distant.[61] Recently, it became more formal and even more distant.[62] They are, after all, political compe- titors and the general suspects Suu Kyi's hand in Facebook's blockade of his (and other military associated) accounts (the 2018 take down of the generals' accounts was perhaps the first ever Western sanction that really hurt them). As for Suu Kyi, behind the façade of a (enforced) "Tatmadaw first" policy, she "is still seething that the Tatmadaw are preventing her from becoming President, where she would play a more ceremonial and less confrontational role than in her present status under the contrived designation of State Counsellor".[63] Suu Kyi's 2018 declaration in Sin- gapore that her relationship with the army "is not that bad" should be read con- versely ("it could be better"), while her description of her three cabinet generals as "rather sweet"[64] was ironic (which was lost to many Westerners), if not a Hello Kitty-styled Asian infantilization. Yet these problems are manageable. Despite "mutual distrust, and at times rising tension" between Suu Kyi and the army, "at the end of the day, the former political prisoners and their erstwhile captors had found a way to work together".[65] Nowadays the Tatmadaw sees the NLD as "decidedly less threatening than it had been a few years before, and far removed from its revolutionary origins".[66] Time did its part: during the five years, neither did the Tatmadaw try to topple the NLD nor did the NLD dismantle the military- constructed system (it only infused adjustments). Previously, political differences overshadowed clearly visible similarities. Among the commonalities are: that both Suu Kyi and the army emphasize the importance of unity, discipline and respon- sibilities; they use moralistic rhetoric to cover their political actions and silence/ criticise political opponents; moreover they are personalistic, hierarchical, and reactionary by nature.[67] One could say, that "the Tatmadaw have found that they need her in order to maintain their status and influence as much as she needs them"; they "need to keep her onside, and she needs them to survive"; and the Tatmadaw "can still cope with her, and she with them".[68] At this time, political expediency plus perhaps growing "similar nationalist leanings" and a "shared Naypyidaw view of the world"[69] trump past and present differences. The Tatmadaw and the NLD may not like one another and staunchly compete for power against each other, yet they grudgingly respect each other and need one another, as they represent "twin authoritarianisms",[70] or, simply, they are Burmese political twins.

Notes

1 *Towards a Peaceful, Fair and Prosperous Future for the People of Rakhine*, Final Report of the Advisory Commission on Rakhine State, August 2017.
2 "Genocide threat for Myanmar's Rohingya greater than ever", *UN News*, 16 September 2019.
3 Conversation with Ye Min Zaw, Yangon, 5 November 2019.
4 Ibid.
5 Interview with Khin Zaw Win, Yangon, 14 November 2019.
6 "Speech delivered by Her Excellency Daw Aung San Suu Kyi on government's efforts with regard to national reconciliation and peace", *State Counsellor Office*, 27 September 2017.
7 Conversation with Bridget Welsh, Kuala Lumpur, 26 February 2020.
8 Conversations in Myanmar, 2014–2019.
9 "Defiant and defensive".
10 Thant Myint-U, *The Hidden History of Burma*, p. 241.
11 Suu Kyi's spokesman on ARSA's October 2016 attacks: "like 9/11 in America". "It is good to be Tatmadaw".
12 Ibid.
13 Conversation with Ye Min Zaw, Yangon, 5 November 2019.
14 James E Hoare, *Extract from the record of a talk by Daw Aung San Suu Kyi at St Antony's College Oxford on 13 November 1979.*
15 "Burma's sectarian violence motivated by fear, says Aung San Suu Kyi", *The Guardian*, 24 October 2013.
16 Popham, *The Lady and the Generals*, p. 256.
17 Conversation with Jerzy Bayer, Berlin, 25 November 2019.
18 "Rohingyas are Bangladeshis, Suu Kyi told David Cameron", *Hindustan Times*, 19 September 2019.
19 "I'm just a politician. I'm not quite like Margaret Thatcher, but on the other hand I am no Mother Teresa either", "Aung San Suu Kyi: No ethnic cleansing of Myanmar Muslim minority", *BBC News*, 6 April 2017.
20 Derek Tonkin, "Aung San Suu Kyi and political realities in Myanmar", *Network Myanmar*, 25 July 2015.
21 Andrew Selth, "Aung San Suu Kyi and the politics of personality", *Griffith Asia Institute Regional Outlook Paper No. 55* (2017), p. 11.
22 Ibid., p. 13.
23 As one of her advisers summarized, "it's a divided society, so stressing human rights and democracy will only heighten disunity and lead to greater instability", "Patience tested".
24 Nick Cheesman, "How in Myanmar 'national races' came to surpass citizenship and excluded Rohingya", *Journal of Contemporary Asia*, vol. 47, no. 3 (2017), pp. 461–483.
25 Jacques Leider, "Competing identities and the hybridized history of the Rohingyas", in *Metamorphosis*, pp. 151–179.
26 "Aung San Suu Kyi defends policies, points to broader investigations", *Nikkei Asia Review*, 21 September 2017.

27 "Rohingya crisis: Suu Kyi says 'fake news helping terrorists'", *BBC*, 6 September 2017.
28 Derek Tonkin, email correspondence, 14 January 2020.
29 Private conversations, Yangon, February 2019.
30 Derek Tonkin, email correspondence, 9 September 2019. For Tonkin, jailing not releasing the journalists is Suu Kyi's "show of intolerance", a "sample of traditional Burmese power in action", Ibid.
31 Kavalam M. Pannikar, *Asia and Western Dominance. A Survey of the Vasco da Gama Epoch in Asian History* (New York, NY: John Day, 1954), p. 110.
32 Interview with Khin Zaw Win, Yangon, 14 November 2019.
33 Derek Tonkin, email correspondence, 9 September 2020.
34 Ibid.
35 "Aung San Suu Kyi comes out on top in ICJ Rohingya ruling", *Nikkei Asia Review*, 8 February 2020.
36 "Aung San Suu Kyi: Give Myanmar time to deliver justice on war crimes", *Financial Times*, 23 January 2020.
37 "Speculation mounts over President U Htin Kyaw's health", *The Irrawaddy*, 19 January 2018.
38 Interview with Khin Zaw Win, Yangon, 14 November 2019.
39 Thant Myint-U, *The Hidden History of Burma*, pp. 222–226.
40 Popham, *The Lady and the Generals*, p. 225.
41 As one of Suu Kyi's advisers told me, when Suu Kyi nominated him to a position, she asked "do you trust me?" Conversation with him in Yangon, 11 November 2019.
42 Interview with Khin Zaw Win, Yangon, 14 November 2019.
43 Headed by Tin Oo, with Hla Pe, Ohn Kyaing, Kyaw Khin and Mahn Johnny as the other four members.
44 "NLD party revamp elevates U Win Myint to no. 2 spot", *The Irrawaddy*, 30 March 2018; "Finally, the NLD embraces succession planning", *Frontier Myanmar*, 4 May 2018.
45 The new members were Tin Myo Win, Aung Kyi Nyunt, Thein Oo, Myint Naing, En Htone Khar Naw Sam and Tin Htut Oo.
46 "Time for Myanmar's new government to get back on track", *The Diplomat*, 12 April 2017.
47 "NLD fires two insubordinate lawyers", *Coconut Yangon*, 6 September 2018.
48 "NLD beefs up CEC, Daw Aung San Suu Kyi remains leader", *The Myanmar Times*, 25 June 2018.
49 Derek Tonkin, email correspondence, 18 February 2020.
50 Interview with Khin Zaw Win, Yangon, 14 November 2019.
51 "Defiant and defensive".
52 Ibid.; "Myanmar intensifies strategic courtship of Beijing", *Bangkok Post*, 8 April 2017; private information; Mon Mon Myat, email correspondence, 11 February 2020.
53 Derek Tonkin, email correspondence, 9 September 2019.
54 Interview with Khin Zaw Win, Yangon, 14 November 2019.
55 Thant Myint-U, *The Hidden History of Burma*, pp. 229–230.
56 Ibid., p. 253.
57 Mon Mon Myat, email correspondence, 11 February 2020.
58 Conversation with Bridget Welsh, Kuala Lumpur, 26 February 2020.
59 "Why Myanmar's military is not planning a coup", *Nikkei Asia Review*, 8 May 2017.
60 Ibid.
61 "Potholes in Myanmar's road to 'democracy'", *Financial Review*, 28 May 2017.
62 Conversation with Bridget Welsh, Kuala Lumpur, 26 February 2020.
63 Derek Tonkin, email correspondence, 14 January 2020.
64 "Myanmar's Suu Kyi says relations with military 'not that bad'", *Reuters*, 21 August 2018.
65 Thant Myint-U, *The Hidden History of Burma*, p. 253.
66 Ibid., p. 253.

67 Khin Zaw Win, "Twin authoritarianisms in Myanmar", *New Mandala*, 13 September 2019; Lubina, *The Moral Democracy*, pp. 191–403.
68 Derek Tonkin, email correspondence, 9 September 2019 and 14 January 2020.
69 Thant Myint-U, *The Hidden History of Burma*, p. 253.
70 Khin Zaw Win, "Twin authoritarianisms".

CONCLUSION: A BALANCE SHEET

March 2020 marked the fifth year of Suu Kyi's governance.[1] She has suffered more failures, than scored gains, retained domestic supporters and disappointed foreign fans. She has not changed much in Myanmar. Her rule has not been a success; on the other hand, it has not been a disaster. Most importantly, she has survived in power and likely will remain at the helm. So – to paraphrase a Chinese saying – as long as she lives, she can do better.

Let's start from the personal; in Suu Kyi's case, political is personal. Aung San Suu Kyi still dominates Myanmar politically. She is the most powerful politician, who controls all aspects of governance but for security and the Tatmadaw's economic satrapies (in other words: she influences all sectors she can). Every important decision must get her approval. Never mind collateral damage such as administrative delays, what matters is that she has oversight. She is feared in the government by civil servants and yet she is adored in the society, particularly by party members. If indeed she believes she "was born to rule",[2] she has reasons to be satisfied. Moreover, she is still the beloved mother of the nation, even if less so than five years ago. She still personifies hope, which holds the Burmese together as a society.[3] Although this is a factor one cannot simply measure or evaluate, it is not irrelevant.

Her image continues to be a commercial brand that glamorizes pictures, calendars, keyrings and souvenirs from Myanmar. Her father is back on banknotes, sirens yet again sound at 10:37 on every 19 July, his new monuments dot the country and his myth is alive and well. Suu Kyi's personal political ideology – that this is all her duty to the people,[4] that she wants to finish her father's job and make Burma free and democratic, that whatever she does, she does for the people at her own personal expense[5] – is widely accepted as truth, even among some intellectuals.[6] It is a story of the mother of Myanmar, who does everything for the children and tries her best to prepare them to live in adulthood (if they fail, however, it will be their fault, not hers).[7] Every success is hers, whereas failures fall on the Tatmadaw,

structural problems, hostile foreigners, karma, bad luck, *force majeure* (or all combined), but rarely on her. Even if more and more Burmese people criticise her, she
still holds a certain amount of immunity.

From this perspective, her situation does not seem bad. If even a veteran critical
expert admits that she "is a woman of destiny, and she knows that she is. Suu Kyi
has spent all her time striving ever since her return to Myanmar in March 1988 and
who can deny that in her own way she has been successful?"[8] – then it is indeed
not bad at all. In such a case, there are no 'four lives' of Aung San Suu Kyi,[9] but
only two: the unfulfilled one before politics and the proper political one.

Yet there is a thorn in her side. She is still not the President. Even if her critics
sometimes go too far in claiming that "she is obsessed about presidency, about
formal aspects of power",[10] her need to achieve the ultimate post is unmistakable.
Becoming State Counsellor was a smart move, but it "sounds silly" to the world: it
"grates with many whenever they hear the designation and is a symbol of the limits
of her power, for Counsellors are but Advisers, and she aspires to be more than
this".[11] She will be faced with a hard battle in her continuing attempt to change
the Constitution, yet given the fact that she is proverbially stubborn, she is unlikely
to crack. As Tonkin stated: "she wants to be President, she can live unhappily
without the final accolade, but this is not likely to stop her striving, by means fair
and foul, to achieve the ultimate prize. This is maybe what keeps her going".[12]

For Myanmar, however, the balance sheet is much more mixed.

Structural problems and negative factors independent from Suu Kyi (US–China
trade war) notwithstanding, she has not delivered well on the economy. Growth
has slowed down, FDI and business confidence has fallen, tourist arrivals have
stagnated. Furthermore, the real estate market is now in trouble. Myanmar's
banking system remains weak, despite some achievements of her government in
cleaning it up. The country still ranks low in doing business: 165th in 2019 (worse
than Laos or Cambodia and a world apart from India at 63rd).[13] The NLD government has failed to execute key reforms and will not do so now because of
electoral logic. The key impediments of doing business in Myanmar – land access,
access to utilities, finance and human capital – have remained the same, not
improving much during the NLD's rule. Little of the NLD's 2016 economic
programme has been achieved.[14]

An ill-disposed devil's advocate may say that at least Suu Kyi no longer questions
people's commitment to the free market.[15] Her previous economic ideas were
quite detached from reality.[16] Apparently, she "historically held the view that she
was lukewarm about foreign investment at all"; allegedly she "even went so far on
one occasion to say she hoped there might never be any further foreign investment
in her country".[17] For similar reasons, she disliked tourism, once declaring that
"providing a smiling service to foreign visitors was demeaning to Burmese", which
really revealed "her innate anti-colonialism".[18] At present, to her credit, at least she
does not disturb the economic sphere.

Yet she does not help it much either. She has some competent ministers and
advisors, both Burmese and Western, but she has proven unable and/or unwilling

to change the bad business environment. It affects all companies. Investors refrain from entering the country or pull out. Businesspeople complain endlessly about the insufficiency of reforms, lack of economic direction (never ending debates on whether to boost tourism or liberalise the retail/wholesale sector?), bureaucratic inertia (e.g. the electricity tariff structure), economic nationalism, the regulatory environment (lack of clarity in mining, oil and gas sector regulations), problems with labour contracts, inadequacy of judicial independence, or existing protectionist policies. The final complaint makes a good case study. In domestic air transportation, the transport ministry rejected foreign airlines – sorry, no Air Asia flights to Bagan – in order to shield the crony-controlled, domestic airlines. Healthcare, retail banking and shipping also remain heavily protected. The insurance market has not opened up yet (which caused Samsung Life to withdraw from Myanmar).[19]

Almost every sector of governance has been in need of drastic reforms and increased resources. Even so, not much has happened in these past five years. Reforms are hampered by the logic of political transformation (the 'let the sleeping dogs lie' policy) and by its dual role in the administration – the policy makes much sense in the political sphere, but what is good for politics is not necessarily good for economics.

Plus there is something else. No vision. In the NLD's Myanmar, just as in the Tatmadaw's Myanmar, there is not only a lack of a comprehensive economic agenda, but worse – there is little if any developmental vision. If at all, it is to follow their neighbours in moving towards a state-dominated capitalism based on export-oriented industrialization. Unfortunately, neoliberal prescriptions clash with bureaucratic habits and socialist leanings, producing chaos, not fusion. Besides, with changing patterns of global economy, very soon "the ladder of export-oriented growth … may be a ladder to nowhere".[20]

It is fair to admit that all these hindrances are not necessarily and not exclusively the fault of Suu Kyi's cabinet. Deep structural problems, a legacy of the Tatmadaw's rule and a worsening global economic climate, would affect every government. Additionally, there are cultural aspects: capitalism has never been popular among the Burmese people, and they have yet to master the hard skills of navigating the stormy waters of global economics. So, these are indeed extenuating circumstances.

This, however, does not absolve Suu Kyi from her own political mistakes. She did not have to promise things she could not deliver. She declared a 'peace first' policy and predictably failed. The situation is now worse than in 2015. This is also the case with the hoped for constitutional amendments. Achieving them was impossible from the outset and expectedly she was unable to do anything. In the same manner she promised to end corruption and – although she still strives to accomplish this goal – success is far, far away.[21] Most importantly, she campaigned to introduce change, but her rule is anything but change. It is a modification of military rule, not a fundamental transformation.

The people of Myanmar expected better government services and lower costs of living. The former did not materialize, the latter is debatable. Suu Kyi, however, does not take responsibility for that. She shies away from everyday governance. She is hardly seen or heard, and even if she (rarely) addresses the public, she does not lower herself to the level of everyday, mundane issues. Instead, the State Councillor offers pedagogical moral preaching about the duties and responsibilities of the citizens, something that takes priority over rights ; that is, about the responsibility of each individual – not the government – to make change.[22] Her rule "was never about (the) government solving people's problems", instead she offered "a life story as an example for others to follow".[23] This is very much a convenient agenda for her: she can levitate 'above politics' and keep her iconic position within Myanmar, but her heavy-handedness and micromanaging style have produced administrative inertia. Many problems lie unresolved as challenges sit in a long queue of issues to be dealt with exclusively by her.

If her governance is a story of disappointment, then why does she remain so popular in Myanmar? From her acclaim it would seem, at least according to norms of electoral democracy, that she has done a good job, whereas the evidence is to the contrary. Why then? How does a leader who governs badly (or so-so at best) continue to enjoy widespread popular support?

I think there are four possible mutually nonexclusive explanations.

The first two are irrational, at least from a Western perspective. Deep-seated Burmese Buddhist cultural patterns, or Maha-Sammata's style of democracy, come first. The Burmese people expect their leaders to be moral. Efficiency comes second, if at all. Suu Kyi, all her vices notwithstanding, is obviously much more moral than any Tatmadaw general, present or former. The second irrational explanation concerns the 'mother of the nation' approach. One does not expect a mother to deliver concrete results. The symbolic bond between Burmese society and their leader gives her immunity, at least temporarily, from delivering results.

Nevertheless, one should be cautious when using these two explanations, as in political science often "what cannot be explained in terms of rationality or logic is expelled into the realm of culture".[24] That is why I prefer the other two rational explanations. The third explication would be that the Burmese people have not yet forgotten the nightmare of the previous military rule. However disappointed they may be with Suu Kyi's governance, she is still preferable compared to the return of military rule – whether in civilian dress or in uniform. She is at worst a lesser evil than the Tatmadaw, and at best a hope that still unites society.

Finally, the last explanation is that her governance is paradoxically not that bad (although that is not much by her merit). Critics admit that she has not disrupted the wider process, started during Thein Sein's governance, of Myanmar's opening up to the world – to external commercial influences, global connectivity and cyber revolution. The people of Myanmar live a better life. Some are much better off, many a little better; they can travel abroad and are no longer cut off from the world. Suu Kyi's successes are here "almost by default", as Tonkin admits, "it is not that she has taken any brave decisions, but rather that she has allowed things to happen – she was never all that much interested in detail".[25] But, she kept "the dreaded hand of the Tatmadaw at bay from the people's daily lives": at present there are fewer arrests – even if these are more often reported than previously – and people "no longer have to watch their words when chatting in the tea-shops".[26] In this regard, her NLD cabinet is a *primum non nocere* government, which continues the positive momentum started during Thein Sein (without admitting it). Supporters argue that there has been developmental progress: better infrastructure (new and improved roads), electrification (access to the grid has reached around 70 per cent of the population), and progress (albeit modest) in education and healthcare (there is greater spending on these sectors in the budget at least). Additionally, there is social progress: less corruption, more transparency ("we can criticize the government but not to the military"), a much reduced network of the Tatmadaw in civil administration, strengthened CSOs and more empowered people who still hope for better in the future.[27] This hope, perhaps, is most important, as it allows civilians to move forward despite everything.[28] Overall, even with the obvious hindrances and disappointments, "things are moving in the right direction in terms of Asian-style democracy".[29]

For these and other reasons, the NLD will most likely win the 2020 elections providing no extraordinary things, such as electoral fraud or a new coup, happen (these are not impossible, but unlikely). The 'boomerang' question that keeps coming back is whether the NLD will score 67 per cent of the seats (or 329 seats) in the Hluttaw? The party is doing its best to achieve that. Unable to repeat its 2015 "change" slogan ("change 2.0" is ruled out), their plan concentrated on promising constitutional amendments in the hopes of capitalizing on the dislike of the Tatmadaw in society. To achieve this, the NLD established a parliamentary commission to amend the constitution, which irritated the military and predictably led to nothing[30]. But at least the policy created an impression of determination: it was all about chasing the rabbit, not catching it. Amending the Constitution is always an adequate electoral slogan in Myanmar, making it a rational winning electoral strategy.

By making accusations about Myanmar at the ICJ, Gambia provided the second electoral engine. The rallying around the flag effect should secure the NLD's victory: the longer and fiercer the world attacks Myanmar (and Suu Kyi), the better her electoral prospects. By doing so, they succour her to win elections. In yet another twist of fate, the West – which had assisted Suu Kyi for two decades – helps her politically yet again, this time by condemning her. The irony is that it is now China that internationally defends Suu Kyi against the West, in a direct reversal of the pre-2011 situation. Chinese support however does not matter as much in terms of electoral victory. Suu Kyi's problem, though, is not with the West. Nor is it with the Buddhist radicals. She neutralised them, at least for now, by outlawing Ma Ba Tha and making Wirathu a fugitive. Dealing with them remains one of her big achievements, although one that is little seen and not appreciated from outside. Her predicament is not even with lesser parties (the 'new third force', 'People's party' or others), as they will be trumped. Her problem is with the ethnic minorities. It is highly unlikely that they will vote for her *en masse* again: they will not make the same mistake twice. Even so, she hopes to achieve partial support and is gambling on the belief that the ethnic vote will be divided. She is working hard to achieve this split in the vote.[31] The first-past-the-post electoral system favours her party, so even with modest support from the Kayins (Karens), Chins, perhaps some Mon and Kachins, maybe Shans (but certainly not Rakhines and probably not Kayahs), she can still manage to get 67 per cent overall. No more is needed.

Therefore, the most likely post-2020 scenario is a continuation of her rule. Some claim she will then challenge the army to secure her place in history,[32] yet this is rather unlikely. More plausible is the continuation of careful tactics to gradually remove the Tatmadaw from power and influence. Maybe she will be able to persuade the military to allow her presidency – she will certainly try hard – but again, this scenario is rather less probable. And even if she somehow manages to do so, this will not change much in the overall assessment of her rule in Myanmar. So far, her governance's score is modest and disappointing though not disastrous. Perhaps the biggest achievement is that she has inadvertently reduced domestic and international expectations: no one waits for miracles now and that is good for Myanmar.[33] The country and its leader deserve to be assessed fairly in rational terms, not by fairy-tale-style categories.

Disappointment with Suu Kyi is now nearly totally in the West. For more than 25 years Suu Kyi and the West spoke the same language, albeit with the same words having different meanings. And then came the shock and disbelief that a genocide might have occurred in a country ruled by a Nobel Peace Prize Laureate. But blaming her for it would be unfair. Claiming that she purposely misguided her foreign supporters and outplayed the West for two decades would be incorrect. One cannot say that she consciously cheated half of the world. The colossal yet mutual misunderstanding between Suu Kyi and the West was due to the fact that she was not a Westernized Burmese (as most in the West believed), but a hybrid politician. Although being anticolonial personally, she unconsciously internalized colonial patterns picked up at schools and during her youth in Burma and India. This has moulded her, while her later socialisation with British elites in the 1960s completed the process. Even if Suu Kyi disliked some (or maybe even many) colonial aspects, she internalized the colonial intellectual superstructure. Burmese postcolonial elites, whose intellectual epigone Suu Kyi is, themselves staunchly anticolonial, emulated colonial patterns in private. And it is precisely this colonial heritage within Suu Kyi that is responsible for her shocking behaviours – from a contemporary Western perspective: Dictatorship in the party (in the colonial world democracy operated only west of Suez), the jailing of Reuters' journalists or restricting freedom of speech. And especially the Rohingya. Her stance on this issues is the most glaring example of a lack of mental decolonization. It shows the enduring post-mortem symbolic violence of colonialism.

The Western world was wrong about Suu Kyi, not because she pretended to be someone else or because of her acquiesce to being misunderstood. No. The West was wrong because it wanted to see in Suu Kyi the brighter face of its legacy in Asia (democracy, human rights etc.). And though it would be unfair to say there was no bright side – there is definitely a lot – the dark side also remains and so does the unaccounted colonial guilt, the burden of creating many Asian structural problems, that hampers Asian countries still now. In this picture, Suu Kyi – a hybrid politician, a product of colonial heritage – is just a local, Burmese example of a wider spectre of Western colonialism's heritage that still haunts Asia.

And, hence it is with other postcolonial leaders she should be compared. In her paramountcy of leadership, she came up to Aung San's level. But, painfully for her, she is not Aung San. She may share charisma and a certain Machiavellianism with him, but he was a much more skilful politician. More importantly, part of his success had to do with the fact that he surrounded himself with competent associates, had good ministers and commanded respect even from his enemies. Given her hybridity, she is perhaps closer to Jawaharlal Nehru, or rather to his post-1947 governance. Obviously she lacks the credentials of his independence struggle – her 'second national independence' may convince her supporters, but is not true. In terms of administrative (in)competences, she indeed reminds us of Nehru. Like him, she is a popular ruler, though not an effective one. Following in Nehru's footsteps, she believes in democracy and does her best to introduce it to Myanmar, just as he tried to do so for India, but she, like him, is personally too autocratic to allow democracy to flourish. Ultimately, like Nehru who (less skilfully) copied British colonial practices, she emulates Thein Sein's reforms, only with less efficiency. So far, similar to Nehru, she does not seem to know how to rule well (though in her case, that may still change). She is even closer to Sirimavo Bandaranaike: a Sinhalese symbol of women's political emancipation who ruled for a long time but not very effectively. Or to Benazir Bhutto, who also capitalised on her father's legacy, constantly struggling with the army and ultimately failing to make a breakthrough in Pakistan. Or to Sheikh Hasina, Suu Kyi's Bengali equivalent (for the good and the bad) – a mirror image minus the Nobel Prize.

If we compare Suu Kyi to leaders in the 1980s, when she started her career, one politician – that she is not at all similar to – comes to mind. Deng Xiaoping. Suu Kyi is much more elegant but she badly lacks two of Deng's features which helped him to make China's spectacular transformation possible. Unlike him, she cannot accept being *primus inter pares* and ruling by advice rather than by command. And, totally dissimilar to him, she cares about the formal aspects of power. These two hindrances originate from her hubristic conviction that she is indispensable and infallible. This is, ultimately, her biggest weakness. If it was less about personal issues, then she might have achieved more. The Tatmadaw might have found it easier to cooperate with her and Myanmar could have been better reformed. But in Suu Kyi's case – just like in many others in Myanmar – it is all about the leader. Ultimately, it is structurally detrimental to this country of great potential, yet weak institutions.

If Suu Kyi wins the 2020 elections her administration will hopefully be better by the very fact of gained experience. She has the talent to stun by her unconventional actions and thus I would not be surprised if she shocks the world yet again – this time by governing well. Yet a breakthrough in Myanmar's fate – say reforms à la Deng Xiaoping or a Korean-style miracle – is impossible. This is not only because the international circumstances are not favourable but, more importantly, because Suu Kyi is a tactician and not a strategist. She has mastered the very Burmese feature of ad hoc actions to perfection. However, she lacks long-term policy strategy; she does not have a developmental vision.

Aung San Suu Kyi may wish to finish her father's job and make Burma great again. But she does not know how to do it.

Notes

1 This book was finished on 1st March 2020, just before the Covid-19 pandemic reached Myanmar. Some political circumstances described in this publication may have changed in the meantime.
2 Derek Tonkin, email correspondence, 9 September 2019.
3 Conversation with Bridget Welsh, Kuala Lumpur, 26 February 2020.
4 "I would like to be seen as a worker. As somebody who has performed what she should have performed, who has done her duty", quoted in Pederson, *The Burma Spring*, p. 486.
5 Thant Myint-U, *The Hidden History of Burma*, p. 252.
6 "What Daw Suu has been trying in 25 years' struggle is similar to her father: to end militarism/authoritarian and to see her country to be 'a free democratic Myanmar'. The situation they both face is quite similar: fighting against Imperialist/Fascist/Tyrant and trying to make peace with different races and religions. That's what Daw Suu takes as 'responsibility toward people' or as her job in politics", Mon Mon Myat, email correspondence, 22 February 2020.
7 "Whether she could achieve what she wants during her rule, after all, it depends solely on the responsibility of each and every citizen to keep the country in a good shape", Ibid.
8 Derek Tonkin, email correspondence, 18 February 2020.
9 According to Timothy Garton Ash, there are four lives of Suu Kyi: youth in the shadow of Aung San, Oxford years, the opposition anti-regime struggle and the post-2012 political life in accordance with Weberian "ethics of responsibility", "The four lives of Aung San Suu Kyi", *The Guardian*, 20 June 2012.
10 Interview with Khin Zaw Win, Yangon, 13 November 2019.
11 Derek Tonkin, email correspondence, 14 January 2020.
12 Ibid., 18 February 2020.
13 *Doing Business 2020. Comparing Business Regulation in 190 Economies*. The World Bank, p. 5.
14 "Myanmar's stalled transition", *Briefing no. 151*, Crisis Group Asia 2018; "A year of despair and despondency", *Myanmar Times*, 28 December 2019.
15 Thant Myint-U, *The Hidden History of Burma*, p. 253.
16 Sengupta, *The Female Voice of Myanmar*, pp. 295–312.
17 Derek Tonkin, email correspondence, 18 February 2020.
18 Ibid.
19 "A year of despair and despondency".
20 Thant Myint-U, *The Hidden History of Burma*, pp. 200 and 257–258.
21 Within society there is (incorrect) perception that the government has done a good job on fulfilling their task to fight corruption, conversation with Bridget Welsh, Kuala Lumpur, 26 February 2020.
22 "The quiet puritanical vision".
23 Thant Myint-U, *The Hidden History of Burma*, p. 252.

24 Simon Philpot, *Rethinking Indonesia. Postcolonial Theory, Authoritarianism and Identity* (London: Macmillan Press, 2000), p. 79.

25 Derek Tonkin, email correspondence, 18 February 2020.

26 Ibid.

27 Mon Mon Myat, email correspondence, 11 February 2020.

28 Conversation with Bridget Welsh, Kuala Lumpur, 26 February 2020.

29 Derek Tonkin, email correspondence, 18 February 2020.

30 In March 2020, already after the book was finished, the Hluttaw once again voted the constitutional amendments down.

31 "Suu Kyi stirs ethnic pot ahead of Myanmar elections".

32 Conversation with a Burmese scholar, Chiang Mai, 7 November 2019.

33 Conversation with Bridget Welsh, Kuala Lumpur, 26 February 2020.

BIBLIOGRAPHY

Ashcroft, B., Griffiths, G., and Tiffin, H. (eds), *The Post-Colonial Studies Reader* (London and New York, NY: Routledge, 2006).

Aung San Suu Kyi, *Letters from Burma* (London: Penguin, 1997).

Aung San Suu Kyi, *Freedom from Fear and Other Writings*, ed. M. Aris (London: Penguin, 2010).

Aung Zaw, *The Face of Resistance* (Chiang Mai: Mekong Press, 2013).

Aung-Thwin, Maitrii, 'Reassessing "Myanmar's Glasnost"', *Kyoto Review of Southeast Asia*, No. 14 (2013).

Aung-Thwin, Michael and Aung-Thwin, Maitrii, *A History of Myanmar Since Ancient Times* (London: Reaktion Books, 2012).

Barker, Chris, *Cultural Studies: Theory and Practice* (London: Sage, 2005).

Bengtsson, Jesper, *Aung San Suu Kyi. A Biography* (New Delhi: Amaryllis, 2012).

Bhabha, Homi K., *Location of Culture* (London and New York, NY: Routledge, 2004).

Blum, Franziska, *Teaching Democracy. The Program and Practice of Aung San Suu Kyi's Concept of People's Education* (Berlin: Regiospectra, 2011).

Bogdanor, V. (ed.), *The Blackwell Encyclopedia of Political Science* (Oxford: Blackwell, 1999).

Bolesta, Andrzej, 'Post-socialist Myanmar and the East Asian Development Model', *Central European Economic Journal*, Vol. 5, no. 52 (2019).

Brooten, Lisa, 'The Feminization of Democracy Under Siege: The Media, "the Lady" of Burma, and U.S. Foreign Policy', *NWSA Journal*, Vol. 17, No. 3 (2005).

Bünthe, Marco, 'Burma's Transition to Quasi-Military Rule: From Rulers to Guardians?', *Armed Forces & Society*, Vol. 40, No. 4 (2014)

Burma's April Parliamentary By-Elections, CRS Report for Congress, 28 March 2012.

Callahan, Mary, 'The Generals Loosen Their Grip', *Journal of Democracy*, Vol. 23, No. 4 (2012).

Carlsnaes, Walter, 'The Agency-Structure Problem in Foreign Policy Analysis', *International Studies Quarterly*, Vol. 36, No. 3 (1992).

Charney, Michael W., *A History of Modern Burma* (Cambridge: Cambridge University Press, 2009).

Cheesman, Nick, 'How in Myanmar "National Races" Came to Surpass Citizenship and Excluded Rohingya', *Journal of Contemporary Asia*, Vol. 47, No. 3 (2017).

Cheesman, N., Farrelly, N., and Wilson, T. (eds), *Debating Democratisation in Myanmar* (Singapore: ISEAS, 2014).

Clements, Alan, *The Voice of Hope. Conversations with Aung San Suu Kyi* (London: Rider, 2008).

Clinton, Hillary R., *Hard Choices* (New York, NY: Simon & Schuster, 2014).

Colvin, David H., Comment on "Democracy Burmese Style – The Great Illusion?", dispatch, Confidential, FAB 014/6, 1 August 1990, "Internal Affairs" FCO, The National Archive, Kew.

Crisis Group Asia, 'Myanmar's Stalled Transition', *Briefing no.* 151 (2018).

Crisis Group Asia, 'Myanmar: Storm Clouds on the Horizon', *Report no.* 238 (2012).

Dittmer, L. (ed.), *Burma or Myanmar? The Struggle for National Identity* (Singapore: World Scientific, 2010).

Duell, K. (ed.), *Myanmar in Transition: Polity, People and Process* (Singapore: KAS, 2013).

Egreteau, Renaud, *Caretaking Democratization. The Military and Political Change in Myanmar* (London: Hurst, 2016).

Egreteau, R. and F. Robinne (eds), *Metamorphosis. Studies in Social and Political Change in Myanmar* (Singapore: NUS Press, 2016).

Fabian, Johannes, *Time and the Other. How Anthropology Makes Its Object* (New York, NY: Colombia University Press, 2014).

Fink, Christina, *Living Silence in Burma. Surviving Under Military Regime* (Chiang Mai: Silkworm Books, 2009).

Fukuyama, Francis, 'The End of History?', *The National Interest*, Vol. 16 (1989).

Ganesan, Narayanan, 'Interpreting Recent Developments in Myanmar as an Attempt to Establish Political Legitimacy', *Asian Journal of Peacebuilding*, Vol. 1, No. 2 (2013).

Ganesan, Narayanan, 'The Myanmar Peace Center: Its Origins, Activities, and Aspirations', *Asian Journal of Peacebuilding*, Vol. 2, No. 1 (2014).

Harriden, Jessica, *The Authority of Influence. Women and Power in Burmese History* (Copenhagen: NIAS Press, 2012).

Hartland-Swann, Julian, 'Burmese Elections: NLD Intentions', Confidential Dispatch, FAB 014/1, 30 May 1990, "Internal Affairs" FCO, The National Archive, Kew.

Hartland-Swann, Julian, 'Democracy Burmese Style – The Great Illusion?', Confidential Dispatch, FAB 014/6, 1 August 1990, "Internal Affairs" FCO, The National Archive, Kew.

Hoare, James E., Extract from the record of a talk by Daw Aung San Suu Kyi at St Antony's College Oxford on 13.11.1979.

Hoogvelt, Ankie, *Globalization and the Postcolonial World: The New Political Economy of Development* (Baltimore, MD: Johns Hopkins University Press, 1997).

Houtman, Gustaaf, *Mental Culture in Burmese Crisis Politics: Aung San Suu Kyi and the National League for Democracy* (Tokyo: ILCAA, 1999).

Jordt, Ingrid, 'Breaking Bad in Burma', *Religion in the News*, Vol. 15, No. 2 (2014).

Koenig, William J., *The Burmese Polity, 1752–1819. Politics, Administration, and Social Organization in the Early Kon-baung Period* (Ann Arbor, MI: University of Michigan, 1990).

Kyaw Yin Hlaing, 'Aung San Suu Kyi of Myanmar: A Review of the Lady's Biographies', *Contemporary Southeast Asia: A Journal of International and Strategic Affairs*, Vol. 29, No. 2 (2007).

Kyaw Yin Hlaing (ed.), *Prisms on the Golden Pagoda. Perspectives on National Reconciliation in Myanmar* (Singapore: NUS Press, 2014).

Kyaw Sein and Nicholas Farrelly, 'Myanmar's Evolving Relations. The NLD in Government', *Asia Paper*, Stockholm, October 2016.

Lall, Marie, *Understanding Reform in Myanmar. People and Society in the Wake of Military Rule* (London: Hurst, 2016).

Laydler, Derek, *Understanding Social Theory* (London: Sage, 1994).

Lee, Ronan, 'Politician, Not an Icon: Aung San Suu Kyi's Silence on Myanmar's Muslim Rohingya', *Islam and Christian–Muslim Relations*, Vol. 25, No. 3 (2014).

Lintner, Bertil, *Aung San Suu Kyi and Burma's Unfinished Renaissance* (Melbourne: Monash University, CSAS, 1990).

Lintner, Bertil, *Aung San Suu Kyi and Burma's Struggle for Democracy* (Chiang Mai: Silkworm Books, 2011).

Lintner, Bertil, *Outrage. Burma's Struggle for Democracy* (London: White Lotus, 1990).

Lubina, Michał, *Pani Birmy. Biografia Polityczna Aung San Suu Kyi* (Warszawa: PWN, 2015).

Lubina, Michał, *The Moral Democracy. The Political Thought of Aung San Suu Kyi* (Warsaw: Scholar, 2018).

Ludwig, Arnold, *King of the Mountain. The Nature of Political Leadership* (Lexington, KT: Kentucky University Press, 2002).

March, D. and Stoker, G. (eds), *Theory and Methods in Political Science* (London: Palgrave Macmillan, 2002).

Maung Maung Gyi, *Burmese Political Values. The Socio-Political Roots of Authoritarianism*, (New York, NY: Praeger, 1983).

Maung Maung, *The 1988 Uprising in Burma* (New Haven, CT: Yale SE Asian Studies, 1999).

McCarthy, Stephen, *The Political Theory of Tyranny in Singapore and Burma: Aristotle and the Rhetoric of Benevolent Despotism* (New York, NY: Routledge, 2006).

Mon Mon Myat, 'Is Politics Aung San Suu Kyi's Vocation?' *Palgrave Communications*, Vol. 5, No. 50 (2019).

Moore, Matthew J., *Buddhism and Political Theory* (New York, NY: Oxford University Press, 2016).

Morland, Martin, 'Valedictory Dispatch to Douglas Hurd', Confidential, 26 April 1990, "Internal Affairs" FCO, The National Archive, Kew.

'The NLD after the arrests', 22 September 1990, FAB 014/1, "*Internal Affairs*" FCO, The National Archive, Kew.

Pannikar, Kavalam M., *Asia and Western Dominance. A Survey of the Vasco da Gama Epoch in Asian History* (New York, NY: John Day, 1954).

Papastergiadis, Nikos, *Debating Cultural Hybridity: Multi-Cultural Identities and the Politics of Anti-Racism* (London: Zed Books, 1997).

Patel, N., Goodman, A., and Snider, N., *Constitutional Reform in Myanmar: Priorities and Prospects for Amendment*, Bingham Centre Working Paper No 2014/01 (London: Bingham Centre for the Rule of Law, BIICL, 2014).

Pederson, Rena, *The Burma Spring. Aung San Suu Kyi and the New Struggle for the Soul of a Nation* (New York, NY: Pegasus, 2015).

Philpot, Simon, *Rethinking Indonesia. Postcolonial Theory, Authoritarianism and Identity* (London: Macmillan Press, 2000).

Pieterse, Jan Nedervenn, 'Globalisation as Hybridisation', *International Sociology*, June 1 (1994).

Popham, Peter, *Aung San Suu Kyi. The Lady and the Generals* (London: Rider, 2016).

Popham, Peter, *Aung San Suu Kyi. The Lady and the Peacock* (London: Rider, 2011).

Reynolds, Craig J., 'A New Look at Old Southeast Asia', *The Journal of Asian Studies*, Vol. 54, No. 2 (1995).

Sarkisyanz, Manuel, *The Buddhist Background of Burmese Revolution* (New York, NY: Springer, 1965).

Selth, Andrew, 'Be Careful What You Wish for: The National League for Democracy and Government in Myanmar', Griffith Asia Institute Regional Outlook Paper no. 56 (2017).

Selth, Andrew, 'Aung San Suu Kyi and the Politics of Personality', Griffith Asia Institute Regional Outlook Paper no. 55 (2017).

Selth, Andrew, *Secrets and Power in Myanmar: Intelligence and the Fall of General Khin Nyunt* (Singapore: ISEAS, 2019).

Sengupta, Nilanjana, *The Female Voice of Myanmar. Khin Myo Chit to Aung San Suu Kyi* (New Delhi: Cambridge University Press, 2015).

Skidmore, M. and Wilson, T. (eds), *Myanmar, the State, Community and the Environment* (Canberra: ANU Press, 2007).

Soe Thane, *Myanmar's Transformation& U Thein Sein. An Insider's Account* (Yangon: Tun, 2017).

Steinberg, David, 'Aung San Suu Kyi and U.S. Policy toward Burma/Myanmar', *Journal of Current Southeast Asian Affairs*, No. 3 (2010).

Steinberg, David, *Burma. The State of Myanmar* (Washington, DC: Georgetown University Press, 2001).

Steinberg, D.I. (ed.), *Myanmar: The Dynamics of an Evolving Polity* (Boulder, CO: LRP, 2015).

Tambiah, Stanley, 'The Buddhist Conception of Kingship and Its Historical Manifestations: A Reply to Spiro', *The Journal of Asian Studies*, Vol. 37, No. 4 (1978).

Taylor, Robert H., 'Myanmar's "Pivot" Toward the Shibboleth of "Democracy"', *Asian Affairs*, Vol. 44, No. 3 (2013).

Taylor, Robert H., 'The Armed Forces in Myanmar's Politics: A Terminating Role?', *ISEAS Trends*, No. 2 (2015).

Taylor, Robert H., *The State in Myanmar* (Singapore: Singapore University Press, 2009).

Thant Myint-U, *The Hidden History of Burma. Race, Capitalism, and the Crisis of Democracy in the 21th Century* (New York, NY: Norton, 2020).

Thant Myint-U, *The Making of Modern Burma* (Cambridge: Cambridge University Press, 2007).

Thant Myint-U, *The River of Lost Footsteps. A Personal History of Burma* (New York, NY: FSG, 2007).

Tonkin, Derek, 'The 1990 Elections in Myanmar: Broken Promises or a Failure of Communication?', *Contemporary Southeast Asia*, Vol. 29, No. 1 (April 2007)

Victor, Barbara, *The Lady: Aung San Suu Kyi: Nobel Laureate and Burma's Prisoner* (New York, NY: Faber & Faber, 2002).

Voicu, Cristina-Georgiana, *Exploring Cultural Identities in Jean Rhys' Fiction* (Berlin: de Gruyter, 2014).

Wallis, J., Kent, L., and Forsyth, M. (eds), *Hybridity on the Ground in Peacebuilding and Development: Critical Conversations* (Canberra: ANU Press, 2018).

Walton, Matthew J., 'Ethnicity, Conflict, and History in Burma: The Myths of Panglong', *Asian Survey*, Vol. 48, No. 6 (2008).

Walton, Matthew J., *Buddhism, Politics and Political Thought in Myanmar* (Cambridge: Cambridge University Press, 2017).

Walton, Matthew J., *Politics in the Moral Universe: Burmese Buddhist Political Thought*, unpublished PhD thesis (Seattle, WA: University of Washington, 2012).

Weber, Max, *The Religion of India* (Glencoe: The Free Press, 1958).

Weber, Max, *Economy and Society* (Los Angeles, CA: University of California Press, 1978).

Winfield, Jordan, *Buddhism and the State in Burma: English-Language Discourses from 1823 to 1962*, unpublished PhD thesis (University of Melbourne, 2017).

Winichakul, Thongchai, *Siam Mapped. A History of a Geo-Body of a Nation* (Honolulu: University of Hawaii Press, 1997).

Wintle, Justin, *Perfect Hostage. Aung San Suu Kyi, Burma and the Generals* (London: Arrows, 2007).

Ye Htut, *Myanmar's Political Transition and Lost Opportunities (2010–2016)* (Singapore: ISEAS, 2019).

Young, Robert, *Colonial Desire. Hybridity in theory, culture and race* (London and New York, NY: Routledge, 2005).

Zöllner, Hans-Bernd, *The Beast and the Beauty, The History of the Conflict Between the Military and Aung San Suu Kyi in Myanmar, 1988–2011, Set in a Global Context* (Berlin: Regiospectra, 2011).

Zöllner, H.-B., (ed.) *Daw Suu's 25 Dialogues with the People 1995–1996* (Hamburg and Yangon: Abera Verlag, 2014).

Zöllner, Hans-Bernd and Ebbighausen, Rodion, *The Daughter. A Political Biography of Aung San Suu Kyi* (Chiang Mai: Silkworm Books, 2018).

INDEX